THE ADVICE KING ANTHOLOGY

THE ADVICE KING ANTHOLOGY

CHRIS CROFTON

VANDERBILT UNIVERSITY PRESS
NASHVILLE, TENNESSEE

First printing 2022

Library of Congress Cataloging-in-Publication Data
Names: Crofton, Chris, 1969– author.
Title: The Advice King anthology / Chris Crofton.
Description: Nashville, Tennessee : Vanderbilt University Press, 2022. | Summary: "A curated collection of the best Advice King columns, with a new introduction by the Advice King and a foreword by Tracy Moore"—
Provided by publisher.
Identifiers: LCCN 2021054505 (print) | LCCN 2021054506 (ebook) | ISBN 9780826504630 (paperback) | ISBN 9780826504647 (epub) | ISBN 9780826504654 (pdf)
Subjects: LCSH: American wit and humor. | Advice columns—Humor. | Conduct of life—Humor. | United States—Civilization—21st century—Humor.
Classification: LCC PN6165 .C76 2022 (print) | LCC PN6165 (ebook) | DDC 818/.602—dc23/eng/20220125
LC record available at https://lccn.loc.gov/2021054505
LC ebook record available at https://lccn.loc.gov/2021054506

Dedicated to the memory of Jim Ridley

CONTENTS

Foreword by Tracy Moore XI

The Coronation of the Advice King XIII

Chapter One. Nashville 1

Chapter Two. Music 41

Chapter Three. Serious Shit 71

Chapter Four. A Little about Me 143

Chapter Five. Politics 163

Chapter Six. Life & Love 185

Chapter Seven. TV & Movies 247

Chapter Eight. Holidaze 271

Chapter Nine. Odds & End(s) 293

Acknowledgments 341

FOREWORD

Tracy Moore

I will happily take credit for pitching the idea for the advice column to Chris Crofton and helping him put out feelers with the *Nashville Scene*. As someone who recruited many writers for the pages of that paper, I knew he had the potential to be one: trenchantly funny, astute, and ranty to a fault are usually the trifecta. That's what we were debating over lunch in Venice that day in 2014, plus our feelings about Nashville—a place I'd since left, and a place he'd left to do comedy on the coast, but would always return to. For every razz I had about Nashville's pitfalls during that lunch, he had an uproarious defense with shrewd tangents that always meandered with noble purpose. Also, musicians such as Henry Rollins and Andrew W. K. were killing it for other papers with wise advice columns of their own. Also, he was broke.

That said, I cannot take the slightest bit of credit for the bitingly funny, philosophical soul-searching infused in his answers to these deceptively simple questions. Why have Nashvillians been priced out of East Nashville? "You were invaded by sociopaths." Should you attend Woodstock 50? "Greta Van Fleet is a group of Civil War reenactors—if the Civil War was Led Zeppelin." What does one do when one marries into cats? "Were your wife's parents divorced?" That is to say, don't read this book for practical advice; there's scant, if any, contained in these pages. What you will find is a blueprint for how to think, not just about Nashville, but about your very existence.

I also can't take any credit for the overwhelming success the column has become, but after reading it for years from afar, I can explain why it strikes such a nerve. Nashville has always had a bit of an identity crisis, and too many competing interests to settle on one. It doesn't always take too kindly to critiques about that. But sometimes it takes a self-deprecating Yankee blueblood from fancy-ass Connecticut to get the job done. To show a town not just where it's losing its way, but how to find its way back to what made it great to begin with—not with judgment, but compassion, and especially, with incisive, big-hearted wit from someone with deep affection for the city who is always willing to cop to his own struggles.

Nashville didn't need to be told what it already knew: that its beautiful neighborhoods have been pilfered by greedy flippers and developers, that its food scene (some of it fantastic, to be sure) has been swarmed by failed restaurateurs from bigger cities pushing the almighty fusion, that its thriving underground music scene has been invaded by just a few too many cheesy rock bands. It needed to be reminded of what it could be and to take a smidge of responsibility for the ways in which it may have (*ahem*) unwittingly played a part in such transformations in its eagerness to be the Third Coast, so as to not let it happen again.

To that end, The Advice King could not have arrived at a more prescient time in what is arguably its most bonkers period of upheaval in recent memory. That it came from an outsider who loves this city as much as its natives should be a reminder to Nashvillians that not all change is bad. Sometimes, it brings tall and skinnies, bachelorettes, and Kid Rock. But sometimes, it brings the best kind of interloper.

THE CORONATION OF THE ADVICE KING

One day in the fall of 2014, at lunch in Venice, California, my friend Tracy Moore suggested that I write an advice column. Tracy was the former music editor for the *Nashville Scene*. She was living in Venice, writing for *Jezebel*. I had just moved to Los Angeles from Nashville. I was not a writer, as far as I knew. I was a musician and a stand-up comedian. Soooo . . . a waiter.

Tracy said I wrote songs and comedy routines, so why not an advice column? Henry Rollins and Andrew W. K. wrote advice columns. As a joke, I said, "What should I call it, 'The Advice King'?"

Tracy texted the idea to *Scene* editor Jim Ridley, right then, at the table.

"Hell yes," Jim replied.

I became The Advice King in about twenty minutes, over lunch in Venice Beach. I was forty-five years old, recently sober, and—as it turns out—I had a lot to say.

CHAPTER 1

NASHVILLE

Priced Out of East Nashville

. . . .

PUBLISHED DECEMBER 2, 2014. One of the first few Advice King columns, and one of the all-time most popular.

Dear Advice King,

I've lived in East Nashville for about a decade now. I've always really liked it over here. I'm an artist (meaning, I work on films and music and writing as much as I can, but I also wait tables), and it's always been pretty easy to find a place with cheap rent. But my landlord is selling my current place, and I have to be out by the end of the year. Everywhere I've looked is way out of my price range. What should I do? Should I move up to Madison, or over to the West Side, or out of Nashville altogether?

Broke as a Joke on the East Side

Dear Broke,

When I moved to Nashville from New York City in 2001, all the fancy people I knew up there said, "Why would you go THERE? What is it? Like, a general store and cows?? HAHAHAHAHA." Little did they know it was a nice place to live. That kind of insecure asshole won't go anywhere that looks different than what they've seen in a style magazine. Nashville was safe from those people, because: A) it's in the South, which people in New York and L.A. think is "sketch" and "random"; B) it didn't have "any good restaurants." Insecure people need the city they live in to have "good restaurants," because what if someone fancy came to visit and they couldn't prove that where they live is fancy too! Now that condos have been built and there's a Whole Foods and Husk,* the condo-zombies think Nashville is a *magical oasis* in the South, the rest of which they still think is "sketch" and "random."

. . . .

* Husk is a new fancy restaurant in Nashville.

"I swear, Larry, you wouldn't even know you were *in* the South. These developers have done a great job. AND there's no income tax!"

The problem is that the insecure people have all the money in this country. Since the ethics have been completely removed from business culture, only super-insecure people are willing to do the immoral shit it takes to make a lot of money. Nice people won't work for Exxon or Dow or Goldman Sachs or a health care system that makes the executives rich at the expense of the sick, so nice people don't have any money. You basically have to be a sociopath to do any of the evil high-paying jobs left, and if you aren't a sociopath, you are a barista. Baristas can't pay the same prices for housing as sociopaths, so the best thing the baristas can do is try to keep the sociopaths at bay. But Nashville *BEGGED THEM TO COME.* Nashville had low self-esteem and wasn't going to rest until it had an ultra-lounge with a bowling alley, too. Well you got it. And so much more! You were invaded by the sociopaths. And as usual, they only care about one thing: appearances. Tear everything down and make it shiny and new, just like in the magazine, just like Brooklyn, just like everywhere.

I remember when some people in Nashville started selling shirts saying "Nashville is the New L.A." in 2006 or something. Waving a red flag in front of a granite-countertop bull, they were.

Nashville will never be Nashville again. Not the Nashville I was lucky enough to live in. The one where most people wore a T-shirt and jeans and were pretty goddamn friendly. The one where people didn't run around in silly hats calling themselves "foodies." The one where people could afford to live, *except for the people who couldn't.* Poor people are always having to uproot as the rich people move in and raise rents. The difference is that now middle-class white people are being priced out. There is no color in America anymore that won't be affected by the giant chasm between the rich and poor. While everybody was porch-drinkin', the 1 percent has been successfully looting this country, and now no town is safe from the sociopath makeover. The best you can do is to hope that these assholes never get interested in YOUR town. But Nashville wanted to be part of the "in" crowd, and never considered what would happen to the rent. Fancy restaurants and boutique hotels are like raw meat to a rich bear. Rich bears can pay un-fucking-limited rent. And once the rich bears found out that the State of Tennessee had no income tax, Nashville was toast. Avocado toast.

American whites will now join the ranks of so many throughout history who have been forced to run from assholes. It's reverse Manifest Destiny, with the world's tiniest violin providing the soundtrack. First go to Madison, my friend, then to Smyrna, then to Columbia, then to the country Colombia, then to that island made of garbage in the Pacific. In the sky above your lean-to on Garbage Island you will see Virgin Galactic flying dickheads from Dubai to East Nashville to get hot chicken, and you will think to yourself, "I should have voted."

Why Don't People Like Condo Developers?

PUBLISHED FEBRUARY 3, 2015. People didn't like them then, and they like them even less now.

Dear Advice King,

I am a condo developer who has many properties in Nashville, some of which I've purchased recently. I buy up old, unused properties, I demolish them, and I turn them into useful spaces for a city with a growing population. So why does everyone hate me and hate what I do? Nashvillians want to be a big, important city. An "It City." It Cities have condos. Why the backlash? I'm only meeting a need.

—William in Nashville

AGAIN WITH THE #@%$IN' CONDOS?!?! Useful spaces for whom, you deluded freak? The middle-class fools who take out loans to buy these overpriced pieces of shit so they can appear successful? You and your cohorts—a slimy cabal of marketers, publicists, lifestyle-branders and bankers—will have already pocketed your fees by the time the foreclosures start. Then you hype another city and do it all again. Why waste your time flipping houses when you can FLIP A CITY? GO BIG OR GO HOME. JUST DO IT. YOU'RE SOAKING IN IT.

This is going to be a pain in the ass to explain, but there was once an economy that made sense. It was a local economy. It was where some guy traded a fish he caught for a night at the inn. It's a regular-size inn and a healthy fish in this scenario, by the way, not a 600-story inn with 10,000-thread-count sheets, artisanal chocolate on the pillow and people "popping bottles" at the rooftop nightclub. The fish was not irradiated, nor was it full of Monsanto Roundup. This was a simple, fair, "healthy fish for a normal room" transaction. Such exchanges of goods and services occurred in towns all over America for hundreds of years. They were fair transactions, so no one got too rich and no one got too poor. The fabled free market at work. Of course there are always a few rotten apples who figure out a way to make more than their fair share. They make outsized profits by "distorting" the market. Plantation owners realized they could make a lot more money if they didn't pay their workers. Slavery was their super-profitable market "distortion."

These days the distortions are more subtle, so that the perpetrators can sleep better at night. Profiteering politicians—in league with the rotten apples—made it legal for American companies to outsource (use foreign labor to make their products). That is a major fucking distortion. In fact, it ruins the whole thing. How are Americans supposed to buy this stuff if they don't have jobs? They buy it with loans—high-interest loans. Double mortgages, triple mortgages, reverse mortgages. How's that working out? Fifty-one percent of American public school children are living in poverty. That's how it's working out.

A really funny thing about greedy capitalists is that they get so mad when you try to set up regulations to make sure there are some jobs, or that loans aren't predatory, that they say crazy things like, "The market will regulate itself," and that the regulations are the "distortions." Nothing makes me madder than dishonest shit like that. They know damn well the market won't regulate itself, because it's they and their fathers before them who rigged it. They just want to make sure it doesn't get unrigged.

Simply put, to make massive profits you have to cheat. You developers keep labor costs low by hiring undocumented or non-union workers and by using building materials manufactured in countries with no labor or environmental laws. This kind of disgraceful behavior is not exclusive to developers—it is worldwide business-as-usual. Endless economic growth (endless ethical economic growth, anyway) is an impossibility. I remember in the early '90s when companies started calling employees "temps" so that they wouldn't have to give them benefits. They had them work slightly less than 40 hours a week so they wouldn't technically be full-time. The money they saved on benefits became "profit," to be divided between executives and stockholders. That is what a healthy person would describe as an immoral arrangement. An outsize-profit-crazed modern asshole sees it as an innovation!

One more important point: America was "developed" on stolen land. The Native Americans were the first American neighborhood association. The "developers" considered their opinion, then murdered them all and did what they wanted. I bet a lot of developers wish they could still murder neighborhood associations. You wanna hear a joke that isn't funny, mister? Why aren't there more black developers? Because they weren't allowed to own land when the country was being divvied up.

Since the paid-off politicians end up approving 99 percent of these projects regardless of what the people want, one small concession should be made: The public gets to name the fucking thing. Good luck selling units in "Conformity Creek" or "Dickhead Central."

Building luxury housing is the opposite of public service. This impoverished world needs affordable housing, not luxury housing. And it's not enough that you are making a lot of money—you want to be liked, too? Start spending some of your ill-gotten gains on a good therapist, William.

The Great East Nashville Train-Horn Controversy

PUBLISHED FEBRUARY 23, 2016. FYI, the horns were NOT silenced.

Dear Advice King,

I live in East Nashville, and lately all these people are showing up on my doorstep asking me to sign a petition about train horns. Some petitions are AGAINST train horns, and some are FOR train horns. Which one should I sign? I wanna be on the right side of the tracks, and history.

—Thomas

OK. This is a real fucking thing, people. The guy who wrote this question is trying to be funny by calling himself "Thomas," but this is a real fucking thing that is REALLY happening in Nashville. Some white person who doesn't like noise bought a house near the train tracks, and now they want the trains to stop blowing their horns. And here's the kicker: This person—from Los Angeles, naturally—bought this house by the train tracks A YEAR AGO.

There are a lot of affordable houses in Nashville that aren't near train tracks, by the way. Thousands of 'em. They just aren't in *East* Nashville. But all the trendy fools who are moving to Nashville from New York and Los Angeles have to live in EAST NASHVILLE, because that's the neighborhood all the magazines talk about. They HAVE TO. What would their lousy friends *think* if they didn't?

Because of the huge demand, East Nashville houses have gotten pretty fucking expensive. EXCEPT FOR THE ONES BY THE TRAIN TRACKS. So this Los Angeles person has a ghoulish thought: "What if I buy a cheap house by the railroad tracks and then use my white privilege to TURN OFF THE TRAIN HORNS?!?" Most people would have a thought like that and say to themselves, "What a terrible thought. I should see a psychiatrist and try to find out why I get these diabolical thoughts. I bet I get them because my parents told me 'NO' all the time." Some people get told "NO" all the time when they are kids, and then when they grow up, they decide they will NEVER TAKE NO FOR AN ANSWER AGAIN. Even if the question is a crazy one, like "Can I turn off the train horns?"

It could also have been the exact opposite situation. This person's parents might have only said "YES." Maybe this person always hated noise. Maybe they said, "Daddy, the birds are loud! Turn off the birds, Daddy!" and their dad got a net and captured all the birds and then built a dome over the house. That would explain a lot.

This person knows that silencing the train horns will make the value of their property go up. It will make the price of houses and rent in that neighborhood go up. When this happens, the people who live near the train tracks now will have to move. Where are they going to move? Why should they have to move?! YOU should move, person. You got there last. You moved into that neighborhood knowing you didn't like trains. Why? Because of diabolical thoughts, that's why. That neighborhood belongs to the people who moved there honestly, understanding—and possibly appreciating—that horns were part of the package. Train horns are EVERYBODY'S, not yours.

One more thing: This isn't free. These anti-horn creeps need $1.5 MILLION in taxpayer dollars to solve this non-problem. That's right, folks—it turns out you can't just "turn off the train horns." Train horns actually serve a fucking purpose. Turns out trains are REAL things that REALLY run smaller things over if those smaller things don't hear a horn and get out of the fucking way. It will cost $1.5 million to put the safety measures in place that would replace the horns. Does this person know that there is serious poverty in East Nashville? Children with empty stomachs live right near those same fucking train tracks, and train horns are the least of their worries. Give THEM $1.5 million. I'm sorry, but this makes me mad.

I bet a large percentage of these people don't even know why trains exist.

East Nashville Anti-Horn Idiot: "Trains are so weird and loud! What do they, like, carry stuff or whatever?"

I can guarantee you that this Los Angeleno's plans don't end with the horns: First ban the horns, then ban the trains, then ban ugly people. I can picture some white asshole in 2019 creating the Facebook invite for Sunday afternoon "Yoga on the Tracks."

Sign the petition to keep the horns, "Thomas." Sign it twice. Hank Williams never wrote a song about yoga.

What Should Go in My Condo Mural?

. . . .

PUBLISHED NOVEMBER 13, 2019.

Dear Advice King,

I've been hired to paint a mural on the side of a new condominium development in Nashville. What should it be? Angel wings? A big bourbon bottle? A guitar with wings? A bourbon bottle with wings?

Thanks,

—Leon in Nashville

"Listen a minute, will ya? Will ya listen a minute? Now listen . . . A lot of people who get up here and sing, I know it's fun, ya know, it's a lot of fun. It's fun for me, I get my feelings off through my music, but listen . . . You got your life wrapped up in it, and it's very difficult to come up here and lay something down when people . . . It's like last Sunday, I went to a Hopi ceremonial dance in the desert, and there were a lot of people there and there were tourists . . . and there were tourists who were getting into it like Indians, and there were Indians who were getting into it like tourists, and I think that you're acting like tourists, man. Give us some respect." —Joni Mitchell at the Isle of Wight Festival, 1970

Joni Mitchell doesn't like tourists—and neither does anyone else. The city of Nashville has been turned over to tourists. There is nothing inherently wrong with a tourist, but if you are trying to do something serious—something deep, something that is important to you—they are the last people you want to have around. Joni was trying to sing her heartfelt songs. Regular Nashvillians are trying to live their lives. Both of these activities require soul and seriousness. Tourists are on a lark, taking a break from their own (possibly serious and soulful) reality. The last thing they are looking for is depth. Mixing frivolous people together with serious people causes extreme discomfort—for the serious people, anyway. The frivolous ones are usually too drunk to notice.

And when I say that "the city of Nashville has been turned over to tourists," you probably think I am exaggerating. I am not. And the reason I am not is because of Nashville's "business-friendly" policy-makers and . . . Airbnb. City leaders being "business-friendly" means you let developers from out of town make over your city with pretty much zero input from actual residents. It means you can build a boutique hotel anywhere except on the grounds of a historic fort—and it turned out even *that* was negotiable at one point. Airbnb means that even though the house next door to you might *look* like a regular house, it is actually a boutique hotel.

Compounding the problem in Nashville is the fact that Nashville isn't that big. Developers have been able to completely change the vibe of an entire city in about seven years. The tourists are ecstatic, and the residents are depressed. That's because in the case of Nashville, THE RESIDENTS are the attraction. There's no ocean. No mountains. There's just neighborhoods. The tourists roam—and reside—on the same streets where regular people are trying to do the soulful, serious business of living their lives. Some of these regular people happen to make music—the music that the tourists are ostensibly in Nashville to hear. But the vast majority of tourists aren't in Nashville to *listen* to music—even if they say they are. They're there to get drunk as shit.

A couple of months ago I was in Nashville visiting my family. As I was leaving the airport, I walked past a flattened "penis" straw on the sidewalk. If you aren't familiar with these novelty straws, they are popular party favors at bachelorette parties. I guess the idea behind them is that the woman getting married won't be able to suck anymore strange dicks once she's hitched so she should . . . suck as many as she can before that? Mostly plastic ones that are on the end of straws? I have no idea, and I don't actually give a fuck—I just think they, and the insipid corporatist party culture that spawned them, are depressing

The point is that Nashville isn't a city known primarily for its music and people anymore. It's a city known for being a great place to get blackout drunk and suck on plastic dicks. A city that is able to support multiple businesses devoted to administering IVs to hungover people.

What's this question about again? Oh yeah, murals. Well, I'm pretty sure a substantial, thought-provoking piece of public art (of which Nashville has a few) would be considered a buzzkill. Condo developers and bachelorettes aren't into social realism—too heavy. They don't want *Guernica*. They are looking for some light subject matter that will serve as an innocuous backdrop for mindless consumption or light subject matter that will lead to an Instagram photo that will act as an enticement to other frivolous people to visit to Nashville and mindlessly consume (or some weird, colorful blobs). I'd go with the bourbon bottle with wings. Paint some guitar strings on the side of the bottle.

By the way, I love Nashville with all my heart. I still consider it to be my home. I love its soulful, serious™ (normal, non-tourist) residents, and its music. That's the only reason I get so fired up about this stuff.

The Fashion House Freaked Me Out—Should I Still Move to Nashville?

PUBLISHED AUGUST 5, 2020. Context: in 2020, the world was in the middle of a deadly, devastating coronavirus pandemic.

Dear Advice King,

Is Nashville still a music city? I saw a news report about a party there, and everyone at the party looked insane. It looked like Gathering of the Juggalos! And no one was taking COVID-19 precautions. Should I move to Nashville? I play country and Western-style fiddle. I don't like Limp Bizkit, and I don't want to die! Thanks!

—Ed in Knoxville

You're talking about the "Fashion House" party. I saw it on the news, too. It looked like Woodstock '99. And I should know, because I was at Woodstock '99. I was working as a production assistant, running videotapes from the stages to the broadcast truck. Woodstock '99—in case you didn't know already—was a disaster. There were multiple sexual assaults, and the event culminated in a riot.

I saw people having public sex at Woodstock '99 in front of cheering, intoxicated crowds. This Nashville "Fashion House" party also included at least one (documented) public sex act.

I love Nashville. The best musicians in the world live there! But Nashville isn't known primarily for music anymore. It is known as a place for tourists to get drunk. And I mean *drunk*. The kind of drunk you don't want to get in your hometown, because you have to *live* there.

Just after I moved to Los Angeles from Nashville, I met a friend of mine (also a recent transplant from Nashville) for coffee. He told me a story that was funny—and sad. He said that when he first arrived in L.A., he was invited to a barbecue. At that barbecue he drank nine beers in three hours—an amount that would hardly raise an eyebrow in Nashville. He said everyone at the party FREAKED OUT. They thought he was trying to kill himself.

I remember reading *A People's History of the United States* by Howard Zinn. In it, he tells the story of Christopher Columbus arriving on the island of Hispaniola (now Haiti and the Dominican Republic). When Columbus had to go back to Spain to get supplies, he left a bunch of his men there. He told them to behave. When he returned, the men he'd left behind were drunk, riding the locals around like horses. That's right, the locals. Not the locals' horses—THE PEOPLE. Why did I bring this up? Because it reminds me of Nashville.

In the Nashville version, the people who attended the "Fashion House" party are like the men Columbus left behind. Maskless boors who fly into a town, get hammered, abuse (infect with COVID, perform desultory analingus on) the residents, and leave. They might not even remember their "visit" to "Music City." To them, Nashville is no different than Las Vegas, spring-break Daytona Beach or Tijuana—a place where it's supposed to be acceptable to act like a monster. A place to ride the locals.*

That old joke about Nashville being a "Drinking City with a Music Problem" isn't funny anymore—it's dangerous. It's time to get back to the goddamn music. Yes, Ed from Knoxville, move to Nashville. Start a band. A really fucking good one.**

. . . .

* Uber, Postmates, Airbnb, and Kid Rock's Big Ass Honky Tonk are all just thinly veiled ways of riding people.

** Sorry in advance for subjecting you to Ed's shitty band.

Can I Rent Out Downtown Nashville Like the NFL Did?

PUBLISHED APRIL 17, 2019.

Dear Advice King,

Why did Nashville rent out its downtown to the NFL Draft? Can I rent downtown Nashville? Can I get some trees removed from a public park for a picnic I have planned?

—Connie, Davidson County resident

Nashville rented its downtown to the NFL Draft because having the NFL Draft in your town improves your town's quality of life, while also giving local youngsters the opportunity to witness an important cultural event.

HAHAHAHAHAHAHAHA.

Nashville rented out its downtown to the NFL Draft because Nashville is "business-friendly." "Business-friendly" is a nice way of saying that you'll do anything for money™. Also, there will be celebrities. Who can resist money and celebrities? "Celebrities and money" is the new "baseball and apple pie." Well, it turns out that even when money *and* celebrities are involved, there are supposed to be limits to what a self-respecting city will do—or allow to have done to it.

Nashville is so goddamn "business-friendly" and celebrity-mad that the city agreed to remove 21 healthy, blooming cherry trees from a public park to accommodate the NFL Draft's giant stage.

This decision made national headlines. And it didn't make national headlines just because people are crazy about cherry trees. For a moment, Nashville's 21 cherry trees came to symbolize all the priceless things (trees, animal species, historic architecture, dignity, morality) that are being lost in this country for nothing more than short-term economic gain.

No one likes to say "short-term economic gain," because it sounds crappy (because it is crappy). So "short-term economic gain" has been replaced with the harmless-sounding—and intentionally misleading—"economic growth." This allows rich tricksters to say stuff like, "Surely you aren't going to stand in the way of my company's plan to turn the library into a microbrewery—after all, it will result in 'economic growth,'" and feel like they aren't technically lying. The question that needs to be asked whenever one encounters this type of bullshit is: "*Whose* economic growth, asshole?"

"Economic growth" is used as the excuse for all kinds of amoral, profitable behavior. The consequences land disproportionately on the poor, while the money ends up (surprise!) in the pockets of the motherfuckers who are always using the expression "economic growth." Everyone else is left with the same amount of money that they had before, and no fucking trees.

Now, to answer your question, Connie. Yes, you could rent downtown Nashville. And I'm pretty sure they'll take down the trees for your picnic if you tell them that some celebrities will be there. I also think Nashville would allow Nissan Stadium to be renamed "Pornhub Stadium" if the bid was high enough.

FUN FACT: Even after a massive public outcry *and* a national shaming, Nashville officials still went ahead and removed some of the trees. And I don't care that they decided to take down less than they originally planned, or that they are going to replant them (which arborists have said is pretty much impossible to do successfully). Ultimately, they did what the National Football League told them to do, and said "fuck you" to their own constituents. The *really* fun fact is that those constituents will probably vote for those same officials again, because . . . "economic growth." God help us.

What's With All the Scooters?

PUBLISHED JANUARY 23, 2019.

Dear Advice King,

Why are there little electric scooters everywhere in my town? Is this supposed to be a good thing? If so, what is good about it? Why is it legal to leave these fucking scooters lying all over the place? How should I proceed?

—Desiree in Nashville

These are excellent questions, Desiree. As a matter of fact, I have the same exact questions! Why *is* it legal to leave these fucking scooters lying all over the place? (Editor's note: It's not, but people do it anyway.) And it's not just happening in Nashville—these scooters are plaguing cities around the world.

I'm sure you've heard the expression "It's all who you know." Well, I don't know if it's *all* "who you know," but it's *definitely* "all who you know" if you plan on getting away with leaving thousands of tacky, for-profit toy scooters on the side of a public road. When a person who doesn't *know* anybody does something like that, it's called "littering."

Here is a short play about the "free" market, called *The "Free" Market.*

THE "FREE" MARKET—A SHORT PLAY ABOUT SHITTY LITTLE SCOOTERS

ACT ONE

CHIEF OF POLICE: Did you leave 50,000 shitty little scooters all over the streets of Nashville?

SCOOTER WEASEL: Yes. I am the young CEO of Flimzee Scooterz™. My name is Larry.

CHIEF OF POLICE: That's littering, Larry! Unless . . . do you happen to know somebody?

SCOOTER WEASEL: My name is Larry Opry—as in "Grand Ole."
CHIEF OF POLICE: Please hold.

Everyone smokes cigar.

THE END

That play was good.

At this point I should explain to those readers whose towns *aren't* littered with these kids' toys recast as "transportation alternatives" what exactly is being discussed here.

A couple years ago, some company called "Bird" dropped heaps of crappy little pay-some-asshole-in-Silicon-Valley-per-ride scooters all over the "fun" areas of a bunch of cities. Last year in Nashville, one of the "fun" areas targeted happened to be East Nashville. The scooter people assumed that since East Nashville had already proven incapable of defending itself against the abominable architecture of out-of-town developers, rents driven sky-high by trust fund kids disguised as saloon pianists and the projectile vomit of Airbnb bachelorettes, it would also prove incapable of defending itself against millions of toy scooters. They were right.

I can guarantee you that if "Bird" had heaped scooters on the lawns and putting greens of Belle Meade, Nashville would have permanently banned them.

After you "activate" these goddamn things with your credit card, you ride them until you arrive at your destination—or are run over by a pedal tavern. Whichever comes first. Then you drop them. And people tend to drop them WHEREVER THEY WANT. "WHEREVER THEY WANT," in case you have forgotten, happens to include THE MIDDLE OF THE FUCKING SIDEWALK. How many people have been disfigured as a result of tripping over these things? Is anyone keeping track?

WELCOME TO NASHVILLE! IT HAS BEEN 0 DAYS SINCE OUR LAST SCOOTER-RELATED DISFIGUREMENT™.

This whole thing reminds me of something I almost forgot! One time I had an idea to leave 200,000 pepper grinders all over Rio de Janeiro. In fact, I just remembered that I actually did it! The mobile-seasoning™

company I founded was called Grindr (we had it first). I personally scattered 200,000 credit-card-activated grinders on the streets of Rio. It took me nine weeks.

Five turns for 50 cents, was the idea. I never found out if it was a GOOD idea, because I got a HUGE ticket for littering before people could start using the damn things. The police chief asked if I *knew* somebody. I thought for a minute and said, hopefully, "Evita?" It turns out Evita isn't from Brazil, and everyone got REALLY mad. Anyway, it took me 200 weeks to clean up the pepper grinders.

My advice to you, Desiree? Attack the scooters with an ax. You are allowed to attack stuff you find in the street with an ax—it's in the fucking street! I attack almost everything I find in the street with an ax. It's one of life's few remaining simple pleasures. Chop chop.

Groaning from the Gulch

PUBLISHED JANUARY 13, 2015.

Dear Advice King,

My wife and I recently relocated to the Gulch Area. After years in L.A. and NYC, we loved the affordability and hominess of everything around here (and no state income tax HIYOOOO!!). We've walked to Watermark, Sambuca, The Turnip Truck, Cantina Laredo, Sambuca again, then all the way down to Subway. Honestly, we're getting a bit bored. Surely there's more to the Gulch than 1.5 blocks and six restaurants? We'd like to go exploring and have heard lots about Five Points in East Nashville. Do they valet?

Thanks,

—Trey and Bev

OK, "Trey and Bev." I know this is a fake question designed to make me yell about a bunch of stuff. How do I know? Because no one is really named Bev, that's how. But guess what. I will take the bait BECAUSE I DON'T HAVE ANY OTHER QUESTIONS.

First softball floating across the hate plate: The hominess and affordability of "The Gulch." I put "The Gulch" in quotes because it is not a real thing. Regarding hominess: The fun thing about upscale McNeighborhoods like "The Gulch" is that they are physical embodiments of the trends of whatever period in which they were pasted together. "The Gulch" was built out of particle board and spit in 45 minutes in 2007. It looks like it. It looks like skinny jeans and bangs and texting. If "The Gulch" feels like home to you, here are some other places you might like to live: A North Korean amusement park, a Mumford & Sons concert, inside a Pumpkin Spice Latte. Regarding affordability: In 2015, making the kind of money you need to have to live in an area like "The Gulch" requires doing something immoral. Have fun at the "block" party with the personal injury lawyers, payday loan tycoons, and that deposed African dictator who calls himself Josh.

Another major drawback to "The Gulch": When the Final Uprising happens, the residents of areas like "The Gulch" will be the first to get it. Have you ever seen *Escape From New York*? One of The Duke of Nashville's offices will be a burned-out Gulch penthouse. His headquarters will be the burned-out Belle Meade Country Club.

Next you're trying to make me mad about Tennessee's lack of income tax. All right, I'm mad about Tennessee's lack of income tax. Because it charges no income tax, Tennessee uses a high sales tax to collect revenue. Poor people have to pay the same amount as rich people, even on food. In 31 states and the District of Columbia food is exempt from sales tax because of the undue burden it places on the poor.

Back to the goddamn "Gulch." It's not very big or exciting, you say? Do you want me to rant about how the "New Nashville" is 90 percent hype, 10 percent actual goods and services? Here is what I recommend to anyone moving to Nashville: Take mushrooms before you get in the car with the real estate agent. Mushrooms make you see the truth. For example, I watched the news the first time I did mushrooms. Guess what. The news is bullshit. If you tour Nashville, on mushrooms, with a real estate lady giving you the "It City" spiel, you will never stop laughing. Ever. The first time that agent says "Brooklyn" or "Los Angeles" while you take a mushroomy gander at the three blocks of marzipan and scrap metal that make up "The Gulch"—the same "Gulch" from the brochure, the same "Gulch" from the *Esquire* listicle, *that* "Gulch"—you will laugh so hard that you may end up in a mental hospital. The real estate tour will be over, that's for sure. That agent will run for her life, leaving you rolling around in the fake gutter next to the fake sidewalk in front of the fake speakeasy. The same thing will happen when that agent shows you the legendary Five Points intersection in East Nashville. Without the aid of mushrooms, your societally conditioned brain may accept the claims of the authority figures—the media, the "licensed" real estate agent—who say the Five Points intersection is the center of an internationally important cultural movement called "New Nashville." You might look at that intersection and accept it. You really might. But if you *are* on mushrooms, you will look around and say, "But uhhhh . . . wha . . . I m-m-m-mean how . . . it's . . . buuuut . . . it's . . . it's soooo uh . . . SMALL. And the, uhhhh . . . biggest thing is . . . A GAS STATION! HAHAHAHAHAHAHAHAHAHAHAHAHAHAHA!" Then the realtor will run away again.

Finally, whoever wrote this letter had the fictional "Trey and Bev" ask if there is valet parking in East Nashville so I would tell them to shove traffic cones up their asses. Shove traffic cones up your asses, Trey and Bev.

Look, I love Nashville. I just don't like the developers who got together with some publicists and invented neighborhoods in order to sell cheaply built condos to trendy out-of-town suckers. Because now Nashville is loaded with trendy out-of-town suckers, and they're all in a shitty mood. Traffic jams full of people who just had the doorknob come off in their hand, angrily looking for "the other stuff" that "there must be." Nashville will become a city of Treys and Bevs, complaining.

Driving in Nashville

PUBLISHED ON FEBRUARY 24, 2015.

Dear Advice King,

I moved to Nashville a couple of years ago counting on relatively mild weather and a good ride to work. Instead I've found a city totally unprepared for inclement weather—heavy rain, occasional ice and snow—and a highway system that even in optimum weather scares the most experienced driver. Most cities advise people to use mass transit, which, except for a few buses, doesn't exist in Nashville. Ironically, a major plan to provide such transportation was recently defeated by the city council. Could this be a conspiracy to discourage a population increase in the "It" city? I need an explanation.

—Melinda Z.

Dear Melinda,

I wish I could tell you that the pasta dish they call a road system in Nashville was part of a diabolical plot. I completely understand why you would be suspicious.

For a couple hundred years, Nashville was an "It City" for buffalo. Nashville roads were laid out by a guy named Mortimer "Buffalo" Braddock. His nickname was "Buffalo" because he loved buffalo. He thought they were endowed with special abilities. He rode around Nashville on a buffalo named Hightower. He once had a buffalo participate in a seance. It was Braddock, at the age of 92 and wearing his trademark pajamas, who decided that the Nashville roads should be based on historic buffalo trails. The problem was that all the buffalo, no matter where they were coming from, ended up at a huge salt lick on the bank of the Cumberland River. Buffalo love salt. You can't have a road system where all the roads go to a salt lick. I mean, I love a salt lick as much as anybody, but I don't want that to be the only place I can go. When the mayor at the time, Spears Wade, found out all his roads were salt lick-bound he fired Buf Braddock, but the damage was done.

It's 2015, and the salt lick has long since been licked. The human herds of today's Nashville like to lick charcuterie plates and pan-seared sea bass. Unfortunately, Nashville's skinny roads are still better suited for buffalo. Buffalo have narrow feet and aren't in a hurry. Foodies drive huge SUVs and are in a big hurry. In 2012 a food writer from Atlanta named Kim Severson wrote an article for *The New York Times* that made Nashville sound like a gourmand's paradise. That was not true (I think people figured the fancy restaurants she mentioned were the BEST fancy restaurants, not the ONLY fancy restaurants), but a lot of people believe shit they read in *The New York Times*, no questions asked. So the hungry, wealthy hordes descended on Nashville, but newspaper articles don't magically transform small Southern cities. A restaurant putting foie gras fritters on the menu has absolutely no effect on the number of snow plows in Tennessee. The number will remain eight. There are eight snow plows, two salt spreaders and one sand truck in the whole state. In the South, people stay home when the roads are bad. Transplants from New York and Los Angeles *lose their minds* if they can't go about their sociopathic business. I would just like to gently remind Mr. and Mrs. Fastpace: YOU LIVE IN TENNESSEE AND NO ONE FORCED YOU TO MOVE THERE. It's not a slow Los Angeles or a New York that always sleeps. It's an ENTIRELY DIFFERENT, COMPLETELY VALID CULTURE, and if you don't like it you should move.

If you would like a harsher reminder that you currently live in Tennessee, here is some red-hot Red State bullshit that recently went down in your new hometown. Public transportation, huh? Definitely seems like a reasonable expectation for a city to have some decent public transportation. Well, it was looking like it might happen for a minute there. A group of sane people, including Mayor Karl Dean, had a reasonable proposal to expand the city bus system. Some rich people didn't like it because it would mean poorer people would have access to the rich people's side of town. In a normal city, the rich people would have had to shut the fuck up because that is an awful reason to oppose something, and the bus system would have been expanded. In Tennessee, where you now live, the Republican-controlled general assembly OUTLAWED THE KIND OF BUS THEY WERE GOING TO USE. The End.

There is no conspiracy. There is no such thing as an "It City." You live in Nashville. Nashville is in Tennessee, and so are you, Melinda.

How Does a Regular Guy Meet Women?

PUBLISHED JANUARY 20, 2015.

Dear Advice King,

It seems Nashville women either want a country singer guy with tight jeans and a goofy hat or some hipster beer-drinking guy with a beard. So let me ask you, Crofton. I'm neither. I'm a regular, non-plaid-wearing guy with hips too big to wear tight jeans. I need some advice. How can a straight-up guy such as myself with a glowing personality and a job snag one of those Nashville women?

Thanks,

—Ben

It's a goofy-hat globe in 2015, my friend. All the world's a Facebook and we are merely profiles. Real people have been sorted, classified and sold back to us as "types." Choose one! Are you Johnny Cash or Paul Westerberg? Are you Emmylou Harris or Lena Dunham?

Which straight-up guy are you, Ben? Andy Griffith? Paul Rudd? Kofi Annan?

Don't get involved in these role-playing games, Ben. There are plenty of normal people out there looking for love. The thing is, even if you dressed up like an extra from *Gangs of New York* and "snagged"* one of these Nashville women, you would end up sad. The kind of lady who wants hats now will want spats later™. People like this change their style AND personality to match their age and reflect current trends. If you date a "Zooey Deschanel" now, she'll turn into a "Susan Sontag" later. "Susan" will leave you for a college professor who matches her new glasses frames. That garage-rock "Mick Jagger"? His "Marianne Faithfull" is going to get tired of having roommates, enter a "new phase" and marry a hedge fund manager. Mick's band is going to break up, and he's going to have to learn to express himself through latte art.

Be especially grateful you're not involved in Americana cosplay—it's a one-way ticket into a Southern Gothic short story. The country-singer guy in the tight jeans is trying to be Merle Haggard, and Merle himself was trying to be a train whistle. The woman thinks she's Sissy from *Urban Cowboy*. More often than not, they're repeating patterns learned from their family of origin. I mean they are literally re-enacting the events that created their own insecurities, and their mom and dad's insecurities, and *their* mom and dad's insecurities before that—the dude is impersonating his alcoholic dad, and the woman gets involved with him as a way to re-do her relationship with her own drunken, emotionally unavailable father. None of the actors in this drama are aware that they are in a play, because they are drunk all the time. Drunkenness was the reason for all the emotional disconnects in their family trees, and drunkenness guarantees the same shit will happen again. When "Tammy Wynette" gets impregnated by "Gram Parsons," the circle is complete (unbroken HAHAHA).

I feel your pain, though. It seems like the people playing dress-up have all the fun. They smile real big in all their selfies, right? They're always going bowling in big groups. Their omnipresent strings of Christmas lights scream, "We are experiencing more warmth than

* Don't ever tell a woman you want to "snag" them, or that you are "happy you snagged them," or that they are the best woman you ever "snagged." You will be alone for life talking like that, hat or no hat, job or no job.

you!" Here's something that should make you feel better: They are being warmed by white privilege, craft cocktails and cocaine. When the metaphorical party is metaphorically over (rehab, race war) these women will never want to see a man wearing a hat again. They will want a straight-up guy with a glowing personality and a job—that's where you come in!

If you absolutely cannot rest until you are involved with one of these troubled, superficial people, I can recommend a plastic surgeon in Green Hills. Dr. Amer I. Canapparel will whittle your hips, seed your beard, remove your chest muscles, and make you gluten intolerant. It's called the "Skinny Genes" treatment. It's an $8,000 outpatient procedure and that price includes a 12-pack of a local microbrew.

Should I Leave My Hometown?

PUBLISHED AUGUST 24, 2016.

Dear Advice King,

When is it time to leave your hometown?

—Eric in Nashville

I'm going to assume Nashville is your hometown, Eric. I know what you want me to do. You want me to yell and scream about floppy hats and mustache wax. No way, buddy. I've been taking anti-rage pills, and now I love floppy hats and mustache wax. And local breweries and macrame classes and "cupping"—all that shit. I love trends! I'm wearing yoga pants and refilling a growler right now!

Have you heard about "cupping"? It's this thing where white people put suction cups on themselves because they have nothing better to do. Growing up in Connecticut in the 1970s, "cupping" was when you broke a cup on someone's head as a prank. In fifth grade I "cupped" my friend Philip with a beer stein while he was bent over the drinking fountain. He had to be in special classes after that. I didn't get in trouble because everyone agreed that I got him fair and square.

Leave your hometown if it sucks, Eric. I left my hometown because it sucked. The No. 1 reason people leave their hometowns is because they suck. No. 2 is mudslides.

My hometown sucked because everybody there was a stockbroker. Stockbrokers always try to convince everyone else to be stockbrokers, too. Being a stockbroker is no fun, you see, and since they aren't having any fun, these stockbrokers decide no one else should get to have any fun either. Misery loves company. Misery also loves COMPANIES™—banks, specifically. When I realized that all the parents in my Connecticut hometown were trying to trick their helpless, idealistic kids into being stockbrokers, I ran for my helpless, idealistic life.

Nashville, Tenn., is not nearly as homogenous and oppressive as the wealthy suburbs of New York City, but it has definitely become MORE homogenous and oppressive in the past few years. Unfortunately, the whole goddamn world is becoming more homogenous and oppressive. Any man on God's green earth with an internet connection knows he's supposed to grow a beard, shave his balls, drink IPAs and watch that show *Stranger Things*. Everywhere you go these days—from the salad bar at Ruby Tuesday to a weather station in Antarctica—you meet the same people, wearing the same clothes, talking about the same things. You can run, Eric, but you can't hide. There is something you can hide from, however—the internet.

Spending too much time on Facebook, for example, will make you think that any town anywhere is full of insecure, narcissistic social climbers. A lot of people ARE insecure, narcissistic social climbers—our survival as a species depends on us all being superficial, narcissistic social climbers, to some degree—but to be reminded of that fact so explicitly, day after day, can be incredibly disheartening. "Everyone in this town is a narcissistic dick," Facebook will make you think. Remember this: Probably only the NORMAL amount of people in your town are narcissistic dicks, but the GIANT, excessively dicky dicks post on Facebook much more than the regular, standard-issue dicks. This will give you the impression that there are more Superdicks™ in ANY town than there actually are.

Make sure you are fleeing your REAL hometown, Eric, and not your hometown reflected in an Internet Funhouse Mirror™. If Nashville is truly overflowing with real, walking, talking, ball-shaving, status-updating, veiny human dicks—and it may be—I recommend Chattanooga.

I Don't Like Hot Chicken

. . . .

PUBLISHED SEPTEMBER 1, 2015.

Dear King,

I don't like "Nashville hot chicken." I don't get it. I think it's prohibitively hot and gross and weird. Am I a bad Nashvillian?

—Bored with the Bird

"Prohibitively hot," huh? Is that fancy talk for "really hot"? Are you sure you are a Nashvillian? You sound like a damn Northeast liberal. What do *you* like to eat, Yankee? Crumpets? I don't even know what a crumpet is because I'm not an asshole, but I'm sure they're not spicy.

I am a real Nashvillian, "Bored with the Bird." Right now I am eating a pork rind-and-motor oil sandwich in a "pita" made out of a supermarket circular. You know how some people eat egg-white omelets? I eat omelets made entirely out of yolks. This morning I had a 20-yolk omelet filled with Miracle Whip and two bottles of Tabasco. I left the Tabasco in the bottles. A motherfucking 20-yolk Tabasco-bottle-and-Miracle Whip omelet. It's called the "Nashville Man" omelet. They sell it at Larry's Pest Control / Diner on Dickerson Pike. I bet you had a bran muffin for breakfast and read *The New York Times*, you elitist scumbag. I read my pocket copy of the Constitution with the 14th Amendment crossed out, and then I drove to my job in my monster truck with Monster Energy stickers on it.

Full disclosure? I'm not a fully fledged Nashvillian. *I'm* a "Yankee Elitist." I grew up in Connecticut. What are people from Connecticut called? Connecticufflinks, I bet. Connecticut isn't known for any kind of food. It's known for . . . ummm . . . uhhhh . . . golf? Golf isn't spicy. If golf was salsa, it would definitely be "mild," and made by a major corporation. Spice racks in Connecticut are used exclusively to display thimble collections. I didn't even know spicy food existed until I went to a party at my Ethnic Studies professor's house in college:

INTERIOR, ETHNIC STUDIES PROFESSOR'S HOUSE, 1988

ME: Ow! These little black balls hurt my mouth! [*Spits food in sink*]
PROFESSOR ORTIZ: First of all, those are beans.

THE END

Here's the crazy thing: It turns out I love spicy food! I also like Gordon Lightfoot! Why the fuck am I mentioning that, you understandably ask? I think most people would say that Gordon Lightfoot is about as spicy as golf. How can I hate golf, love Gordon Lightfoot *and* like spicy food? *AND* love Nashville and be from Connecticut? *AND* live in Los Angeles?! *And* consider myself a Nashvillian? AND HATE HOT CHICKEN??

There are no rules, "Bored." You don't have to eat horrible shit to be a real Southerner, a real Nashvillian, or a real man. Hot chicken won't make you anything except sick. The white bread alone will kill you, never mind the lard. You'll end up with a Monster Energy sticker on your dialysis machine.

Homesick for Seattle

PUBLISHED SEPTEMBER 29, 2015.

Hi King!

I moved to Nashville a couple years ago, and I LOVE IT. But every time I go back to my hometown (Seattle), I come back to Nashville feeling a little sad that it's not home—and moving back to the Pacific Northwest isn't an option right now, for a variety of reasons. Any tips on how to continue settling into a not-so-new city and get over the homesick blues that probably should've worn off by now?

—Suzy From Seattle

Before I get into this, I just wanted to let everyone know that the Advice King now listens exclusively to the Survivor album *Vital Signs*. Survivor had two singers. Did you know that? The first one, the guy who sang "Eye of the Tiger," wore a beret. I bet they kicked him out because he wore a beret. The second one, the guy who sings on *Vital Signs*, did not wear a beret, and is cuter than the beret guy. The beret guy, Dave Bickler, must still be proud of his beret, because his Wikipedia page says, "In addition to his wide vocal range, his street-wise image included a trademark beret,"* and you can edit your own Wikipedia page, so he would probably take that part off if he didn't still think berets were cool, which they aren't. The cuter guy who sings on *Vital Signs* is named Jimi Jamison—formerly of the bands Target and Cobra (true). He probably got the job by approaching the guitar player Jim "Spaghetti Fingers"** Peterik after a gig and saying, "First of all, smokin' set. You wanna

* Fun Fact: Berets looked "street-wise" in 1982, because the NYC subway patrol group The Guardian Angels wore them.

** I'm pretty sure I'm the only one who calls him this.

bump? Dude, you've got bodacious chops, but you'll never be truly huge with a singer named 'Dave Bickler.' He wears a fucking beret. One of the other guys wears shorts! You'll be playing 'Eye of the Tiger' at county fairs for the rest of your life. My name is Jimi Jameson. Sounds nice, right? I don't wear a beret, and I wear leather pants when I fucking JOG. And here, touch my hair. See? Take my card." (His card said, "JIMI JAMESON—Rock Vox.) Jimi's phone rang the next day.

Go back, Suzy. Nashville has enough people. I bet you miss the Space Needle. And grunge. Would you classify Survivor as a "proto-grunge" band? I do. Why can't you move back? The highways are running, planes are flying, U-Haul is renting. What gives? To properly answer this question, I need to know the "variety of reasons" you can't move. Since I don't know them, I am going to guess them: You opened a vintage clothing store in East Nashville. The store is called Hopalong Suzy's Va Va Voom Vintage. You figured you'd come to town and sell overpriced sundress/boot "combos" to all the sociopathic transplant trust-fund square dancers, then head back to Seattle with your ill-gotten gains. I bet you thought you'd be buying a fancy new umbrella with all that dough. Then I guess you planned on sucking down a REAL NORTHWEST BLAH BLAH BLAH WHATEVER double espresso and going to a grunge concert at the Space Needle. I hate to rain on your parade (although I bet you love rainy parades), Suzy, but *you're not the only person who thought of that.* Now you can't move until you've sold all your charming crap. Right?

Sorry Suzy, there's a sundress surplus. Say that five times fast.

Did you know that some Nashville vintage stores actually sell "combos" now, like fast-food-value-menu style? Like, I'll take a No. 1 with a large cowboy hat? Well, they do. I happen to know a famous singer whose name rhymes with Reven Wyler who had a last-minute music-style change and needed a rodeo belt buckle and some turquoise in a hurry. He got it from a DRIVE-THRU (!) vintage place in East Nashville en route to his red-hot gig at The Bluebird. It has pictures on the sign just like fast-food places, but Western shirts instead of hamburgers. He got a No. 5—"The Larry Gatlin" with a side of pinky rings. NOT ONION RINGS! PINKY RINGS!

I'm kidding around, Suzy! Welcome to Nashville! My real advice? Drink a lot. XO

Should I Use Elite Daily's Nashville Instagram Captions?

. . . .

PUBLISHED MAY 31, 2019.

Dear Advice King,

I just read an article about Nashville on a website called Elite Daily. It tells you what captions are good to use for your Nashville travel photos. I'm visiting Nashville soon, and I was wondering if you think it's a good idea to use those suggested captions for my Nashville Instagram posts.

—Lauren in Madison, Wisc.

Did you know that you said "Nashville" FOUR times in that stupid question, Lauren? I wish Nashville was called something different so people would stop saying it so much. I bet people wouldn't say "Satan's Crotch" or "Herpesville" over and over.

"Tina's celebrating her 40th in Herpesville! Save the date!"

Do you know the story about Greenland and Iceland? Supposedly Iceland was called "Iceland" as a trick so no one would want to move there—Greenland was the icy one. I don't know if that's true, but I think Nashville should try it. "Music City" is much too attractive-sounding. How about "Brown Recluse City"?

I don't feel bad for saying your question is stupid, because I am 100 percent sure that you are not a real person, Lauren. No real person would ever actually consider using Elite Daily's "Nashville Instagram caption suggestions." And if a real person *did* make the mistake of using any of Elite Daily's "Nashville Instagram caption suggestions," they would no longer qualify as a real person after doing that.

What the hell is "Elite Daily" anyway? I just read the "about" section on their website. It says that "Elite Daily" is part of the "Bustle Media Group." Bustle Media Group says it is "the largest premium publisher reaching millennial women." According to Bustle Media Group, millennial women turn to them for "impactful conversation." What is a premium publisher? And why does everybody say "impactful" five times a goddamn minute all of a sudden?

Here's a short play about the apocalypse called Modern Conversation:

MODERN CONVERSATION

MODERN DOPE NO. 1: Nashville.
MODERN DOPE NO. 2: Hot chicken.
MODERN DOPE NO. 3: Premium hot chicken.
MODERN DOPE NO. 1: Elite premium impactful hot chicken.
MODERN DOPE NO. 2: *Game of Thrones.*
MODERN DOPE NO. 3: Hot chicken Nashville *Game of Thrones* hot chicken. Celebrity.

Ocean boils, sky falls.

THE END

I never even HEARD the word "impactful" until 2018. After that, it seems like I heard it 250,000 times. Remember a couple years ago when nobody could stop saying, "putting a thumb on the scale"? Remember a couple weeks ago when Notre Dame burned down?

Anyway.

Let's talk about Elite Daily's premium impactful Instagram caption suggestions! The pitch (from their website):

> Throughout the week, you flip through your calendar and mark down your plans. You make a note for when you're going to a spin class with your best friend, or have a coffee date with your mom. You put cute waffle stickers on the weekend mornings you're going to brunch, and palm trees on the ones you're going on vacation. There's one sticker that really stands out amongst the rest, though, because it's a pair of cowboy boots. Let me take a wild guess: You're heading down South with your BFFs, and need some captions for visiting Nashville and following your wanderlust this summer.

First of all, WHO THE FUCK OVER THE AGE OF 13 PUTS STICKERS ON THINGS?!?! Certainly no one I would classify as "premium."

Here are Elite Daily's suggested Nashville photo captions. Seriously:

1. "Wanderlust and city dust."
2. "Nashville looks so good on you."
3. "It was love at first beer flight."
4. "When in doubt, go on a girls' trip."
5. "Live like a local."
6. "This is the most brew-tiful place I've ever been."
7. "Stay in your magic, babe."
8. "We're fueled by coffee and country music."
9. "Take time to do what makes your soul happy."
10. "This city is as sweet as a peach."
11. "Start each day with a grateful heart and a good itinerary."
12. "I followed my heart, and it led me to Nashville."
13. "More bouquets and cowboy boots, please."
14. "Keep on dreamin', even if it breaks your heart."—Eli Young Band, "Even If It Breaks Your Heart"
15. "Let your dreams stay big, your worries stay small." —Rascal Flatts, "My Wish"
16. "Funny how a melody sounds like a memory."—Eric Church, "Springsteen"

17. "Always stay humble and kind."—Tim McGraw, "Humble and Kind"
18. "Live a little, love a lot."—Kenny Chesney, "Live a Little"
19. "Cowboy take me away."—Dixie Chicks, "Cowboy Take Me Away"
20. "I believe in the beauty of Nashville."
21. "We owned the night."—Lady Antebellum, "We Owned the Night"
22. "With you, I'd dance in a storm in my best dress, fearless."—Taylor Swift, "Fearless"
23. "Life changes, and I wouldn't change it for the world."—Thomas Rhett, "Life Changes"
24. "She'll be here until she runs. Some just have to chase the sun."—Kenny Chesney, "Wild Child"
25. "Dear, Nashville. You're my absolute favorite."
26. "Peace, love, and the land of country music."
27. "You either love Nashville, or you're wrong."
28. "I'm in a Southern state of mind."
29. "Eat, drink, and celebrate everything in Nashville."

Here are my 29:

1. "I am drunk."
2. "I am drunk."
3. "I am living proof that American public schools are underfunded."
4. "Mural is big painting."
5. "I am drunk."
6. "I love stores."
7. "We are drunk."
8. "I was drunk."
9. "I'm a pony or something. I look like a pony. I'm drunk."
10. "We got drunk."
11. "Waiting in line is a big part of life."

12. "I am drunk."
13. "Taylor Swift is a celebrity."
14. "I am drunk."
15. "Nashville is made of drinks."
16. "Cowboy boot means drinking."
17. "She got drunk."
18. "I got drunk."
19. "I am drunk and in a line."
20. "I move to Nashville because drink."
21. "Random people got mad at us."
22. "Brunch is drunk."
23. "Day drunk also drunk."
24. "Why I like mural?"
25. "Drunk."
26. "We got drunk."
27. "Taylor Drunk."
28. "I throw up."
29. "Drunkville."

Impactful?

Leaving Las Vegas

. . . .

PUBLISHED APRIL 7, 2015.

Dear Advice King,

I moved from Nashville to Las Vegas about four years ago as a result of a cost-of-living-to-career-opportunity calculation. I'm making a decent living in Las Vegas, and it's very affordable to live here. Also, I met a great girl here. The problem is, I hate almost everything else about this town. I feel that this town is soulless, and I'm worried that I might get stuck here.

Should I try to convince my girlfriend that we should move back to Nashville, even though it would likely mean a significant pay decrease and increase in housing costs? Or should I just try to make the best of it here?

Thanks for the advice.

—Andrew in Las Vegas

Sure thing, Andrew! I must confess, though, that practical advice is not my strong suit. I base all my life decisions on what my spiritual adviser Mr. Morgan tells me. Mr. Morgan is my neighbor *and* he's a licensed parrot astrologer. My readings are free. All I have to do is buy Mr. Morgan his cigarettes and cook him steaks and rub his feet and drive him to the dog track. Mr. Morgan's also a "dome diviner," and he says he can tell from looking at my forehead that I was a roll-top desk in a past life.

Condo-fied Nashville isn't exactly soul central these days, but it's a regular Wattstax compared to the Gathering of the Juggalos that is Las Vegas. Las Vegas is *advertised* as the place to go if you want to behave badly. Considering that people in 2015 already have the manners of rabid ferrets, I can only imagine the horror when they decide to "loosen up." Living at ground zero for YOLO Yo-YoS™ has to take a serious psychological toll. And what if you want to have kids? Forty percent of children raised in Las Vegas grow up to be hit men, 30 percent run puppy mills, 22 percent are prop comedians, and 8 percent are roulette wheel greasers. Do you want to end up the father of a prop comedian?!

One last terrifying statistic: Sixty percent of Las Vegans have lost at least one limb to a card-shuffling machine. (To be fair, 14 percent of Nashvillians have "dobro legs"—it's like polio except with way more yodeling.)

A "cost-of-living-to-career-opportunity calculation"? Sounds pretty fucking soulless, Andrew. Follow your heart back to Tennessee™.

Should I Start a Food Truck?

. . . .

PUBLISHED APRIL 20, 2016.

Dear King,

Are food trucks just a passing fad? Me and my friend Eddie are considering starting one. Is it a good idea? Thanks!

—Stu, Nashville

Food trucks are on the way out, Stu. Why? Global fucking warming, that's why. No one's going to want to eat a $12 tofu taco in a parking lot next to a running truck when it's 100 degrees Celsius. Even without global warming, food trucks' popularity will eventually fade, as more and more people realize that they are simply trucks with food in them. None of this means that you and Eddie can't make some money in the next few years, before the shit goes down. Here's how:

Food trucks are a classic symptom of "Candyland Syndrome." Candyland Syndrome occurs when the distribution of wealth in a country is so lopsided that the economy ends up based entirely on rich people paying money to have whimsical experiences. Also called "The Hot Air Balloon Economy" or "The *Chitty Chitty Bang Bang* Model," this type of an economy is a real bummer for the low-wage workers providing the whimsy, so . . .

No. 1: Make Sure Your Prices Are High

The people who eat at these trucks are the same people who can pay $3,000 a month for a one-bedroom, so GOUGE 'EM. Don't use decimal points on the prices, though. In the 2016 Artisanal Fantasy Neighborhood prices are allowed to be high, but THERE ARE TO BE NO DECIMAL POINTS. A side of sorghum kale is "11." The Bolivian sea bass is "45." ("But Bolivia doesn't even *have* an ocean!" Believe me, it doesn't matter.) A scoop of rhubarb black bean ice cream is "14."

No. 2: Use Gimmicks

Regular people don't want gimmicks. Regular people are at home cleaning their guns and thinking about the "gimmicks" in their mortgage contract. Your clientele—Caucasian "day-drinkers" wearing Native-American headdresses—want every day to feel like another day in the Lollipop Forest, and they LOVE gimmicks. I think using a hearse for your "truck" would be a good idea. And sell something that begins with "H." Alliteration is whimsical as hell. Ham. Sell ham. "The Ham Hearse." Dress up like clowns. Rig one of those accordion boxing gloves under the hood and "check the oil." The crowd will love this.

"Let's get stoned and get ham from the hearse where that worker clown guy gets punched! Life is rad and easy!"

Say the ham has "fair trade sea salt" on it.

No. 3: The Medicine Show Angle

The dominant aesthetic in Candyland Syndrome-affected neighborhoods is "old-time carnival chic"—picture the tattooed lady eating "cotton pork" (like cotton candy, except pork). Old-time carnivals always had a medicine show. Rich people want to live forever. See what I'm getting at, Stu? Involve some kinda health bullshit. Put a scoop of probiotic powder on anything you sell for an extra "8."

Here is another thought: If you can cold-press juice, why can't you cold-press other stuff? I still think rich people would eat rocks or wood if you marketed them right. "Cold-pressed oak." "Pacific Northwest Pebble Salad." Sounds nice, right?

MENU

Hearse Ham with Fair Trade Sea Salt .... LARGE 21
LARGER 38

Teak Chips.. 11

Cotton Pork .... Market Price

BEVERAGES

Towel-Harvested Grass Dew.. 13

Granite Tea.. 9

CHAPTER 2

MUSIC

Should I Go to Woodstock 50?

PUBLISHED APRIL 3, 2019. Woodstock 50 was canceled, for reasons that will become obvious.

Dear Advice King,

Should I go to the 50th anniversary of Woodstock?

—Elise in Pontiac, Mich.

HAHAHAHAHAHAHAHA!

Sorry.

Finally, a festival for people who like Jay-Z and Hot Tuna. And there's going to be "glamping." Do you know what "glamping" is, Elise? It means glamorous camping. It costs extra. You'll feel like you never even left Starbucks. A tent is already set up for you, and the inside looks just like a trust-fund kid's studio apartment in Bushwick, Brooklyn. Nothing says "back to the garden" like an IKEA lamp.

At least in 1969 every socioeconomic class was stuck in the same fucking mud—not that very many classes were represented. The original Woodstock's audience was mostly middle-class and upper-middle-class white kids. It was never intended to be a free concert, and tickets were expensive.*

FUN FACT: I was at Woodstock '99.

It's true. I worked the whole festival, as a production assistant. I was in charge of running the videotapes from the cameras at the stages back to the "production truck." That's right, videotapes. I know all the kooky young millennial Hot Tuna and Country Joe and the Fish fans reading this are like, "What's a videotape?" It's a real thing, you crazy kids—look it up.

* $18 in advance, $24 at the gate—the equivalent of $120 and $160 today.

When I worked at Woodstock '99 I saw Michael Lang often. He wore khaki shorts and a polo shirt, and sat around on a golf cart. For those of you who don't know who Michael Lang is, he was one of the organizers of the first Woodstock, and he's been in charge of the brand ever since. If you've ever seen the Woodstock movie, he's the "hippie" wearing the leather vest with nothing under it, riding a motorcycle.

Well, at Woodstock '99, the "hippie" was backstage drinking Pellegrino while a sea of drunken, dehydrated murderers (aka Korn fans) stood on a disused military runway and screamed "show your tits" at Sheryl Crow (true).

In 1999 it was Sheryl Crow and Korn, in 2019 it's Imagine Dragons and John Sebastian. If anybody's taking the brown acid, IT'S THE BOOKER, AMIRITE?

While I'm sure that Woodstock 50—or whatever they're calling it—will be physically safer than Woodstock '99, there will be no way to avoid being irreparably harmed by one particular musical performance. James Hetfield's son Randy's Americana band? Paul McCartney's long-lost daughter Daphne's neo-soul outfit? A Janis Joplin hologram? SHA NA NA? Even worse: Greta Van Fleet.

Greta Van Fleet is the corpse of Woodstock, a corpse that has been beaten for so long that it has risen from the grave in the form of four bleating toadstools who call themselves a band. They're more like Jann Wenner's Muppets. I call them The Four Hobbyhorsemen of the Apocalypse™.

Greta Van Fleet is a group of Civil War reenactors—if the Civil War was Led Zeppelin™.

Greta Van Fleet, and other acts like them, are the horrifying product of a 50-year disinformation campaign waged by the baby-boomer generation. Those goddamn boomers had a good time during their youth. They also went to a fun concert (Woodstock). No harm done, right? Here comes the horrible part: For some reason this lousy generation decides that its youth (the 1960s) was the BEST AND MOST CONSEQUENTIAL YOUTH EVER, and that the good concert they went to just so happened to be—by a total coincidence—THE BEST AND MOST CONSEQUENTIAL CONCERT EVER.

Here comes the *really* bad part: The baby boomers ended up in charge of a relatively new medium called television. Through television, they fed subsequent generations a steady diet of nostalgia—and not nostalgia for the youth of these subsequent generations, but rather nostalgia for their own youth, the 1960s. Over and over. This weaponized nostalgia has been delivered so relentlessly and effectively that no one from later generations has been able to produce anything—artistic or otherwise (e.g., kids named Dylan and Cash)—that doesn't reflect some aspect of the baby-boomer generation's self-created, self-serving mythology. Boomers take these regurgitated references as proof that they were right—their generation must be the most important generation ever! If it wasn't, why would it still be on TV all the time?

Whew.

Don't go to Woodstock 50, Elise.

Should I Join the Mainstream Country Machine?

PUBLISHED SEPTEMBER 8, 2015. You'll have to imagine the photos—or come see me on my book tour and I'll give you the links. :) Also, this column is probably best described as Florida Georgia Line, uhhh, "fan fiction."

Dear Advice King,

I'm a working musician in Nashville. Some of my more successful friends in the music industry say that if I want a good gig—like with Florida Georgia Line or something—I need to go to one of those big megachurches to network. I'm still traveling in a van and sleeping on floors, and I don't know if that is appropriate for a 33-year-old man. I also detest megachurches. What am I to do?

—Playing for Pennies

I don't know what "Florida Georgia Line" is. Hold on while I google 'em . . . DEAR GOD.

These guys are musicians?! THESE guys? THIS guy?! What is that hairdo called? A "camel toe"? They look like pro wrestlers or magicians or Realtors-to-the-stars or the ghosts of people who died in ATV accidents.

I found an old promo picture of "Florida Georgia Line." It's from the early 2000s when they were performing in the Orlando area as a rap rock duo called "Dubble Trubble." A reggae-fied version of Sammy Hagar's "I Can't Drive 55" was their first "hit," peaking at No. 67 on Orlando's ZINC-FM local chart in 2004. More Florida Georgia Line trivia: The Country Music Association barred the band from making music for six months in 2012 after one of the members of their DJ squad—a man named "Barn Door B"—tested positive for anabolic steroids. The test was administered following a complaint from Luke Bryan that Mr. Door B seemed "extra strong" and "like, too strong," when the two were oil wrestling at country music executive Scott Borchetta's holiday party. The CMA now requires all "bro country" artists to be randomly tested for performance enhancing drugs.

Steroids? DJ squads? Isn't country supposed to be roots music? If these are the roots, the tree must be a neon dildo.

Speaking of neon dildos: Joel Osteen. I know he looks like a mentally ill dentist, but he's actually a megachurch pastor. He also wears his hair in a "camel toe." He is also "ripped." Does Mr. Osteen use the same stylist as that Florida Georgia Line guy? Perhaps he's getting his steroids from the same guy who supplied Barn Door B? That may be why your "friends" are telling you to go to megachurches! Something is afoot! I think Osteen and Florida Georgia Line are running a steroid smuggling operation. The drugs are transported in a Florida Georgia Line wardrobe case marked "WALLET CHAINS" and distributed through Osteen's network of drive-thru confessionals. The feds are getting too close for comfort, and you are meant to be the patsy, "Playing for Pennies."

I don't know which one of those guys is "Florida" and which one is "Georgia," but if you join that band, one day either Florida or Georgia (I'm pretty sure Florida is the one with the bob) will say, "Hey 'Playing for Pennies,' keep an eye on this box of wallet chains while we get the oil changed on the bus. We'll be right back, dude." That's when you'll hear the sirens.

It's a long way to the top if you wanna rock 'n' roll, "Playing for Pennies." Stay in the van and stay true to yourself. Steer clear of mega churches and men with really white teeth.

Am I too Old to Go to Bonnaroo?

PUBLISHED JUNE 4, 2019. "GRiZ," "AJR," and "NGHTMRE," are the names of actual artists that performed at Bonnaroo in 2019. U2 performed at Bonnaroo 2017. Barry is still in that tree.

Dear Advice King,

I am 40 years old. Should I go to Bonnaroo?

—Ken in Bowling Green, Ky.

I don't care what you do, Ken. But I don't think you're gonna like the lineup. Are you a big fan of "GRiZ"? Or "AJR"? Oh wait, you're probably going to see "NGHTMRE."

I just googled these fools. AJR looks like an undernourished Jonas Brother. One AJR guy (J?) wears the same winter hat in all their press photos. GRiZ is a go-go-dancing male computer programmer (some people insist on calling these people "DJs"). Your favorite band, NGHTMRE, is actually NOT a band—it's ANOTHER go-go-dancing male computer programmer. Why aren't there any female laptop go-go people? Is that one with the Mickey Mouse head a lady? What happened to Lady Sovereign?

I had high hopes for NGHTMRE—I thought if it wasn't a metal band it would at least be a doom rapper. Is there such a thing as a doom rapper? What kind of rapper was "Lil Peep"? Mumblecore? I thought mumblecore was the movies where those skinny white people talk all day. Is "Dogme 95" a rapper?

You can see why I won't be at Bonnaroo.

If you're not going for the music, you must be using Bonnaroo as a justification to do drugs. That's a great idea—on paper. Have you thought this through, Ken? Do you really want to be "tripping balls" at a Post Malone concert? Do you even know what a "Post Malone" is? Do you want to find out when it's already too late? Don't risk it. I think this Post Malone man's "music" was written by the CIA specifically to put elderly acid heads into mental wards (less liberals on the street). Have you ever seen the movie Midnight Express?

Maybe you're not planning on doing acid, or mushrooms—or even smoking weed. Maybe you actually want to hear some of today's top "artists." That doesn't solve your problem. You still have to deal with the KIDS, Ken. The fucking kids.

These kids WILL NOT be sober, my man, and the shit they are taking in 2019, well . . . let's just say you better make sure your tent is made of some thick-ass material. These fuckers take bath salts FOR BREAKFAST. Do you know what bath salts are, Kenny? GOOGLE IT. Also, have you ever wondered what's inside those goddamn backpacks young adults wear? Krokodil, that's what. Krokodil and Game Boys. Google "krokodil" if you're feeling feisty. DO NOT DO AN IMAGE SEARCH.

Do you have any idea what effect electronic music has on a teenager taking these types of things? Well, it doesn't make them any LESS dangerous, that's for fucking sure. My 42-year-old friend Barry spent the entirety of the 2017 Bonnaroo at the top of a tall tree, hiding from a roving "bath-salt gang." The U2 song "Where the Streets Have No Name" really brought out the worst in them—they were licking the sides of his tree and screaming "SALTS! SALTS!" Barry told me that he owed his life to Nintendo. "Those Game Boys were the only thing that seemed to calm them," he said.

Have fun!

Should I Go to a Bro-Country Bar?

PUBLISHED JANUARY 9, 2020.

Dear Advice King,

My wife and I are going to Nashville on vacation. We're thinking about hanging out in a bro-country bar. Would you recommend?

—Eli in St. Louis

What? Why? Do you need to get herpes in a hurry? Are you trying to see how sad you can get? Guess what I call Florida Georgia Line. Florida Georgia LINES. Get it? *SNIFF* Get it?

By the way, the last time I mentioned Florida Georgia Line in this column was in 2015, when I said that they looked like "the ghosts of people who died in ATV accidents."

FGL House* is *not* a good name for a bar. Sounds more like the name of a rehab facility—which is ironic, since YOU, my dear advice-seeker, are obviously in need of SOME kind of rehab (brain?). Healthy people do not want to go to these places.**

Do "Florida" or "Georgia" ever poke their heads into the ol' FGL House to babble incoherently about Oprah? Is Florida the guy who shot the bear in a cage? Or is that Georgia? Is it true that Florida had to be rushed to the hospital after a jalapeño-popper overdose?

Who is Luke Byram? I'm gonna google him. Oh my Lord God. He's a JC Penney model that does some kind of "fiddle rap" with Republican

* FGL stands for "Florida Georgia Line," which is the name of a "bro-country" band. "Bro-country" is a special type of country music that sucks.

** If you wanna have some fun, check out the customer reviews for these places. Here's an excerpt: "We stopped by during the day for drinks. It was not busy at all, and it was easy to get in and out. However, we paid $18 for one drink. In addition, I went to another bartender (because the one on the rooftop was so rude) and asked how much a double amaretto sour was. She said $10. The prices were inconsistent throughout the bar."

I only have one thing to say: DOUBLE AMARETTO SOUR?!?!

talking points for lyrics (i.e., self-sufficiency, objectifying women, heavy petting in trucks). And his name isn't Luke Byram. His name *is* Luke, but he's also named "Bryan." Luke AND Bryan, the Republican fiddle rapper. I think he's Christian, too. I wonder what happens at his bar—drunken hip-hop abstinence? I bet he lives on a golf course. He looks like one of those fiddle-Christian hip-hop golfers.

I'm just guessing, so settle down. I don't actually know anything about Christians or golf or Republican fiddle rap.

I know Jason Aldean looks like a duck hunter. I do know that. He's supposed to look like he "works as hard as he plays." He doesn't need any stinking health insurance. All he needs are guns and whiskey and ducks and his family.

Why are country musicians and Republicans OK with all their taxes going toward weapons instead of health care? And how come it isn't socialism to subsidize farmers? Oh well. I'm gonna keel over dirt-poor in a duck blind from undiagnosed high blood pressure while listening to corporate propaganda set to song by rich, healthy, Christian golfers. Just like Jesus did.

If dying of treatable diseases ain't country, I'll kiss your ass.

Do not go to those bars, Eli. All you and your wife are going to do in those bars is argue. Save money by getting drunk in your hotel room and arguing there.

Party Psychic Crofto the Magnificent™ predicts:

There will be a band in every one of those bars that looks like 5 Finger Death Punch. They will all be playing a nu-metal version of "Whiskey River." You are going to have 95 Bud Lights and decide that the bass player is flirting with your wife. You are going to get hit with a bass guitar, your pants are going to fall down, you are going to start crying, and you are going to get tased. These things will not necessarily happen in that order, but they will happen. You will wake up at 3 p.m. the next day with no memory and no money. Your stomach will contain a huge amount of discount cheese. You will find this out when you barf. Your wife left Nashville on a bus in the middle of the night. With the bass player. You were right—they were flirting. When you look at your phone you will have 410 new messages from your mother.

Sleazy Record Execs

. . . .

PUBLISHED MARCH 31, 2015.

Dear Advice King,

My girlfriend has made plans for us to go out with her boss and his wife for dinner. She works for a sleazy record company exec with an ego the size of Mars. How do I make it through an evening of his insufferable bullshit without saying something that could put my girl's job in jeopardy?

Thanks,

—No Filter

There are still sleazy record company execs? What are they selling? They certainly aren't selling records. The No. 1 record on the *Billboard* charts this week sold 88 copies. They must be selling all their leather couches and glass-top coffee tables and J. Geils Band gold records on Craigslist.

The only people who still pay for music are people who don't know how to steal it with computers. Did you know that? Did you ever wonder why modern pop music sounds like it could only be appreciated by a child? That is because it is meant for children. Children don't know how to use computers to steal music. Ed Sheeran is a Muppet. Adam Levine is a Muppet with herpes. Taylor Swift is a birthday pony.

You know who else can't steal music? People with no money. They don't have computers. It is no coincidence that country music is the only musical genre that still sells physical copies—today's country music panders to the poor. The lyrics are a mix of right-wing talking points and celebrations of escapist behavior—drinking, drug-taking, shooting guns and casual sex.

The right-wing bullshit tells them that being poor is noble and fun: "Some folks sit and wait on the government check / Some of us have the sun beatin' down on our neck" —Billy Currington's "Lil' Ol' Lonesome Dixie Town"; and "Ain't no line around the corner, no security / No velvet rope, no dress code, everybody's VIP / You can wear your hat, dance in your bare feet / No credit card, no roll of cash, just BYOB" —Dierks Bentley's "Back Porch." And the party instructions sell alcohol and keep the for-profit jail industrial complex thriving: "DRINK IN OR NEAR YOUR TRUCK, SON" —Every Country Song on the Radio. Blake Shelton's "Boys 'Round Here" even gives a not-so-sly and super-awful shout-out to the meth crowd: "Yeah, the girls 'round here, they all deserve a whistle / Shakin' that sugar, sweet as Dixie crystal." You can try to tell me that's just about sugar, but it's fucking not.

Glorifying dysfunction helps keep people dysfunctional. The less functional the public is, the more likely they are to buy CDs.

"Hey Randy, pick up the new Florida Georgia Line CD when you're out. They have an awesome new song called 'Natural Light, Hot Cheetos and Jesus.' And get some Natural Light and Hot Cheetos, too. And pregnancy tests. And come right back because I need the car to go to court."

"Man, my friend Onion said we could get that for free on a torrent."

"Your friend Onion bought a Taurus?"

"Do what now?"

I *am* a musician and would obviously prefer for people to pay for music, but trying to keep the poor poor—and drunk—is not the right way to do it. Act like adults, music biz people, and figure out a new model for selling *art*, because right now you're selling advertising.

Oh yeah, ADVICE. OK Mr. "No Filter" Man, can you *really* not control yourself? Be polite for your girlfriend's sake. Be polite for your girlfriend's money's sake! If it helps, remember that this guy's big ego is just how he compensates for the self-hatred that comes from working in the fading, artless industry I described above.

The Grammys

PUBLISHED FEB 1, 2018. Almost all of this column is bullshit, obviously, BUT during the 2018 Grammys "the head of the Grammys" Neil Portnow actually said, essentially, what I said he said. As a result, Portnow was forced to "step down" from his position. FUN FACT: This is one of my favorite columns.

Dear Advice King,

I missed the Grammys. Can you give me a recap?

—Alex in Austin, Texas

I didn't watch it either—and this does NOT qualify as an "advice" question—but I think recapping a show I didn't see sounds like fun!

A note about the Grammys before I begin. The same mega-conglomerates that own the TV network that broadcasts the show also own the record companies that own the "artists" who are getting the "awards." Winning a Grammy is a lot like the Big Mac winning Sandwich of the Year at the McDonaldys. If you like Big Macs, you'll love the Grammys™.

ADVICE KING 2018 GRAMMY RECAP WITHOUT SEEING THE SHOW

The show was supposed to be hosted by a hologram of deceased record executive Ahmet Ertegun. In the opening number, Ertegun's ghost came out in an old-school breakdance tracksuit shooting musical notes out of his fingers. Everyone was really excited, but there was a malfunction and the hologram started saying John F. Kennedy speeches from the Cuban Missile Crisis and then its head disappeared so they had to unplug it.

The Grammy people may be a lot of things, but they're not dumb. They know holograms can be unreliable, and a James Corden was backstage in a box ready to go. Once the Corden was inflated, the show began.*

FULL DISCLOSURE: I know a little about what happened on the show from reading the news.

After the Corden did a karaoke version of Jewel's "Who Will Save Your Soul" with Neil deGrasse Tyson and David Duchovny in a Prius that said Bed Bath and Beyond on it, Bono from U2 rode out on a horse that said Samsung on it to give the award for Best Country Artist.

The nominees for Best Country Artist were Sting, Bono and hologram Stevie Ray Vaughan. Hologram Stevie Ray Vaughan won for "The Sky Is Crying"—which came out in 1991. Stevie was able to thank his mom, Uber, Amazon and Gulden's Mustard before his head disappeared.

Best New Artist was next. The nominees were Led Zeppelin and Neil deGrasse Tyson. Neil deGrasse Tyson won. I thought it was weird that there were only two nominees. Aren't there usually more than that?

Sting got a Lifetime Achievement Award for still having hair in the front.

Bono came back out and did a card trick.

The man in charge of the Grammys came out and said that no girls were nominated this year because they didn't do any good music.

Bono shot a toy gun and a flag came out of it. The flag said #GIRLPOWER.

Sting duetted with Shaggy on his 1987 song "Englishman in New York." By the way, THIS IS THE FAKEST SOUNDING THING IN THIS WHOLE FAKE RECAP AND IT'S FUCKING REAL.

According to the NME, Shaggy and Sting have recorded an "island-themed record" that "reflects their mutual love of Jamaica." God help us.

Some other stuff happened that I don't feel like describing, and

. . . .

* That same night, another James Corden was hosting a silent auction in the Sultan of Brunei's sex dungeon. The other James Corden was in storage. There are three "James Cordens."

then it was time for the most important award of the night—Album of the Year. The nominees were Chipotle, Goldman Sachs, the Wendy's dollar menu, David Duchovny and that U2 record with "It's a Beautiful Day" on it.

Elon Musk handed the envelope to Jann Wenner who handed it to Lorne Michaels and he handed it to Dr. Phil who handed it to Tom Brady. Ryan Seacrest took the envelope from Brady and tore it open. Goldman Sachs won again, and I kicked the TV into the fireplace.

Advice? DON'T WATCH THE GRAMMYS.

How Do I Get Famous?

. . . .

PUBLISHED MAY 4, 2016.

Dear Advice King,

How do you get famous?

—Sue in Temple, Texas

Famous? In Temple, Texas? Grow a huge gourd.

I only chose this question because I wanted to write "Grow a huge gourd" in a column. It's a lot of fun to write that. I bet I could sell T-shirts that say "Grow a huge gourd." It would be written in all caps, with a period.

GROW A HUGE GOURD.

I just realized I am stealing this design from "GO HIKE THE CANYON" T-shirts, but "GROW A HUGE GOURD" is better because it will make people feel like they're being "sustainable" and "supporting" vegetables, whatever that means. Americana people would DEFINITELY buy them. Put a tractor graphic on that thing and *CHA-CHING*. Make it out of some fabric that allegedly has coconuts in it. Kacey Musgraves would wear one.

"Kacey Musgraves." Look at that name for a while. I bet "Kacey" and her publicist came up with that name in four hours using a dry-erase board.

REJECTED KACEY MUSGRAVES NAMES:

Randi Mustrage
Musky Ribcage
Sase Civilwargraves*
Sevargsum Yesak**

How's it going, Sue? Are you famous yet? I can't think of a single famous person named Sue, so you must not be. Maybe you took out the ol' dry-erase board and you're famous under a different name. Maybe you call yourself "Gazebo Meringue" ("Gaz" for short), you just finished filming *Batman vs. Superman vs. Gallagher* (Seth Rogen plays Batman), and you were at the Met Gala last night wearing a dress made out of enough fabric to clothe every orphan in Budapest.

If I get Kacey Musgraves and "Gov't Mule" and The Rusty Mountain Rumblers to wear my GROW A HUGE GOURD T-shirts at Farm Aid and I start an Instagram and post pictures of different scarecrows all around America wearing them, I bet I could get famous. Do you know who "Famous Amos" is, Sue? He made cookies. He got famous by being the mascot for his product, like Chef Boyardee or Steve Jobs. If these GROW A HUGE GOURD shirts take off, I bet I'll end up in the VIP tent at the Stagecoach Festival doing coke with Chris Robinson and Mr. Clean.

I wouldn't really need to travel around and find scarecrows, either. I could shoot the whole "Scarecrows Across America" campaign in

. . . .

* "Sase" is pronounced "SAY-zee." It was a popular girls' name in the 1960s and '70s, adapted from the acronym for "self-addressed stamped envelope."

** Kacey Musgraves backward. They decided it sounded too "Norwegian Black Metal."

a studio with a green screen. I could hire some stylists to make the 'crows. I'll crowdfund the whole fucking thing by saying it's all about "sustainability" and "vegetables."

OK, Sue, there ya go. If you can't get famous after a step-by-step tutorial like that, I'm afraid you probably don't have what it takes to make it in show business.

I'll throw you a few free T-shirt ideas because I am a nice guy:

"GAME OF BONES"—A play on the name of the popular television show *Game of Thrones*. There is a picture of a dog sitting on a throne made of bones on the shirt.

"THE PLAYING DEAD"—Text written in the style of popular television show "The Walking Dead." Picture of dogs playing dead on shirt.

"MAD DOGS"—Dogs dressed like 1960s advertising executives.

"NAMASTE" - Must be written in comic sans font.

How Should I Spend My 40th Birthday?

PUBLISHED FEBRUARY 8, 2017.

Dear Advice King,

How should I spend my 40th birthday?

—Justin in Indianapolis

I wonder what the lead singer of Survivor, Jimi Jamison, did for his 40th birthday. The *second* lead singer of Survivor, I should say. The first lead singer of Survivor was Dave Bickler. Dave Bickler was fired from Survivor in 1984, when he was 31 years old, because he had "vocal fold nodules." He should have been fired way before that, in my opinion, because he wore a beret.

Jimi Jamison, the second lead singer of Survivor, turned 40 in 1991. At the time, Survivor was on indefinite hiatus. Did Jimi Jamison let that stop him? No fucking way. He started "Jimi Jamison's Survivor" and successfully toured the world. I bet Jimi Jamison spent his 40th birthday on the phone with French concert promoters talking about fog machines.

I know what you're thinking. You're thinking, "What is all this shit? I just wanna know if I should go to the craft beer place and THEN the craft cocktail place, or the other way around!"* I hear you, buddy. I got drunk on all my birthdays from 1984 until 2011. I had a birthday tradition where every year, at the end of the night, after the cops got me to come in off the porch where I had been loudly telling the neighbors about the Bilderberg Group, I would "fall asleep" in the backyard holding a lot of cheese.

I am challenging you to be a better person, Justin. Do you think you're at the mountaintop? Is it all downhill from here? Here's how I see it: It takes 40 years to reach spiritual BASE CAMP™. You are now at a STARTING POINT™. If you get your shit together you might have a shot at THE SUMMIT™.

THE SUMMIT™ is a revolutionary personal power webinar created by me and Darnel—a guy who works at the gym I go to. It's revolutionary for a bunch of reasons, but one *big* reason is because it's the first webinar ever that is NOT on the web—it's on DVD!

BASE CAMP™ is the 20-DVD starter set. After you have completed BASE CAMP™ you move to STARTING POINT™ (50 DVDs) and finally, THE SUMMIT™ (100 DVDs). Each DVD is filmed with the latest HD (heavy duty) technology, and everyone who buys BASE CAMP™ gets an HQ (high quality) visor. All DVDs at all levels are $20 and are six hours long. The background music is by me and Darnel's funk band "mIND oVER mATTER." All purchases include download codes for the latest "mIND oVER mATTER" release, "THE S.U.M.M.I.T.," and automatically register you for their mailing list.

. . . .

* Beer then liquor, never sicker. Liquor then beer, you are still pretty fucking sick. Don't drink schnapps, you'll get caught in traps.

I forgot to mention that "SUMMIT" is a badass acronym: "S.T.A.R. ULTRA MEGA MAXIMUM TRUTH." The "S" in the SUMMIT acronym has its own acronym: "START TALKIN' AND ROCKIN'." So, from the top, it's "START TALKIN' AND ROCKIN' ULTRA MEGA MAXIMUM TRUTH." The only way to find out how to do that—and to find out the SECRET acronyms for the words "THE" "MEGA," and "TRUTH"—is to buy all 170 DVDs and start THE CLIMB™.

OK, now you're like, "I wanna get those DVDs, but why did you talk so much about Survivor at the beginning?"

I'll tell you why, Justin. Because Jimi Jamison was 40 years old when he started "Jimi Jamison's Survivor."* He made his move, now it's time for you to make yours.

Cancel those dinner reservations and clean your DVD player. See you at THE SUMMIT™.

HAPPY BIRTHDAY!!!

Quitting Your Band or Living the Dream

. . . .

PUBLISHED APRIL 14, 2015.

Dear Advice King,

I'm at a crossroads. I moved to Nashville to study and play music, and I've been in a band for five years. I like playing in this band a lot, but we haven't had a whole lot of success, and I'm stuck. Should I quit the band, focus on my day job and stop with the pipe dreams of being a rock star? Or should I quit the day job and give it a real shot—more touring, more focus on recording, et cetera.

—Brent in Bordeaux

. . . .

* I also listen to Survivor when I write these.

When you say you're at a crossroads, you probably mean Five Points, that legendary East Nashville intersection where you can trade your soul for an overpriced ice cream cone. Also, I heard the devil (Ryan Seacrest) stopped accepting musicians' souls—there's no money in it. The last soul he accepted was from the singer of Puddle of Mudd in 1999.

Brent, huh? That's not a very rockin' name. I bet there are three guys named Brent in that band "fun." You like that band, Brent? I sure hope not. You don't happen to have a snappy little haircut and a snappy little shirt that's all snapped-up and snappy little rolled-up trousers and shiny brown shoes, do you? Please focus on your day job if that's the case. There are enough emasculated dandies making "music" already.

You know what else there are enough of? Slack-jawed, "psychedelic" garage bands. "Psychedelic" used to describe a particular style of music: Pink Floyd, The 13th Floor Elevators, Spiritualized, The Flaming Lips. Now "psychedelic" means your songs have anemic melodies and the vocals are fuzzy so you can't hear the lousy lyrics. And you wear a flat-brim baseball hat with squiggly neon things on it. It's no wonder these bands release 28 albums a year and still don't make an impression—quantity is no substitute for quality. Five mediocre songs don't equal one good one. If it worked that way, Greg Kihn would be in the Rock and Roll Hall of Fame.

Put some time into your lyrics, kids. There are a lot of cute boys and girls playing three chords in this world (Three-Chord Cuties™), but the expression is "three chords and the truth," not "three chords and a baseball hat with squiggly things on it." Either today's bands are treating lyrics as an afterthought, or they simply haven't had enough life experience to write them. Don't put the microphone cart before the have-something-to-say horse, fools.

I've been playing music for almost 20 years, Brent, so let me tell you how it works: You definitely won't make any money, you will develop a drinking problem, and your girlfriend will call you childish at some point in every argument.* If you can quit, you should. If you MUST play—and all the best must—try your best to buck the trends.

. . . .

* You will not have a good comeback.

What Kind of Music Video Should I Make?

PUBLISHED SEPTEMBER 14, 2017.

Dear Advice King,

I'm in a band, and we're making our first video! What kind of video do you think we should make? Thanks!

—Teri in Austin

I'm listening to Survivor's *Vital Signs* again, Teri. "Broken Promises" is playing right now:

We had dreams, visions and plans
Into the night, out of our hands
Letting our passion fulfill our demands
I remember those songs on the radio
The jasmine, the wind in your hair

Is it just me, or are rock-band lead singers 1,000 times more sensitive to jasmine than regular people? I couldn't identify the odor of jasmine if I was standing in the middle of a 10-foot-high field of the stuff. I would probably guess basil.

If song lyrics are a reliable indicator—and I think they are—the world, and girls especially, reeked of jasmine in the 1970s and '80s.

What does "Letting our passion fulfill our demands" mean? Obviously "passion" means intercourse—but what were the "demands"? I guess it means they both "demanded" intercourse? Sheesh. Doesn't sound very romantic. "Jasmine and Demands" is a great name for a power ballad!

"Jasmine and Demands"

VERSE:
My heart won't ever mend
I thought you were my friend
With a helping hand to lend
This road has no end
And there are flowers in the jug
CHORUS:
Jasmine (check!), demands (check!)
Your love is a homer to the upper deck
And I miss you baby, I miss your jasmine and demands

It only took me six hours to write that song, if you can believe it—and you can have it! Public domain. I'm not kidding. Match that poetry up to some music and make it rain! You're welcome, rockers.

Sorry, Teri, I got way off track. It happens a lot when I listen to Vital Signs.

OK, videos. Whatever you do, don't make a video like the one Survivor made for "I Can't Hold Back" off their album *Vital Signs*. Have you ever heard of that record, Teri? It's pretty good. Anyway, in the video, some normal woman who works in a bookstore turns into a sex maniac with giant hair when she hears the Survivor song "I Can't Hold Back." Like, she's acting normal and wearing glasses and working, and then "I Can't Hold Back" starts playing and there's an explosion and all of a sudden she's not at work and she's horny as hell and she has no glasses (horny AND blind!), dancing around in Spandex and spike heels at a Survivor concert. The male viewer is supposed to be like, "If I play my pal Nancy 'I Can't Hold Back' then she'll finally let me out of the 'friend zone'!" I guess the female viewer is supposed to be like, "Never listen to Survivor because you'll lose your job."

At the end of the "I Can't Hold Back" video, you find out the whole thing was a daydream that Survivor's singer—and ACTUAL big-haired sex maniac—Jimi Jamison was having while he was in the bookstore staring at this lady like a psychopath. In the pop culture of the '80s and '70s and '60s and '50s and '40s and '30s and '20s—and every other time in recorded history—male sex psychopaths were presented as charming rascals for some reason. I think I know the reason, but I have to finish this column TODAY.

Since you live in Austin, I'm going to go out on an extremely solid limb and say you're in an "Americana" band, Teri. Put on your best gingham 'n' spurs and have your manager Josh "film" you (on his iPad) walking around a part of town that has a lot of murals in it. Fake laugh a lot and knock off each other's cowboy hats, snap each other's suspenders, etc. Then put it in slow motion. At the end of the video have a barista write your band's name on top of a latte.*

Should I Get a Tattoo?

. . . .

PUBLISHED JUNE 16, 2015.

Dear Advice King,

Should I get a tattoo? All my friends have them, but I can't think of anything to get.

—Tony

I'm listening to Journey's *Greatest Hits* as I answer this, Tony.** Seems appropriate. "Only the Young Can Say."

. . . .

* "Gingham 'N' Spurs" would look great on top of a latte. Public domain!

** Just thought I'd let y'all know that when that Journey album ended, YouTube slid me directly into Air Supply's *Greatest Hits*, and I never looked back. I think I am listening to Air Supply B-sides right now. I'm probably the first non-German person ever to do so.

Only the young can say
They're free to fly away
Sharing the same desire
Burnin' like wildfire

Good stuff. Rock 'n' roll lyrics are always a safe bet for a tattoo idea. I have a bunch of Grateful Dead quotes on my butt cheeks. Maybe you should get "Only the Young Can Say" on your foot. In Sanskrit! And then someday an Indian person can tell you it actually says "FOURTH FLOOR: LINGERIE, MEN'S HATS."

Shit! I'm showing my age! You don't want to get a tattoo of a Journey quote. What was I thinking? You would want a quote from a current band, like Blink 182. Get "All the Small Things!" on your toes. One word on each toe, and an exclamation point on the last toe. Words are best on feet and necks. Arms are for portraits: Marilyn Monroe, Jesus Christ, George Jefferson, etc.

A nice back piece would be a food truck, but instead of a pita full of aioli or whatever, the guy inside is holding out a Yin Yang symbol wrapped in wax paper. Oooh! "Gluten-Free Pimp" in comic sans would be great for your neck!

Do you know why I'm listening to Journey, Tony? Because the first time I saw tattoos was at 1980s rock concerts I attended. Back then, tattoos were mainly popular among the working class. Rich people snickered at the "kind of people" who would be "stupid enough" to get a tattoo. "Don't they know they'll eventually get tired of it?! *So* dumb, those people." I liked those tattoos. They came from the heart. A girlfriend or boyfriend's name, a unicorn, a rose, an electric guitar, the Tasmanian Devil holding a mug of beer.

Like they do with every culture, rich white people finally got around to appropriating tattoo culture, and as usual, they took all the fucking fun out of it. They either take their tattoos more SERIOUSLY to show that they are smarter than poor people—pretentious quotes, esoteric images—or they treat them as a trendy fashion accessory. "A tattoo sleeve would look great with this blouse!" The thing I like about this particular fashion accessory is that these rich fools are stuck with these metaphorical mock turtlenecks for life. You can take off a choker, but you can't take off that tattoo of a choker, Chelsea.

Another thing to consider, Tony: I don't really have Grateful Dead quotes on my butt cheeks, but I very easily could. When you are young, you think you know everything. I was pretty convinced I liked the Grateful Dead for about three months in 1986. Unfortunately, those three months happened to include the day I submitted my quotes for my high school yearbook. It was my senior year, I was 18, and this was my big chance to let the world know my deepest thoughts. Here's what I put:

"Then God way up in heaven, for whatever it was worth, thought he'd have big ol' party, thought he'd call it planet earth." —The Grateful Dead

"There's a fine line between relaxation and irresponsibility."

The first quote could not represent my worldview less, and that second thing is something I made up that I thought was really smart. Imagine if any of that idiocy was tattooed on me! The horror!

The only tattoo I seriously considered getting as a youngster was the Pabst Blue Ribbon logo, and I am now a recovered alcoholic. Are you picking up what I'm laying down, friend? Comprende? Capiche?

My advice to you is to have fun! Get a tattoo if you want one! Don't get it on your neck! Be careful what you choose!

Are My Kanye-Hating Friends Racist?

PUBLISHED FEBRUARY 17, 2015.

Dear Advice King,

Did you watch the Grammys? They sure managed to bring out the worst in the Internet! What amazed me was the virulent justifications that

some folks used to negate the artistry of some who appeared. It's almost as if people have one set of standards for judging art made by aging white dudes and another set of standards for everyone else. How do I explain to my friends that people making music outside of the Anglo-American-heterosexual-male vernacular can still be considered artists? Like, without calling them racists and sexists and shit, even though they probably are.

—Yeezus of Suburbia

I did not watch the Grammys, because I am a grown-ass man, but I heard Clive Davis named Beck employee of the month. I went back and watched Kanye West's performance. Not his best. Sounded like an improvised Seals and Crofts song. I am a fan of both Beck and Kanye, and I like Beck's new record a lot. However, Beck was at the height of his fame in 1996 and it is 2015, so him winning is like if Engelbert Humperdinck won Album of the Year in 1996. Alanis Morissette's *Jagged Little Pill* won Album of the Year in 1996. Coincidentally, that album was inspired by her relationship with . . . Engelbert Humperdinck!

Beck means as much to a 20-year-old today as Three Dog Night meant to me in 1989. I was listening to Public Enemy in 1989. Remember when Three Dog Night and Public Enemy toured together? That was weird. The "Three Dog Night of the Living Baseheads" tour of 1992—Flavor Flav yelling "Yeaahhhhh boyeeeeee" during "Old Fashioned Love Song," Chuck Negron burning the American flag as part of the "Welcome to the Terrordome" / "Joy to the World" finale. But I digress.

Kanye West has been pissing off racists for a while now. Remember "George Bush doesn't care about black people"? That RULED. I wish more artists did shit like that. Corporations control almost every broadcast microphone in America, and artists who use their access to yell into these microphones should be encouraged, not torn down. The last thing this uptight post-9/11 world needs is more conformity. Sometimes Kanye is annoying and sometimes Kanye is amazing, but aren't both of those better than being Sam Smith?

HISTORICAL CONTEXT FOR WHITE PEOPLE WHO THINK KANYE SHOULD "HAVE BETTER MANNERS": The first Grammy ceremony was held at the Sturgis Pretzel House in Letitz, Pa., in 1868. "Taps" beat out "The Star-Spangled Banner" and "The Man on the Flying Trapeze" for Song of the Year, and all the other categories had to do with agriculture. George Leybourne (writer of "Flying Trapeze") approached the stage during Captain John C. Tidball's acceptance speech (Tidball received the award on behalf of the song's author, Brigadier General Daniel Butterfield, who was recording "Taps: Excursions" in Miami) and said something along the lines of, "I'M GOING TO LET YOU FINISH." Tidball slapped Leybourne with some gloves, they dueled at dawn, and Leybourne never played the piano properly again.

That last paragraph is complete bullshit. But if that *had* happened, everyone involved would have been white. You know why? Because black people didn't get fucking awards. For anything. If you don't know history, then you might really be confused by Kanye West's behavior. Kanye wants to be recognized as a great artist. He believes he has to be 10 times as talented as a white man, and 10 times as loud about that talent, in order to avoid being overlooked. This belief is supported by the facts. Black musicians have been purposely denied proper compensation and credit for their work since the beginning of the entertainment industry. In vaudeville days, black singers and players were called "entertainers" and "comedians"—to be considered a "musician" or an "artist," you had to be white. With the advent of recording came "race records," crooked contracts and stolen royalties. Kanye wants to make sure that he—and other black artists, like Beyonce—get their due. He has every reason to suspect that they won't.

This Grammy ceremony was for the year 2014, the year of Michael Brown and Eric Garner. There are no black actors or directors nominated for Academy Awards. Beyonce loses Album of the Year to a white man whose heyday was two decades ago. Kanye West gets upset and expresses himself nonviolently WITH A SMILE ON HIS FACE. White people tell him to "behave." Fuck that. They *are* racist, and you should tell them so.

The Merits of Collecting Vinyl

. . . .

PUBLISHED APRIL 21, 2015.

Sir King of Advice,

My parents always said I should put my money in CDs. I followed their advice for most of the '90s, but now I think vinyl is a better investment? I really want to be able to leave my kids some sort of inheritance. At the moment, it consists of about 1,300 albums and 45s. There are so many great used record stores here in Nashville, but I'm wondering if I should diversify my assets?

Much thanks!

—The Dude @TheDailyVinyl

I hope you are kidding. Your parents told you to put your money in what?! How much of your money? All of your money? What do you have in your "portfolio"? The Offspring? Paula Cole? Your kids must think you are crazy. "Dad keeps talking about how someday we're going to get his copy of *Blood Sugar Sex Magic* in the original jewel case. I think maybe we should put him in a home."

"Jewel case." HAHAHAHAHAHAHAHAHAHA.

Vinyl is definitely a better investment, but it's not going to put your kids' kids through college or anything—unless you have 1,300 copies of The Beatles' *Yesterday and Today* "Butcher" covers. Just because you have a vinyl record and it's "old" doesn't mean it's worth much. Enough Boz Scaggs records were produced to fill six Grand Canyons. Eighty percent of building materials used in the United States today contain part of a Boz Scaggs LP.

I saw a copy of Michael Jackson's *Thriller* at a yard sale marked "RARE—$20." There are a lot of words one can use to describe a vinyl copy of Michael Jackson's *Thriller*, but "rare" is not one of them—there are, quite literally, millions of them. That record is about as hard to find as a lying politician, or a stand-up comedian wearing a zip-up sweatshirt. Just because something is old doesn't mean it's rare. If there were as many Chippendale sideboards out there as there are *Thriller* LPs, that little handsome guy from *Antiques Roadshow* would be out of work. I just found a copy of *Thriller* on eBay for 99 cents.

Don't get me wrong, I'm not putting down vinyl. I love listening to music, and I *especially* love listening to music on a vinyl record. I love it because it has liner notes and big pictures to look at and it sounds great. I love it because one time the John Denver record *Back Home Again* fell out of my van and I ran over it and it still played fine.* I love it because there are two sides. You listen to one side, and then you listen to the other side, and then you can pick your favorite side and listen to that one again. Then you can talk to your friend about what side they like, and the two of you can make lists of "perfect album sides" and request them from radio stations. (Records are like sandwiches, they're better when cut in half.)

I love vinyl records because they used to come with a poster sometimes, or a fan-club sign-up sheet, or a roach clip. The Ozark Mountain Daredevils wallet that came with *Men from Earth* is in my back pocket right now. Brian Wilson wanted to include a gift certificate for a live alpaca in every copy of *Pet Sounds*. Capitol said no because of the potential liability from the spitting.

There *are* other things to invest in besides music. You know that, right? There isn't a single used record store on the *Forbes* 500. If your 1,300 vinyl records are nothing but Moby Grape test pressings and Beach Boys albums that came with real animals, your kids will be rich. If you have 1,300 copies of the Steve Miller Band's *Greatest Hits*, well, so does everybody.

Fuck the money, Dude. The music you love—on CD or vinyl—will be a wonderful thing for your children to inherit.

. . . .

* If you ran two copies of Vaughn Meader's *The First Family* through the Large Hadron Collider I bet afterward they'd both still play.

Speed Songwriting

PUBLISHED OCTOBER 7, 2015.

Dear King,

I've been writing songs for a while. I'll write one or two good ones a year when the inspiration strikes, but I have trouble finishing them. Recently I discovered a "speed songwriting" course that claims to help you finish more songs with more commercial value. Do you think if I take this course I'll be able to get a publishing deal?

—Roy in Dickson

Hmmm. I poked around the ol' Internet, and it seems the world's preeminent speed songwriter is a guy named Graham English. His website says he is a "funky pop/rock songwriter and jazz-trained keyboard player. "Funky pop/rock" being played by a jazz-trained keyboardist? Just reading about it makes my skin crawl. He also says people who "can't even write grocery lists" can write 365 songs a year. He doesn't mention anything about who he thinks would like to hear those songs. Jack Johnson fans, maybe?

JACK JOHNSON'S GROCERY LIST:

BRONZER
VIAGRA
COCONUT WATER

Graham English says if you join his email list he'll send you "some funky vibes." Gross. I'm sure those "funky vibes" (I can't believe I had to write "funky vibes" twice. Three times!) could be better described as "relentless spam." I still get "funky vibes" (four) like 20 times a week from that storytelling outfit The Moth because I made the mistake of signing their mailing list in the year 2000. I figured they'd go out of business at some point.

Graham English claims to have "shared the stage with rock legends Cheap Trick and jazz legends like Grover Washington Jr. and James Moody." I guarantee you he was a roadie. I also find it extremely suspicious that Mr. English does not seem to have written any notable songs—or *any* songs, for that matter. The only video on YouTube of English shows JUST HIS HANDS playing "Christmas Time Is Here" on a keyboard. At the time of this writing, it has 2,901 views. FYI, "Christmas Time Is Here" is an instrumental number written by Vince Guaraldi.

Here's the good news, Roy: *I'm* a famous songwriter. I wrote America's unofficial national anthem "Dickerson Pike." Don't give your money to some guy who's afraid to show his face on YouTube—give it to me! I promise not to send you any "funky vibes" (five). I will send you a 90-minute audio cassette called *Money Sings*. It costs $199.99. That may seem like a lot, but how much would you pay to have a 90-minute conversation with Francis Scott Key? Ten million dollars? This tape is the same thing, except you save like 9 million dollars. Here is a little taste of what you'll get:

10 WORDS THAT HAVE TO BE IN A ROCK SONG IF YOU WANT IT TO CHART

1. ROCK
2. NIGHT
3. HOT
4. STREET
5. LOVIN'
6. RIDIN'
7. STREET
8. STREET
9. CITY
10. CAR

Order now!

CHAPTER 3

SERIOUS SHIT

What about Guns?

PUBLISHED 6/28/2016.

Dear Advice King,

What kind of guns should I get, and how many?

—Pete in Nashville

Hi Pete! Great question! It depends on what kind of damage you want to do to your brother-in-law. If you really want him dead, get an AR-15. If you just want to maim him, get a .22-caliber pistol. I know what you're thinking. You're thinking, "I'm not going to use my guns to shoot my brother-in-law! I like Gary! I'm going to use my guns to shoot home invaders and terrorists!" That's what everybody thinks when they buy a gun, Pete. They all imagine they're going to be stopping crimes and foiling plots 24/7. They're totally pumped for their whole new life of hiding in the shadows, checking perimeters, screwing on silencers, doing somersaults and throwing really nice lighters into gasoline trails. Maybe they'll stop so many crimes that the president of the United States will call them and see if they want to be on SEAL Team Six! And they'll say, "Thank you, Mr. President, but I'm just going to stay here in Sheboygan and run this puppy mill. I'll just continue to shoot criminals locally. Yes, I'd be happy to be your secret crime consultant. Anything for my country. OK, bye!"

Here's the bad news, Pete. People who buy guns don't end up as heroes. They end up shooting their brother-in-law. In this scenario, you are the shooter. You shoot your brother-in-law, Gary.

Gary is married to your sister Nancy. Gary and Nancy's basement has flooded on a Tuesday at 11:30 p.m. in September. You have a pump in your garage, Pete. Gary knows about the pump because he gave it to you for your 50th birthday. It's a beaut. Gary has a key to your garage because he feeds your parrot when you go on vacation. It's a school night, so you and your wife Blanche and your two kids Spike and Raylene and the parrot are all asleep. Gary doesn't call ahead because he doesn't want to wake you all up. Gary comes over, opens the side door to your garage with his key, and tries to find the light switch. You wake up. It sounds like someone is IN THE GARAGE. "ISIS HAS ARRIVED IN SHEBOYGAN," you think. You also think, "THIS IS MY TIME TO SHINE." You grab your gun from underneath the nightstand, put on your night vision goggles and head downstairs for your date with destiny. "Will I get a ticker-tape parade?" you wonder.

This is the part where your choice of weapon matters.

If you bought the AR-15, Gary is totally fucking dead. And one of your neighbors is dead, too, because nine of the 20 bullets you shot went through the wall of your garage. Two of those went through your neighbors' bedroom window. If you bought the .22, Gary is merely paralyzed.

Feels good, right? Just like you pictured it. The president should be calling any minute.

OK, so maybe it doesn't go down quite like that. Maybe you don't kill your brother-in-law. Maybe your 8-year-old daughter accidentally shoots herself. Maybe you accidentally shoot yourself. Maybe your wife reaches under the nightstand to answer the phone and . . . same goddamn difference. Fantasy turned tragedy.

So you say, "I keep it locked up. I'm not stupid." Now you hear a noise and you're fumbling with a LOCK AND A GUN in a panic and this time you shoot your son. The noise was a squirrel on the roof. If you have guns around, somebody is going to get shot, Pete. If there are no guns around, no one is going to get shot. Why is that so fucking hard to understand, Wayne LaPierre?*

Fun Fact I: The NRA is a death cult.
Fun Fact II: No one I know has any guns.
Fun Fact III: No one I know ever gets shot.

. . . .

* Wayne LaPierre is the paranoid, death-obsessed National Rifle Association spokesman.

I used to have neighbors in Nashville who had two sons and lots of guns. No home invaders ever came for them, and no ISIS fighters. One brother accidentally shot and killed the other brother when they were both drunk. The boy who was killed was 18. The family moved away after that, heartbroken, utterly destroyed.

Have you ever considered that no one is coming for you, Pete? Would that make you sad? Does the thought that no one is planning to attack you make you feel lonely? Do you imagine that you would feel better if you were able to shoot a robber and get your name in the paper? Are you sure that it would feel good to kill someone, even if that person was a "robber"? Have you ever read anything? Have you ever read anything about war? Did you know that killing people—even "bad" people—makes human beings feel HORRIBLE? Who tells you who is "bad" and who is "good"? God? Henry Kissinger?

Perhaps you get your ideas about killing and guns and terrorism and heroism from Hollywood movies. If you are getting your information about killing from Hollywood movies then I can understand why you might think that killing a "bad guy" would make you feel complete, BUT YOU ARE A GROWN MAN CAPABLE OF COMPLEX THOUGHT, SO I EXPECT A LITTLE MORE FROM YOU PETE.

Hero/redemption fantasies are the engine that powers the gun industry. These fantasies have nothing to do with actual threats; they are born of an acute existential dread—existential dread that comes from the spiritual and physical isolation inherent to modern society. The irony is that the "terrorists" are dealing with the same dread by the same means. Gun violence is a side effect of a worldwide anxiety disorder. The violence is escalating because people feel impotent in the face of a global corporate hegemony and the money-hoarding of the executive class, and alienated by increased interaction with digital devices and the accompanying decrease in interaction with their fellow man. I feel anxious, Pete, but I do not label my anxiety "terrorism" or "immigrants" or "robbers" and attempt to medicate it by buying guns. I exercise regularly, see a therapist, and do my best to challenge corporate power. I haven't shot a brother-in-law yet.

How Can I Help Protect a Woman's Right to an Abortion?

PUBLISHED MAY 16, 2019.

Dear Advice King,

How can I help to protect a woman's right to an abortion? Why are lawmakers attempting to take away a woman's right to an abortion? The Supreme Court already ruled on this. Abortion is legal. It's the law. Why is this happening?

—Concerned in Boston

People are trying to take away a woman's right to an abortion because of misogyny and politics. In that order. You may say, "What about religion?" I am filing "religion" under misogyny in this case.

I am certainly not the first person to make this observation: If men could get pregnant, abortions would be as easy to get as an oil change. As easy to get as Viagra.

More than 6 million children in America don't have consistent access to food RIGHT NOW. Migrant children are in cages at the border RIGHT NOW. This abortion fight has nothing to do with ACTUALLY caring about children. Oh, I know it's about caring about children in the abstract sense. Everybody says they "care about children." But they don't TAKE CARE of the children once they are born. The woman who got pregnant has to take care of the child.

Forcing a woman to have a baby is FORCING THE WOMAN TO TAKE CARE OF THE BABY. A man can decide if he wants to help take care of the baby or not. Nobody can make a man take care of a baby. The man can leave the woman with the baby HE MADE and go get someone else pregnant and decide he doesn't want to take care of that baby either. A man can do that over and over. And men do.

And then these anti-abortion people say that someone will adopt the child. Except when someone doesn't.

AND abortion has already been illegal! We've been through this—the results are already in! Women will continue to get abortions! They will just have to go through hell to get them. And that's what this is really about—putting women through hell.

In the Bible story, EVE was the dumb asshole who ate the apple that doomed humanity. What more do you need to know about how Christians feel about women? Of course, it's not just Christians that think women are the root of all evil, but Christians are the main ones pushing that narrative in America. And I'm not saying EVERY Christian thinks women can't be trusted around "snakes" and "fruit," but why aren't they allowed to be Pope? Why aren't women allowed to be anything important in most religions?

Because religion is a racket set up by men to control women. Men are jealous maniacs who want women to BE AT HOME while the men themselves are not at home. It's as simple as that. Men invented the burka, for God's sake (no pun intended). Legal abortion gives women more sexual freedom, which makes men uncomfortable—even though men have COMPLETE SEXUAL FREEDOM. When you get mad that somebody else gets to have what you have, you are A FUCKING ASSHOLE. When you make a law to take that thing away from the other person, you are something much worse.

Here's a crazy thing. Many of the male lawmakers who are trying to ban abortion so that they can get the support of the coveted "people who want to control women" voting block are known to have pushed their own partners to have abortions!

And religious women who are stuck at home taking care of their kids while their husbands "have to work late" are angry that they are being lied to—and cheated on—by men. So they want ALL women to have to suffer the same. Misery loves company.

How can you help, "Concerned"? Vote. And stop voting for men who look like Mike Pence or some slight variation of Mike Pence. Stop voting for grown men who part their hair like they're in a fifth-grade class picture—it's a 1950s-style smokescreen to cover up the fact that they are scum. Ted Bundy parted his hair.

Should I Get the COVID Vaccine?

PUBLISHED APRIL 14 2021.

Dear Advice King,

Should I get the COVID vaccine? It's not [fully] FDA approved, which worries me. Also, I don't like the government telling me what to do. And I have heard that there's a microchip in it. Do you have any thoughts on the microchip thing?

—Ryan in St. Petersburg

Of course you should get vaccinated, you dope! The FDA?! First of all, both the Pfizer and the Moderna vaccines have been given emergency use authorization.

Also, if you want to talk about FDA-approved drugs, here are some of the possible side effects of an FDA-approved antidepressant called Abilify:

ABILIFY may cause serious side effects including:

- Increased risk of stroke and ministroke has been reported in clinical studies with oral aripiprazole of elderly people with dementia-related psychosis and can lead to death.
- Neuroleptic malignant syndrome (NMS), a serious condition that can lead to death. Call your healthcare provider or go to the nearest emergency room right away if you have some or all of the following symptoms of NMS: high fever, stiff muscles, confusion, sweating, or changes in pulse, heart rate, and blood pressure.
- Uncontrolled body movements (tardive dyskinesia). ABILIFY may cause movements that you cannot control in your face, tongue, or other body parts. Tardive dyskinesia may not go

away, even if you stop receiving ABILIFY. Tardive dyskinesia may also start after you stop receiving ABILIFY.

- Problems with your metabolism such as: High blood sugar (hyperglycemia): Increases in blood sugar can happen in some people who receive ABILIFY. Extremely high blood sugar can lead to coma or death. If you have diabetes or risk factors for diabetes (such as being overweight or a family history of diabetes), your healthcare provider should check your blood sugar before you start receiving ABILIFY and during your treatment.

Death and uncontrolled body movements! Thanks FDA! (In the FDA's defense, once you are dead, you are no longer bipolar.)

What made me think of Abilify, you ask? After taking it, my father developed tardive dyskinesia.* He got the COVID vaccine though, and he's fine. Well, fine except for the tardive dyskinesia he got after taking Abilify—that's permanent.**

Soooo . . . even if and when the FDA fully approves the vaccine, that does NOT mean that it wouldn't kill you, Ryan. And the FDA has approved it "for emergency use." It's not as if your Libertarian neighbor Cody made it out of egg whites and hydroxychloroquine. By the way, I think Libertarians should have to manufacture their own vaccine. They hate taxes, ergo they hate public health. United States taxpayer money helped develop and distribute these vaccines. If there's anything a Libertarian hates more than taxes, though, it's being consistent—they'll be the first ones in line to get the goddamn shot.

As far as "not liking the government telling you what to do," are you aware that the FDA is the government? Also, what is your position on drivers' licenses? If you are against them, I admire your commitment to "not liking the government telling you what to do." Have fun catching

* 100 percent true.
** 100 percent true.

polio from the unvaccinated 8-year-old who just ran you over with his Porsche.

Now, for the fun one: Microchips. Are you out of your fucking mind, Ryan?! MICROCHIPS?! Do you have any idea how many ways you are already being tracked?! Do you use credit cards? Do you send emails? Do you have a cellphone? Do you text? Do you use social media? DO YOU HAVE A FITBIT? DO YOU USE "ALEXA"?!

The government doesn't need to waste its time putting chips in our goddamn vaccines, THEY KNOW WHERE WE ARE. Jesus. FACEbook. FACIAL recognition. Notice how they both have "face" in them?

Ancestry.com? More like, "Thanks for giving your DNA to TheCops.com." 23andMe? More "23CopsandMe." FamilySearch.org? More like, "IGaveGrandmasDNAtoaCop.org." Etc.

Here's the truth, Ryan: The vaccines are good. The vaccines help. You wanna know why I am so certain? Because the government doesn't want you dead. You are worth more to the government alive. The government wants you to WORK, and the government wants you to CONSUME. Dead people can't staff Amazon warehouses, and dead people don't order from Amazon. And as I have already established, dead people don't buy antidepressants.

You know that economy politicians want to open so badly? It's built on the backs of people. Live, depressed people.

Take the vaccine first, then question your beliefs, Ryan.

Will Addiction Always Be an Issue for Me?

PUBLISHED DECEMBER 9, 2020. The line in the play where I say, "This wasn't on my 2020 Bingo ca" is a reference to a popular 2020 Twitter rhetorical device. "This wasn't on my 2020 Bingo card," was a saying that meant, "I didn't see THAT coming." If you are reading this in the distant future, and you have no idea what Twitter is, I envy you.

Dear Advice King,

I've been sober for a couple of years, but lately I've noticed an uptick in some other compulsive behaviors that concern me (internet, TV, food, etc.). Do I have to accept the fact that this will always be an issue, or is there a way for me to be completely free of all addictions?

Thanks for your help!

—Marla in Boulder, Colo.

Get a green lamp. Or a yellow lamp. It's honestly hard for me to say what color lamp you should get without knowing the color of everything else in the room.

Shit! I tried to answer the question without reading it again.

I'm in the same spot, Marla! And I wish I were better at taking my own advice, which is . . . GO EASY ON YOURSELF! That's right, go easy on yourself. It's easier said than done, I realize. If I'm not paying attention, I'll shame myself all day long.

THE ADVICE KING AT HOME—A SHORT PLAY

Interior, cluttered living room. An IKEA clothing rack purchased two years ago remains sealed in its box. The box leans against the wall at the rear of the stage, and is lit rather dramatically.

The Advice King is drinking coffee, watching a man metal-detect on YouTube.

THE ADVICE KING (TO HIMSELF): Why did you eat so many M&Ms, you dummy? Why do you keep checking Instagram, you dummy? You are desperate for approval, you dummy. Aren't there about 1,000 things you could be doing right now, you dummy? Etc.

Unassembled IKEA clothing rack bursts from box and attacks Advice King.

THE ADVICE KING: ARGGGGGHHHHHH!!! AHHHHHHHHH!!! THIS WASN'T ON MY 2020 BINGO CA

World explodes.

THE END

FUN FACT: All the best plays end with the world exploding.

When I quit drinking in 2012, it had nothing to do with shame. I quit because I was tired of being helpless. For years, I had been unable to help anybody move. Yes, move. As in, load stuff into van, drive van someplace else, unload stuff—that kind of move. I mean, I would *say* I was going to do it, but I wouldn't show up. And whoever I was supposed to help move KNEW I wasn't going to show up, because they knew ME. They knew I would be hungover, and asleep. I was completely helpless—I couldn't help myself, and I couldn't help others.*

Marla, if life were a ship, it would be slowly sinking. Now the sinking ship has a pandemic on it! The pandemic has caused a mental health crisis! This is an all-hands-on-deck situation. I don't care how much TV you watch, or how much Instagram you look at, or how much you

* Please do not interpret this passage to mean that I want to help YOU move.

eat—and you shouldn't either. AS LONG AS YOU CAN SHOW UP FOR YOUR SHIFT IN THE CROW'S NEST. Can you wake up for your shift in the crow's nest? Are you strong enough to grab a bucket and start bailing? (Ship metaphor suspended.)

What I mean is, can you answer the phone when a friend in need calls, and offer help? I can.

I watch A LOT of YouTube, eat too many peanut-butter-filled pretzel nuggets, smoke an occasional cigarette, and check Twitter incessantly. BUT I TRY NOT TO DO THE THINGS THAT RENDER ME HELPLESS. But when I falter—or when you do—let's go easy on ourselves. SHAME DOESN'T HELP™.

ONE MORE: Pick your battles, so you will be FIT for battle™.*

What Does Sobriety Do to Your Brain?

PUBLISHED FEBRUARY 21, 2019.

Dear Advice King,

What is the recovery process of the brain during early alcohol sobriety?

—Sarah in Nashville

Hi Sarah! I'm going to assume that you are quitting drinking. You wouldn't be quitting unless it was affecting you negatively in some way, so . . . CONGRATULATIONS! I'm sending you all the love and encouragement I've got in me. I'm pretty sure this question is a version of the one that I asked myself over and over when I was quitting drinking: *When will I start to feel better?!*

* These are love battles. Come armed with hugs, kisses, pep talks and casseroles.

As far as what exactly happens in the brain in the early stages of recovery, I'm not entirely sure. I'm no scientist—I'm an alcoholic. But I'll tell you what I have experienced.

Alcohol was a constant in my life for 25 years. I got drunk almost every day during that time. That's more than two decades of self-imposed disorientation. And when I say "disorientation," I mean disorientation. My brain was soaking in a chemical marinade. I spent 25 years guzzling clinical depressants, while simultaneously wondering—often aloud, often in therapists' offices—why I was clinically depressed.

CHRIS CROFTON'S SPICY HOMEMADE BRAIN MARINADE RECIPE

Nine any-size cans Pabst Blue Ribbon
Three big shots Jack Daniel's

If these ingredients aren't available, you may substitute a similar quantity of "whatever booze you can get your hands on."

Now for the good news: All you have to do to feel better is drain that marinade out of your head!

The hardest part of recovery from alcohol is the first few months. Your body throws a tantrum because it's not getting the chemicals it has come to expect. I was nervous, I had trouble sleeping, and I went through a deep depression. But I did not drink. I thought to myself that if I had survived 10,000 hangovers, 5,000 panic attacks, nine hospitalizations and a stint in jail, I could make it through a period of extreme discomfort.

Allow me to reiterate: In the early days of sobriety, you will not feel good. And you will be tempted to take a drink. If you do, you will be right back on the goddamn merry-go-round. If you don't, your body will begin to heal. As time passes, you will feel stronger—and less anxious! I discovered that the "anxiety" I was drinking to alleviate was mostly caused BY THAT SAME DRINKING.

The best way to keep yourself sober is to go to a place where you can get advice from people who know what you are going through, because they have been through it themselves. That place for me was a 12-step meeting. In my first year of sobriety, I attended a 12-step meeting almost every day. It was INVALUABLE. I cannot recommend 12-step meetings enough. I asked the people there if I was doing the right thing. They said yes. I asked them if it would get better. They said it would. And it did. And it *kept* getting better. And it *keeps* getting better.

It turned out that 25 years of being drunk had taken away my self-respect. Being sober gave me that back. By the grace of God (or, in your case, whatever you decide to call your higher power), I will never have to experience its absence again. I wish the same for you, Sarah.

How Do I Avoid Succumbing to Cynicism?

PUBLISHED NOVEMBER 11, 2020.

Dear Advice King,

I've been in such great spirits these past few days. How do I keep the good mood going for as long as possible, without succumbing to the usual fear and cynicism?

Thanks for your help!

—Nicole in Lansing, Mich.

Did you happen to catch Dave Chappelle's *Saturday Night Live* monologue? It's not important that you watch the whole thing—it's the last two minutes that are amazing.

The point that Chappelle made in those last two minutes was SO IMPORTANT, and so insightful. He said, essentially, that white people need to stop acting aggrieved, and start acting grateful. He argued that

Black people are better at finding joy in life than white people, even when their lives have been made extremely difficult—ON PURPOSE, BY WHITE PEOPLE!

Black people were brought to America against their will. They were enslaved for hundreds of years. They were terrorized by the Ku Klux Klan. They were lynched. They endured Jim Crow. They were redlined. Their leaders were assassinated. Redlining was a policy instituted by the Federal Housing Authority that denied federally insured mortgage loans to people in "redlined" areas. The areas were actually outlined in red ink. These areas were mostly "inner city" African American neighborhoods.

White people owned Black slaves. White people *were* the Ku Klux Klan. White people lynched. White people enacted Jim Crow. White people set up the redlining. White people (mostly) did the assassinating.

White racists love to speculate as to why "Black people aren't doing better." They arrogantly muse about the "absence of Black fathers." Redlining was a FEDERAL POLICY. Black people were denied upward economic mobility on purpose.

In America, white people have relentlessly and systematically oppressed Black people, yet it's white Americans who are always threatening to "move to Canada" whenever something doesn't go their way. And it's white people who GO BERSERK when they are asked to do something as simple as putting on a mask during a pandemic.

Cheer up! Nothing is guaranteed. Not only is nothing guaranteed, but sometimes things are denied to you on purpose! The world is not fair, and then you die. There is a reason life has been described as a "vale of tears" and not a "five-car garage." Good spirits are best achieved through a shift in perspective.

Heed the words of Dave Chappelle! Lower your expectations, and heighten your forgiveness.

Should I Play the Stock Market?

PUBLISHED JUNE 24, 2020.

Dear Advice King,

I've never invested in the stock market, but it seems to be doing very well despite the seemingly grim economic reality. Does this mean it's foolproof? Did I make a mistake? Please advise!

—Missing the Boat

Put the bacon in the microwave with three paper towels underneath it and three paper towels on top. After it's done cooking, give it an initial pat-down with six more paper towels. Place the bacon on a bed of eight paper towels for final draining. Before you serve it, give it one final squeeze with six more paper towels. Serve! Altogether, to make six slices of bacon you need 250 paper towels.

Damn it! I did the thing where I try to answer the question without reading it. I guessed (incorrectly) that you asked how many paper towels you need to make six pieces of bacon in a microwave.

Oh no! I wish the question was about bacon. It's about the stock market!

I've never invested in the stock market either, "Missing the Boat." I've always been one of those hand-to-mouth motherfuckers. Like most Americans, I don't have any "extra" money to gamble. Like most Americans, I rarely go to the dentist. The dentist and the stock market are for Fox News and MSNBC hosts. I bet Nancy Pelosi goes to the dentist after she eats all that ice cream. Mitch McConnell can afford the dentist, and not only can he play the stock market, he—and everyone else in Congress—can insider-trade without fear of prosecution!

I call the stock market THE THEFT THERMOMETER. It's not foolproof—far from it. IT'S PROPPED UP.

It's a pyramid scheme that collapses every few years (seems to happen about every 10 years). When the pyramid falls, it's the average (often employed!) citizens who end up living in their cars. The Federal Reserve prints money and hands it to the pyramid's architects (banks, giant corporations) so they can start it all over again. FUN FACT: When it's time for social services to be funded, these same people who just gave unlimited zero-interest loans to oligarchs—and the oligarchs who received them—have the gall to talk about "fiscal responsibility." It's "fiscal responsibility," foreclosures and living in cars for us, and free (zero-interest loans, the Federal Reserve buying worthless corporate bonds) money for them.

Do you realize that if you give billions of dollars of zero-interest loans to the wealthy—without any conditions—they will take that money and invest it, stash it offshore, shove it up their ass—and STILL lay off employees. That's right, the recipients of this free money aren't even required to put the money toward their employees.

IF ONLY the only thing all this corruption led to was people having a lot of cavities and being unable to invest in the stock market! What do unhappy, unemployed, broke people do with their spare time? They try to forget they are unhappy and broke, that's what. One way to do that is with drugs (opioid epidemic)—another way is by looking for someone to blame.

The actual blame lies with the Federal Reserve Bank and the (overwhelmingly white) oligarchs it caters to. But Fox News, MSNBC, CNN and Rush Limbaugh have split this country down the middle so successfully that these unhappy broke people blame . . . *other* unhappy broke people! And if you can't figure out on your own which group of powerless people you—also a powerless person—should attack, the president of the United States has issued a handy list: immigrants, liberals, Black Lives Matter activists and Antifa. Anyone but the real culprits.

The real problem is that 1 percent of the world's population has half the world's money. That should be the headline every day. Until that changes, everything will remain broken. EVERY DAY THAT SHOULD BE THE HEADLINE. You cannot fix this country without redistributing wealth.

Now, "Missing the Boat," if you have already gone to the dentist, and you have some money left to buy stocks, here are some tips:

ADVICE KING STOCK TIPS

1. Dog food. There's no way around it—dogs are eating. And from where I'm sitting, I don't think they have any intention of stopping. Buy a few shares of Alpo, and thank me later.
2. M&Ms. The worse things get, the more of these I eat.
3. Poster board, magic markers, long sticks, tape. People are going to need a ton of these for the foreseeable future.
4. Fireworks. I don't know why, but these are year-round now.
5. Amazon. That's right. In case you haven't noticed, the entire economy is run by a delivery service. Never a good sign. Rome was run by a delivery service right before it fell.

Tipping on a Cup of Coffee

PUBLISHED JUNE 9, 2015.

Hi King!

How much should I tip on a gourmet coffee? Well, I guess they are all gourmet now, except for Mapco. So I guess my question is, how much should I tip for a regular coffee at Mapco?

Thanks,

—Louie

Hi, Louie. Now that the Advice King column has been nominated for an award, I have fans from all over the world. For the benefit of "Royal

Watchers" (that's what Advice King fans call themselves) reading this in Singapore, Palestine or Namibia, Mapco is the name of a chain of gas stations / convenience stores found mostly in the Southeastern United States.

I found a website with some comments from Mapco workers about their experiences working for the company. Overall, they had very nice things to say. Mapco customers get their own cup of normal coffee and bring it up to the cashier to pay for it. The cashier wears regular clothes. He or she doesn't have to wear an antique butcher's apron or a train engineer hat. There is no milk-steaming, pouring-over or "Where were these beans sourced?" type baloney. Well, that's good. Nobody wants to wear a train engineer's hat or have to talk about where coffee beans come from. Sounds OK so far . . .

Unfortunately, the fact that Mapco employees had such nice things to say about Mapco is not nice at all—it is frightening. The starting salary for a Mapco cashier appears to be about $8.25 an hour. Sure, that's a dollar more than the U.S. minimum wage of $7.25, but it's still GARBAGE. That's $330 a week if you are working 40 hours. And most of these workers don't get a 40-hour week, because that would qualify them for benefits. They are scheduled for 33 hours instead, and the stockholders and execs pocket the money that should have gone toward employee X's health care. Mapco's executives make millions annually, btw.

Also, Mapco employees occasionally get pistol-whipped at work by robbers. Mapco executives almost never get pistol-whipped. They get deep-tissue massages on Turks and Caicos.

SHOUT-OUT TO MY "ROYAL WATCHERS" IN TURKS AND CAICOS!!!

If you work a 33-hour week as an occasionally pistol-whipped cashier at Mapco, you make about $272 before taxes.

"So you take home $220. As long as you're not the type that needs to eat food, you'll be fine. Don't tell me you're one of those greedy, entitled, unskilled, unworthy people I heard about on Fox News who thinks a hugely profitable corporation should pay their workers enough to cover rent *and* food?! You should listen to a Joel Osteen sermon or read *Atlas Shrugged* immediately." —Old white guys with money who benefited hugely (directly or indirectly) from the G.I. Bill, their gender and the color of their skin. They happily use Medicare, and collect Social Security.

The same white guys who say the kind of shit in the above paragraph happen to run this country and its media. They are anti-union because they want to keep wages barbarically low and deny health care, and anti-tax and anti-government because they don't want to have to help the people they have impoverished and sickened. Sick and impoverished people already feel bad about themselves, even though they shouldn't, and these fuckers take every opportunity to make them feel worse. Social programs have been renamed "entitlements" to make the poor feel guilty for needing them, and to make everyone else angry at the poor. Rich white Fox News anchors (I use the term "news anchor" extremely loosely) say "entitlements" about 600,000 times a day. Fox News is essentially an app. An app that keeps taxes low by making people hate the poor. Nothing to do with news. Not a goddamn thing.

ANYHOO, to help make up for the poverty wages paid by Mapco—and many, many, many other American companies just like it—and to help build the self-esteem of workers who think jobs with poverty wages are all they are "entitled" to, I suggest a $50 tip on every Mapco coffee purchase.

Projecting Success

PUBLISHED MAY 12, 2015.

Dear Advice King,

I go to Nashville State and my grades are great, but sometimes I worry that isn't enough. I keep noticing I don't look like successful people. Or people that "project success." Will I ever land my dream job without a crazy hat or conceptual haircut?

I recently edited my hair to serve my agenda.

—*Paul*

Depends on your dream job, Paul. If you want to work in the septic business, you can wear whatever you want. You can even wear a marijuana-leaf do-rag—unless you're trying to break into management. If you are applying for a management position at a septic company, you should cultivate the "state trooper at a barbecue" look: Put your phone in a holder on your belt (a really fucking big Android phone, ideally), and wear a polo shirt, khakis, wraparound shades and mustache. A sensible "brother-in-law" mustache, by the way, not some hipster conversation piece. People expect the septic organization they choose to keep their shit *ON LOCKDOWN*. Like shit policemen. Oh, that reminds me: Once you get your outfit together, remember not to say "shit" in the interview. Say "solid waste."

My cousin Lonnie didn't get past the first interview because he said "shit" too much. He wasn't even applying for a management position. He just wanted to be a "tank monkey." He sent an email afterward and asked if he didn't get the job because of his "Bikini Inspector" shirt. They said no, the shirt was fine, since he wasn't going for a management position. They just said, "You should try to avoid saying 'shit' and 'piss' in a job interview, even if it's for septic work."

What was the question? Oh yeah, "projecting success."

Are you studying hands-on septic work, pest control or grave-digging at Nashville State, Paul? If not, you sure as hell better have the right haircut—and the right *jawline*—for today's horrible job market. In 2015 America there are 500 applicants for every position. If you have the wrong head (like, actual skull), you are probably out of luck. There used to be jobs for regular-looking people, and they still have them in other countries. They were called "MANUFACTURING JOBS." A master machinist could get hired even if he had a hump. Do you see any lawyers, hedge fund managers, restaurateurs, craft brewers, fashion designers, PR agents or HMO managers with humps? Of course not. All the money in the United States has been stolen from the lower classes using high-interest loans. The new "economy" consists of attractive people passing the loot back and forth.

Why are all these people good-looking? Because passing ill-gotten money around is *not* a hard job. There is plenty of time left to fuck your co-workers. And when these creeps are done fucking all the attractive co-workers they hired, they move on to fucking the employees of the craft brewery they frequent.

These days, the American job market isn't so much a rat race as it is a rat beauty contest™. You better slick that hair, put lifts in your shoes, suck on a mint, and maybe even put some putty on your nose before your first interview, Paul.

How Do We Escape the Impending Climate Apocalypse?

PUBLISHED JULY 9, 2019.

Dear Advice King,

Is there anywhere we can go to escape the impending climate apocalypse?

Thanks,

—Barb in Los Angeles

Move to a hill, or become friends with someone who lives on a hill.

I'm the last person you should be asking about this, Barb—I'll be dead four days after the shelves at Trader Joe's are empty.

I think it's pretty funny that the automobile was invented a little more than 100 years ago, and it is threatening the existence of the ENTIRE HUMAN SPECIES, and people are like: "There's nothing we can do, because we already have them and they're really fun. Plus we already paved everything."

"HERE LIES THE HUMAN RACE. THEY LOVED TO RIDE AROUND."

One million years from now—when the world is run by giant hyper-intelligent cockroaches who wear pants and ONLY TRAVEL ON FOOT—cockroach professors at cockroach colleges are going to teach classes about how fucking stupid we were. They will focus on the late 19th century through the death of the human species, in 2140. This period, referred to by the cockroaches as the "The Paving Period"—or "The Clown Meltdown"—will be extremely funny in retrospect.

Here is an example of how I imagine futuristic-cockroach academics will talk about us:

HUMAN HISTORY 101—ANTENNA UNIVERSITY, PROFESSOR IMA ROACH

Hello class. Ronald, please take off your hats. Thank you.

So in this course we are going to discuss the decline and fall of the "drivers," also known as "humans." Humans thrived on earth for a long time. They were walking around and having fun. Then they invented motorized carts. They called these motorized carts "cars" for short. [Class laughs.] No, it's true. [Class laughs.] The basic idea was, with the motorized carts, you don't have to walk anymore—you can go places sitting down. So everybody got really fat. [Class laughs.] No, it's true. [Class laughs.*] These fat people liked rolling around on these carts so much that they paved the whole earth so they could roll on it better. [Class laughs.] That sounds funny, but they really did it. And then they found out that the smoke that was coming out of the "cars" was causing the earth to get hotter, but they decided that since they had already paved the whole earth it would be too much trouble to unpave it, so they all burned and drowned. [Class laughs.] No, it's true.

Ronald, what are you licking? Is that sheetrock? Did you bring enough for the whole class? Put it away. Thank you.

. . . .

*The laugh of the hyper-intelligent cockroach sounds a lot like a modern sheep, except about 15 times louder: *BAAAAAAAAA BAAAAAAAAA BAAAAAAAAAA.*

The richest humans piled into "spaceships," which were, essentially, sky cars, and tried to drive to Mars. [Class laughs.] We all know how that turned out. If you aren't familiar with the story, watch the movie *Sky Titanic*, starring Roachonardo DiRoachrio. And THAT, my handsome friends, is why we walk. [Bell rings.] OK, for next week I want five paragraphs on "selfies."

What Should I Bring to Antiques Roadshow?

. . . .

PUBLISHED FEBRUARY 19, 2020.

Dear Advice King,

Hello Advice King! Longtime reader, first-time writer! I live in Ohio. Antiques Roadshow is coming to my area soon! Antiques Roadshow is a PBS television show. You bring stuff that you think is valuable to a convention center, and professional appraisers tell you what it's worth. What should I bring down there?

—Trevor in Columbus, Ohio

Michael Bloomberg's candidacy is a prime example of what happens when antitrust laws aren't enforced. You end up with a billionaire—a "former Republican" billionaire who endorsed George W. Bush at the 2004 Republican convention—buying himself a spot on the presidential debate stage. AND HE'S RUNNING AS A DEMOCRAT. Michael Bloomberg is one of the 10 richest people in the world, and anybody alive in America right now who is experiencing Bloomberg's relentless, all-encompassing, mind-numbing, Orwellian, self-funded advertising blitz can vouch for that. I farted this morning and a Bloomberg commercial came out. My cat tried to meow but it was a Bloomberg commercial. In related news, my parakeet keeps saying "stop and frisk."

Under the current campaign finance rules, the more money you have, the more political power you have. And anybody who tries to tell you otherwise is insane or lying. Billionaires are destroying democracy. Antitrust enforcement could help restore it.

I did that thing where I try to answer the question without reading it again. It turns out you DIDN'T ask what happens to democracy when you don't enforce antitrust laws. Thank goodness! That column would be *soooooo* boring. Even just a couple of paragraphs would be intolerable.

I appreciate you explaining how *Antiques Roadshow* works, Trevor. I think most people are familiar with *Antiques Roadshow* though. Maybe not. What do I know about people? Do any of us really KNOW anything, Trevor? Sorry. I'm drinking coffee at 1 a.m. so please bear with me.

The problem with this question is that I don't know what you have, so how am I supposed to know what you should bring? Are you rich? Rich people can bring almost anything down to the ol' *Antiques Roadshow* and they'll be "pleasantly surprised" by how much it's worth. To illustrate this point, here's a short play I wrote called *Rich Guy at Antiques Roadshow.*

RICH GUY AT ANTIQUES ROADSHOW

RICH GUY: I brought in a painting that my mom had hanging in the bathroom in the basement. It fell in the toilet at some point so that's why it has that big stain on it. My great-great grandfather invented the sextant, which was a navigational tool, so I'm wondering if it has something to do with him since it's a picture of an old boat. I'm trying to decide whether I should throw it away because I already have a ton of other great paintings without stains.

APPRAISER WEARING SPATS: [Visibly quivering] Sir, this was painted by Moby Dick. This was actually painted by the white whale from Herman Melville's famous book. There are no other known paintings by Moby Dick—or any whale, for that matter. It is worth $680 million, and it was an honor just to stand near it.

RICH GUY: Ho ho ho. What a pleasant surprise. I guess I won't throw it away then.

THE END

And here's a play I wrote about what happens when people who aren't rich bring stuff to *Antiques Roadshow*. It's called *Person Who Isn't Rich at Antiques Roadshow.*

PERSON WHO ISN'T RICH AT ANTIQUES ROADSHOW

PERSON WHO ISN'T RICH: My Uncle Onion left me this weird old ceramic bottle that says "Pennsylvania" on it. He won it in a card game. It apparently belonged to a soldier from the Revolutionary War. It says the soldier's name on it. His name was "Jim Beam," which is funny because Jim Beam is also the name of a famous whiskey that I was drinking just now, when I was waiting in line.

APPRAISER WEARING JODHPURS: [Visibly distraught] This is a decanter made by the Jim Beam whiskey company to commemorate the United States Bicentennial celebration. The Bicentennial was in 1976. This jug is from 1976. It says "Pennsylvania" because that is where the Declaration of Independence was signed. Approximately 250 million of these are known to exist. It is worth between 0 and 2 dollars. May God have mercy on your soul.

PERSON WHO ISN'T RICH: That's cool. Which line do I get in to collect the money?

THE END

Good luck, Trevor!

Should I Buy a Fidget Spinner?

. . . .

PUBLISHED JUNE 14, 2017.

Dear Advice King,

Should I get a "fidget spinner"? I see them in gas stations, but I don't really know what they are. It seems like everybody is always talking about them.

Thanks!

—Liz in Torrance, Calif.

I don't know what a "fidget spinner" is, Liz. I have heard about them too. Hold on for a sec while I look into this . . .

HOLY SHIT. They are the stupidest things ever. A "fidget spinner" is a little plastic thing that you spin around in your hand. That's it. It spins around. You spin it, and it spins. THE END.

It has ball bearings, so it doesn't make much noise. "Hey Betty! Check it out! This plastic thing is cool! It spins around and it doesn't make much noise!" God help us. Please. IF THERE IS A GOD, IT IS TIME TO SHOW UP NOW. HEY GOD, THINGS ARE WAY PAST FUCKED, SO IF YOU WANNA SHOW UP, NOW WOULD BE A GOOD TIME. THE WORLD IS COLLAPSING AROUND OUR EARS AND PEOPLE ARE SPINNING SHIT AND HUNTING POKEMONS HELP HELP HELP HELP.

Nothing.

I have a sneaking suspicion that planet Earth is God's fidget spinner.

I guess "fidget spinners" are the modern equivalent of Rubik's Cubes, except dumbed down for the pea-brained texters we politely refer to as "today's youth."

I'm kidding around! Today's youth isn't pea-brained! They're just shy . . . or something. Every generation needs a way to pass the time. For mine, it was smoking cigarettes. "Fidget spinning" is much healthier than smoking cigarettes, but smoking looks cool. "Fidget spinning" makes you look like a moron. Imagine if James Dean "fidget spun" instead of smoking—I bet he wouldn't have gotten a single part. "Hey Larry, you wanna hire James Dean?" "You mean the moron?"

Call me crabby, but I think, historically speaking, this might not be the ideal time to recreationally spin stuff.

Don't get me wrong: It would be great if everybody spinning little plastic things made campaign finance reform happen. Maybe if we spun REAL hard, these greedy scumbags would raise the minimum wage, and cut defense spending in order to pay for decent schools and clean drinking water and health care for all. Maybe they'd stop calling social programs "entitlements" on purpose to make them sound bad, and stop acting like fucking kings and queens instead of elected public servants. But it's not going to work. The immoral executive class of this sad world pays the lowest wages they can get away with and uses their outsized profits to bribe politicians. In the long run, all these fuckers are planning to escape this planet on Elon Musk's Mars Express. That's why they don't care about the environment—they're not planning to be here! Tickets for the Mars Express are going to be REAL fucking expensive. Like, IMMORAL EXECUTIVE CLASS AND PAID-FOR POLITICIAN expensive. We're all going to be left down here to drown like rats. Rats in rowboats, sailing the seas of oil sludge and fidget spinners.

Light up a cigarette, Liz, and light up the switchboards of the Mars-bound assholes we politely refer to as "Congress."

Also, don't buy things you see in gas stations.

Dealing with Depression

. . . .

PUBLISHED NOVEMBER 10, 2015.

Dear Advice King,

How do I stop being depressed?

—Joe

I received this question a week ago, and I was going to give a silly answer like, "See an IMAX movie every day!" Then something terrible happened that made me reconsider. My friend Craig Smith, who suffered from depression, committed suicide. Craig was a comedian and a bartender at a dive bar called Springwater in Nashville. He was a father. He was a tree surgeon. He was a promoter; a promoter who promoted others as much if not more than himself. And he was a good friend to many, many, many people.

I spent a lot of time at the Springwater. For the first few years I was in Nashville I was there just about every day. Musicians, eccentrics, criminals and people with physical and mental disabilities all mixed together, enjoying live performances on the small stage, drinking and taking drugs. The Springwater regulars amounted to what felt like a family—an extremely diverse and accepting one. I loved it. It felt close the way I imagine a community feels during a war—everyone coming together and making the best of it. What I didn't realize at the time was that it *was* a wartime community. It, and every other dive bar "community," is under siege—besieged by the tragedies and losses that inevitably accompany a lifestyle defined by alcohol and drugs. These tragedies bring the community closer, but the patterns that lead to the tragedies continue uninterrupted. Craig drank, and he is gone. I'm sure many of Craig's friends will honor him by drinking, and put themselves at risk of dying, and then their friends will honor them.

My father has severe depression. His sister Mary suffered from depression and alcoholism and committed suicide. I began showing signs of depression when I was about 17. I had started drinking when I was 14. When I drank, I felt good. The days I didn't drink, I felt really low. I decided that I would drink every day. I only allowed myself to drink at night, so during daylight hours I felt awful. All I wanted to do was sleep—and I did. During college I started sleeping until 4 or 5 p.m. I went to see the school psychologist. That was the first time I was advised to quit drinking—the first of hundreds of times to come. I couldn't imagine quitting. What would I do? Who would I hang out with? Also, I wanted to be an artist. Artists drink, right? I read *No One Here Gets Out Alive*. I continued to drink for the next 25 years. But I never stopped experimenting with therapy. I saw a social worker at a public health clinic in my early 20s, and when I got a job with benefits I saw the first therapist who helped me make real progress. She got me to take Zoloft. I was afraid it would "affect my creativity." It did not. There were times that I was so depressed suicide crossed my mind, and I believe Zoloft has helped keep me safe. I am mentioning all this to let you know, Joe, that therapy and medication can be extremely helpful, and that even if you don't have much money, there ARE options. For example, psychologists get medicine samples from the drug companies. I was able to try many different medications (a lot of which made me feel horrible) before settling on Zoloft. And if you go to a therapist and you don't like them, TRY ANOTHER ONE. Trying one therapist does not mean you've "tried therapy" and it "didn't work." If you get one bad haircut, do you swear off barbers? No. You go to another barber.

"I tried haircuts, but they don't work." —a maniac

I went on Zoloft in 1997, but I continued to drink until 2012. Every therapist I saw told me to stop. Alcohol is a depressant, they would say. It just didn't seem true to me. Every time I took a few days off from drinking I would feel horrible, and I would only start to feel good again when I drank. I went on panic-attack-induced ambulance rides, to rehab and even to a mental hospital, but it still seemed to me that the only time I was not depressed was when I drank. So I kept drinking.

I quit drinking with the help of a 12-step program. I learned that long-term alcohol abuse affects your brain chemistry. I learned that even if you take a month off from drinking you will still be depressed. You will be depressed from the drinking you did for all the months before that month. (The most I ever took off was three days.) I learned that if you stay sober for six months some really interesting things happen. Your brain starts to change, and with it your mood. And it keeps getting better. The transition period is difficult. You will be dealing with the fallout from all the years of havoc you have wreaked on your brain, and time is the only thing that will heal it. That transition period is when a 12-step program is a tremendous help. It's a community just like a bar community. It is LITERALLY a community made up of the regulars from bars. Dysfunctional people from all different walks of life hanging out and loving each other. The difference is that the people in a 12-step community are loving each other to life—bar communities love each other to death.

Joe, if you are prone to depression, you have a brain that needs to be handled with care. Self-medicating is like throwing gasoline on an already unpredictable fire. The fire is your brain, and the guy throwing the gasoline is drunk. (Hey, still a better metaphor than that egg thing.) No one I have ever met was more fearless than Craig Smith. He wasn't afraid of psychic pain—he lived with it. He wasn't afraid of physical pain—he did this. He wasn't afraid to be honest—he was compulsively honest. He wasn't afraid to be loving—he was unabashedly affectionate. In that video he said his life was "a shambles" and he was "in the market for transcendence." I know how that feels. I felt that way for 25 years. I took my fearlessness and threw it into risky partying. A lot of depressed people do. It turns out the path to transcendence is through sobriety, exercise and medication. To take that path requires just as much courage as self-destruction does, but the reward is life itself. Craig was more than courageous enough to have made it, and I wish I could have helped him. If only we had all known. If only.

I loved Craig, and will miss him so, so much. Depression is dangerous, Joe. Address it. No one here gets out alive, sure, but let's all try to hang around as long as we can.

Is Universal Health Care Socialism?

PUBLISHED SEPTEMBER 18, 2019.

Dear Advice King,
I told my family that I thought universal health care sounded like a great idea. My dad told me that he didn't raise me to be a socialist, and kicked me out of the house. Is universal health care socialism? Is socialism bad? I'm so confused! Help!

—Todd in Cincinnati

To put it bluntly, your air-conditioning unit doesn't have enough BTUs. BTUs stands for "Booming Thunder Unbelievables."

Sorry! I'm still trying that thing where I answer the question without reading it.

Hi Todd!

Your dad is confusing socialism with communism. Socialism just means "everybody owns it together." We have plenty of socialist stuff in America already. Anything funded by taxpayers is essentially, by definition, "socialist." Roads and bridges and traffic lights are socialist. The fire department and the police department are socialist. The United States military is socialist, for fuck's sake.

Socialism is NOT communism. The hospital corporations and drug companies have been feeding Cold War cartoons into your dad's brain. They want him to think that with universal health care, his regular doctor will be replaced by Joseph Stalin.

But . . .

FUN FACTS: Taxpayer money is routinely used to build privately owned sports stadiums. Taxpayers give nearly $700 billion a year to the military. Taxpayer money propped up the (private?) banks after they almost collapsed due to the frauds they were perpetrating against those same taxpayers.

What kind of capitalism is that? Certainly not the "pure" kind that rich people act like they can't violate—except for when they can, which is anytime they fucking feel like it, as long as it benefits them. The thing about the banks is truly exceptional, however. Defrauded people paying to save the banks that just fucked them? That's definitely not capitalism. That's not socialism either. *That* actually sounds like worst-case-scenario communism.

ONE MORE FUN FACT: Sick people in America are often forced to "crowdfund" to pay their medical bills. "Crowdfunding" is a made-up expression that means "asking your friends for money when you won't be able to pay them back." What "enhanced interrogation" was to "torture," "crowdfunding" is to "begging." It sounds nicer—but that's still what it is.

Tell your dad that it's 2019, and Joseph Stalin can't be his doctor, because Joseph Stalin is dead. But ask him a question: Does a country that spends public money to fund private enterprises (stadiums, corporate tax breaks) and build a gigantic military while the citizens pay their medical bills with GoFundMe pages sound THAT much different from Soviet Russia?

The Soviet Union was just an oligarchy with Marxism as set-dressing to justify why everybody was poor except for the people in power (*something something proletariat*). America is an oligarchy now, too. Six men own half the country's wealth. Capitalism has become the set-dressing to justify why everybody is poor except the people in power (something something bootstraps). GoFundMe is nothing more than a high-tech bread line.

If the banks get health care, we get health care™.

I love this country, and we can do better. Health care is a human right. Profiting excessively from health care is immoral. Medicare for all. PLEASE VOTE.

Where Is My Venti Mocha?

PUBLISHED JULY 7, 2021.

Dear Advice King,

Starbucks is running out of everything. I'm so used to being able to get what I want, when I want, that I don't know what to do when I can't. I yelled at the girl behind the counter. I know it's not her fault, and I felt awful. If I don't have a venti mocha every morning I can't function! Why is this happening? How do you make a venti mocha at home?

—Peggy in Palm Beach, Fla.

Sounds like you have VENTI problems, Peggy. At least they're not "Trenta." Trenta is the largest size at Starbucks. You could baptize a baby in a Trenta. I bet some Starbucks loon has done it. I bet the baby's name was "Spinach and Feta Wrap."

This is a good question, Peggy. It brings up a lot of shit. Uniquely American shit.

Americans have forgotten that mocha is a thing that somebody has to make and then deliver to Starbucks. Mocha cannot be conjured—even by yelling. Someone has to put mocha in the Starbucks, or it will not be there. Mocha is a substance—not a right. Do you see what I'm saying, Peggy? The Declaration of Independence doesn't say anything about mocha.

We need cocoa to make chocolate sauce, Peggy. We get most of it from Africa. It arrives in America via the "supply chain." Most people in America (including me) do not ever think about this "supply chain," because it usually runs smoothly: You go to a job you hate and fuck around on Facebook all day, and in return you get a direct deposit every two weeks. You go to Starbucks, put your little plastic bank card into the little plastic card reader, and receive a giant mocha! Then you go home and get on Facebook. Repeat until death or the rapture. OHHHHH SAAAAY CAAAAN YOUUUUU SEEEEEEE . . .

The supply chain was interrupted by COVID-19—which is pretty funny since a ton of Americans think the pandemic was invented by Democrats to mess up Trump's presidency. (But if that were true, why would it affect the global supply chain? Is the whole globe working for the Democrats? Are African cocoa farmers Democrats?)

The fact is, Americans really don't acknowledge that other countries exist. Not only do Americans think mocha comes out of the air, they also think America is the WHOLE WORLD. If you think America is the whole world, it's gotta be pretty hard to get your head around the idea of a "global supply chain." To you, that just sounds like "American supply chain." Which means you're like, "WHERE'S MY FUCKING MOCHA?! IS THE MOCHA TRAIN FROM CINCINNATI DELAYED BECAUSE A DEMOCRAT IS DRIVING IT?!?"

Americans need a little gratitude in their attitude™.

Peggy, YouTube has plenty of instructional videos on how to make a mocha at home, but—and I realize this probably sounds crazy—YOU WILL NEED MOCHA.

Mocha is real. The pandemic is real. The supply chain is real. Other countries are real. You can't eat a debit card, and you can't eat a gun.

Should I Study Journalism?

. . . .

PUBLISHED FEBRUARY 7, 2019.

Dear Advice King,

I really want to study journalism, but there have been so many layoffs lately. Should I do something else? Thanks!

—*Geraldine in Yonkers, NY*

You should do something else. Let me think what other jobs there are . . .

This should be a recurring feature—"WHAT JOBS?!"

WHAT JOBS?!

1. Uber
2. Lyft
3. Uber
4. Barista
5. Lyft
6. Fracker
7. Pundit
8. Grubhub

Almost all news outlets rely on corporate sponsors to exist. In addition, most of those news outlets are OWNED by big corporations.

Corporations have no interest in journalism. Corporations have no interest in the truth. Corporations would drill for oil in your grandmother. After "fracking" your grandmother to death, the president of Shithead Oil would say that Shithead Oil had no choice because of "an obligation they have to their stockholders." Any time I commit a crime in the future I am going to say I did it because I had an obligation to my stockholders, and they will let me go.

Corporations sponsor journalists for the same reason they sponsor politicians—so they will be able to influence their work. See: Sinclair Broadcasting.

The First Amendment is alive and well in Uber and Lyft, though, I'll tell you that. I've had some of the wildest conversations in those things. As an alternative to journalism, you could drive for a ride service and talk to your passengers exclusively about the importance of overturning Citizens United and how universal health care is a moral imperative. Just for fun, I'm going to tell you about some things I learned from an extremely lively Uber driver I rode with recently.

First, he told me that he had invented a new-and-improved MP3 player. I was like, "Cool." Then he was like, "Do you wanna hear it go?" And I was like, "Sure." I then heard The Doors song "Love Her Madly" LOUDER THAN I HAVE EVER HEARD IT. (I smoked a lot of pot in suburban 1980s Connecticut, so that's really saying something.) He kept yelling, "Listen to the clarity!" while he was weaving all over the road. I thought I was going to die. There were probably worse ways to go, I figured. At least I got to experience the song "Love Her Madly" the way it was *meant* to sound—which is, apparently, loud as shit with a Greek man screaming "listen to the clarity" over it.

After he was finished demonstrating his new-and-improved MP3 player—the one that big corporations are trying to keep off the market because it is too good (which I 100 percent believe, btw)—he said he had immigrated to America from Greece in the 1980s. He said he came to America to FIND JIM CROCE. He was not kidding. Since that was before the internet, he had no way of knowing that Jim Croce had died years earlier. That's what he said. Even without an internet, there must have been a way to find out if Jim Croce was alive or dead before you moved to another country to find him. (A private detective? *People Magazine*?) But ANYWAY.

He learned English from Jim Croce songs. And he learned to play guitar by playing along to Jim Croce songs. He asked if I would like to hear some of his original songs. I said yes, because by that point I was already in pretty deep. It turned out his songs were pretty good! Do you know how rare that is? He actually had talent. I told him his voice reminded me of Cat Stevens. That made him really excited. He fully turned around to look at me (on a highway) and yelled, joyously, "EVERYBODY TELLS ME THAT!!!" and started weaving all over the road again.

All of this happened in 15 minutes.

If journalists had *half* this Uber driver's sense of urgency, we would have already addressed global warming, and begun redistributing the wealth.

Try to dodge the big corporations, Geraldine. Do what some friends of mine in Nashville have done, and start your own publication. Or do what my brother Gregory—himself a laid-off journalist—does, and run a cool website.

Or write a politically charged advice column for an amazing alt-weekly.

Should I Start Doing Comedy?

. . . .

PUBLISHED NOVEMBER 22, 2017.

Dear Advice King,

There is an open mic at the sports bar inside the Clarion Inn every other Tuesday in Cookeville, Tenn., where I live. Is this where I should start comedy?

—Daniel in Cookeville, Tenn.

Sure. I don't care. "Start comedy" wherever you want. So many people are "starting comedy" these days that the words "starting comedy" have lost all meaning. They just sound like two noises.

"My nephew is starting comedy!" sounds like, "My nephew is blooping blorpy!"

SOME FOOL IN A HOODIE: "I'm thinking about starting comedy!"

WHAT I HEAR: "I'm blooping blorf blapping bloopy!"

Are you 26, Daniel? Or 24? Or—*shudder*—even younger? Most people "starting comedy" are, like anyone starting out in any profession, young. But being a stand-up comedian is not a normal profession—it is an art form that requires life experience, talent and endless practice. "Being funny" is only about 50 percent of the gig. The other 50 percent is figuring out how to successfully repackage one's natural "funniness" for presentation on a stage—alone, with a limited amount of time.

Let's assume you *are* funny, Daniel—and that is an extremely rash assumption. You still have to have stuff to talk about. This is why I asked how old you are. When you are 22 years old, you don't know about anything, so what the fuck are you going to talk about? And even if you *do* know some things, I doubt you have a fully developed perspective on those things. And even if you have what *you* believe is a fully developed perspective on those things, that perspective will become more nuanced with age—it could even transform completely.

When I first started doing comedy, I talked almost exclusively about a bad breakup. Because I was 24, this bad breakup felt to me like one of the most significant events in all of human history. My girlfriend had cheated on me, and I was mad. And drunk. So I was mad and I was drunk. I was the drunk comedian who was mad at his ex-girlfriend. I thought I was doing a really good—possibly groundbreaking—comedic job. I most certainly was not.

Twenty years later I realize that my drinking made having a successful relationship with *anyone* impossible—so now I talk about that. It turns out comedy audiences would rather see me honestly appraise my own faults than watch me yell about how it's all somebody else's fault.

But there is something much more significant than a limited perspective that makes stand-up comedy particularly hard for young comedians today. They are the first generation of adults who grew up with social media.

Social media rewards conformity—literally. Kids who use Facebook learn quickly that restating a prevailing opinion is rewarded with lots of "likes." Going against a prevailing opinion invites bullying and even "unfriending." I know ADULTS who get upset if they are "unfriended"—imagine how a teenager must feel. Social media's message to a young person is crystal clear: Keep your original thoughts to yourself, and there won't be any trouble.

Comedy is meant to challenge "prevailing opinion," not reflect it. There's not a damn thing funny about people congratulating each other for thinking the same thing—that's what church is for. It's the differences of opinion, the original thoughts—the stuff social media discourages—that form the basis for good comedy.

Most "comedy" shows today consist of young people saying things that they hope the audience will agree with. The comedian is "posting" out loud. The laughter and applause are "likes." It's live-action social media, and not only is it not funny—it's frightening.

If you do "blip bloppity," Daniel, make sure to speak your mind.

Investment Advice

....

PUBLISHED NOVEMBER 3, 2015.

Dear King,

Does it make more sense to focus on making additional payments on a mortgage, or instead try to increase my 401K contribution? The stock market seems like it's at a point where it may not do much better than offset our mortgage interest, and in fact may do much worse. Also, how do you feel about this new generation of robo-investors like Wealthfront or Betterment? Trendy fad or here to stay? Thanks!

—Sawyer in Franklin

HOLY FUCK. "Sawyer"?! Jesus. A guy named Sawyer *would* ask a question like this. Fun fact: I grew up in Connecticut surrounded by people like "Sawyer." Rich white dudes. Dudes named Sawyer and Tucker and Hunter and Brooks and Chandler and "Stopher." That's right, "Stopher." Derived from Christopher, pronounced like the frozen dinner. My name is Christopher. If I ever get into a situation where I need to sound like a pompous ass, I've got "Stopher" in my back pocket. These names are intended to call to mind a historical period when the world was fancier and more "civilized." I believe this ultra-violent and xenophobic, super-sophisticated period has a name—the European Colonial Period.*

It happened from the 1500s until the mid-1900s. That was when white people named Phineas and Alistair ran around the globe "discovering" countries that already were full of people. After enslaving the locals and draining the land of its natural resources, they knighted each other. It's still happening. It's called "globalism" now. Sounds better. Corporations are the new colonizers, but PR firms had them tone down the names and outfits so it's not as obvious that they are shit-people. The community liaison for Exxon Mobil calls himself "Larry" now—not his real name, "Sawyer Twiddlington III." When "Larry" (known around the office as The Earl of Stouffer) says he "discovered" oil in Nile Delta—which the locals have known about for centuries and left in the ground on purpose—he isn't wearing jodhpurs and a pith helmet and twirling his mustache. He's wearing a polo shirt and pleated khakis. These modern fuckers twirl their mustaches ON THE INSIDE.

The women from this crowd are named things like Eliza and Mildred and Peyton. Those are supposed to be old-time-Caucasian-classy too.

Interior: Skull and Bones frat house, Yale University. Chandler is drinking out of Geronimo's skull with a straw.

TUCKER: Hey Chandler. Who is that topless chick doing the keg stand?
CHANDLER: That's Hester Plymouth Rock Manifest Destiny Alcott.
TUCKER: She just puked.

Anyway, Sawyer, you racist scumbag,** I have no idea what your question is about.

I know what kind of talk that is, though.

. . . .

* Extremely white Fox News host Megyn Kelly's kids are named "Yates," "Yardley" and "Thatcher." No joke.

** It's OK! This isn't even a real person!

That's the kind of gibberish Wall Street types use to make their useless gambling sound legit. The free market collapsed in 2008. The Federal Reserve printed fake money and gave it to their friends. Today's stock market is a SUBSIDY. A high-speed, insider-traded SUBSIDY for the well-off. I can't wait until the fraudulent mortgages fueling this current round of condo madness destroy everything AGAIN. Will Americans tolerate a SECOND bailout? I'm excited to find out. In the meantime, anyone with a brain should vote for Bernie Sanders.*

Also, re: "Trendy fad or here to stay?" All fads are trendy, by definition.

Wedding at an Antebellum Plantation

PUBLISHED MARCH 24, 2015.

Dear Advice King,

My friend wants to get married at an antebellum plantation. How do I explain to her why that is a terrible idea?

—Sally in Inglewood

First of all, John Q. Public, in case you don't know why it's a terrible idea to get married on an antebellum plantation, google "SLAVERY," asshole.

NOW . . .

Good luck. She must be *really* dumb. Why are you friends with someone that dumb? Does she know what "antebellum" means? She probably thinks it means "deluxe." She's not going to want to hear what it really means. She's going to get mad at you and say you are being

* I have received a number of questions about whether I support Bernie Sanders. I do.

"negative" when you tell her. Americans are used to doing whatever they want whenever they want, and any person who gets in the way of that is called a "hater." The valid information conveyed by a "hater" (the history of plantations, in this case) is labeled "negativity" by the person who is made uncomfortable (i.e., forced to think) by that information.

Sally, pretend your friend—let's call her Linda—wants to invade Iraq in 2003 instead of getting married at an antebellum plantation. Linda has a good old-fashioned American "gut feeling" that the war is going to be easy. You will be playing the role of a "General Eric Shinseki-esque realist" (General Shinseki is the hater who had the nerve to suggest that invading Iraq might be difficult) opposite Linda's "Cheney-o-pathic" type in the following playlet:

[CURTAIN UP]

Two women sit in the restaurant of a country club eating salads with grilled chicken on them. Each has a glass of Chardonnay.

LINDA: Sally, I'm going to invade Iraq, and I would like your help. I think if we can just get all the girls who play doubles on Thursdays and some Range Rovers . . . "My belief is we will, in fact, be greeted as liberators. . . . I think it will go relatively quickly . . . [in] weeks rather than months."*

SALLY: I think we are going to need more people than just the doubles girls, Linda. Aren't you concerned that sectarian warfare might erupt between the Shiites and the Sunnis?

LINDA [IRRITATED]: Am I concerned if it will be sunny? Nectarine warfare? What the hell are you talking about?! Just drink your wine and nod your head like a good friend is supposed to! Do me a favor and put a note on the bulletin board by the pool that says the Thursday doubles girls are invading Iraq next week and that everyone should cook something. It'll be a potluck invasion! I'm so excited!

. . . .

* Dick Cheney in 2003.

SALLY: Linda, we can't invade Iraq in tennis dresses. I don't think you've done the proper . . .

LINDA [VERY ANGRY]: *SHUT UP, SALLY!* I'm tired of all this!! What has gotten into you?! I can't believe I used to think you were cool!

Linda stomps out.

THE END

In real life, General Shinseki and Dick Cheney aren't friends anymore. Dick stomped out of the country club without finishing his salad. See, Dick *REEAAALLLY WANTED* to invade Iraq—he already had his dress picked out and everything.

"A *TRUE* friend would be supportive of my decisions, not try to make me feel bad about them. Don't hate, Shinseki!"*

What does all this have to do with you and Linda, you ask? I'll tell you. Anyone insensitive enough to have a wedding at an antebellum plantation is either ignorant, entitled or racist—and they're probably all three. Ignorance breeds racism and entitlement, entitlement breeds ignorance and racism. The ignorant, entitled, racist architects of the Iraq War didn't like inconvenient facts that interfered with their plans, and I doubt your moronic friend will be interested in anything you have to say that might complicate her ignorant, entitled, racist wedding.

My Son Is a Gun Nut

PUBLISHED MARCH 10, 2015.

Dear Advice King,

I have a young adult son who is a smart, funny and seemingly well-adjusted person, but is rather obsessed with guns and lately has been

*Dick Cheney in the Advice King's imagination.

saying he wants to go off the grid and live in the woods in preparation for some kind of Armageddon. I make light of it because I feel that if I counter him strongly, he will be more resolved to go to that extreme. He has a loving family and support system, as well as having been provided all of the tools he needs to earn a living and make his way in the world. What's a worried mother to do?

Sincerely,

—*Vexed Liberal Parent*

First of All, THIS CAN'T BE A REAL QUESTION. I NEED REAL FUCKING QUESTIONS!!! No actual liberal mom would say cutesy stuff like, "What's a worried mother to do?" if her son was moving to the woods. Seriously. Please. OK, now . . .

Hmmmm, a well-adjusted gun nut? The bar for being well-adjusted is set pretty low these days. And "rather obsessed." That sounds nice, "rather obsessed." Ted Bundy was "rather obsessed" with sorority girls. No bigs. Just kidding, *your son is a loon.*

Or maybe I'm just uptight. Is moving to the woods the rural-Tennessee equivalent of going to the prom? You don't happen to live in Beersheba Springs, do you? In Hornbeak the prom is chasing a weasel with a hammer. What is a "young adult," by the way? I am assuming you mean a teenager. If you are talking about a 30-year-old, you and his father should tackle him and stuff him in a laundry bag as soon as you are finished reading this sentence. If he's a teen, where is he getting the idea that Armageddon is nigh? Is he playing too much *Call of Duty* or *Assassin's Creed* or *Green Beret Hootenanny*? JUST KIDDING AGAIN.

I can't blame any young person exposed to Fox News or "conservative" talk radio for heading for the woods. I put "conservative" in quotes because "trying to scare the shit out of everybody" is not a political position; it's a way to steer dollars toward defense contractors, security contractors, gun manufacturers, gun dealers, Walmart's camping department and Michael Chertoff's nude body scanner concession. If, as a side effect of this moneymaking scheme, the entire

U.S. population is terrorized (this is the *real* terrorism in America) and has to buy psychiatric medication, all the better for Big Pharma. If a few nervous types get *way too fucking scared* and go on shooting rampages, well then that just means the police need tanks and everybody needs more guns and more meds and it keeps going and going. The "conservative" economy is bloody, depressing madness. Literally. I am not saying that the "liberal" politicians aren't complicit in this fear jamboree, and I know the two-party system is just a monster with two heads, but there are *some* sane "liberals" and there are zero sane "conservatives." ANYHOO . . .

So you are thinking maybe the thing to do is to pretend you are supportive of your funny, smart, well-adjusted survivalist? But how?

"Hey Mom, I am going to move to the woods with a bunch of guns."

"OK, don't be home too late!"

(I want to know what kind of jokes this guy does. Are they all related to Armageddon prep? Like, "Larry is only planning to establish a 30-foot perimeter around his foodstuffs! HAHAHA." Or, "You're not going to take down one of the Four Horsemen of the Apocalypse with a .22! Can you imagine . . . HAHAHA. Mom, I mean, just . . . Larry thinks . . . HAHA . . . picture the Horseman being like, 'What was that, a bug?' . . . HAHAHAHA . . . I mean . . .")

You must counter him strongly, Vexed Liberal Parent. The world isn't ending—it just sucks—and what good would a gun do if it were? Your weapons expert/comedian should know this better than anyone. Alert him to the long history of people thinking that Armageddon was coming—and I mean *long*—and being wrong. Let him know that thinking Armageddon is coming and deciding to move to the woods is just a maniac's version of taking guitar lessons. Tell him that if he is really concerned about the state of the world he should try to change it for the better, not go hide.

Should I Get Right with God?

. . . .

PUBLISHED SEPTEMBER 16, 2020.

Dear Advice King,

My mom used to say that we all need to "get right with God" before we die. Now that we're clearly in the End Times, it actually feels relevant. But how do I "get right with God" if I'm not even religious? I don't know what to do!

—Anonymous Heathen in Los Angeles

Great question, Anonymous Heathen! I agree with your mom! It's always a good time to "get right with god"—but it depends very much on which "god" you mean. I'm pretty sure your mother intended for you to "get right" with the Christian version of God. Christians believe that God is a vengeful man with a beard who watches humanity from above, judging their actions—and threatening retribution.

The God your mom is talking about allows people to act like assholes their whole life as long as, at the last minute, they ask for forgiveness. That's right, the God the Christians conceived promises that even the world's biggest dicks can get into heaven as long as they ask for forgiveness before they die.

Call me crazy, but that sounds suspiciously like a god invented by some folks who wanted to be able to break all the rules and not get in trouble. I don't believe in gods who issue "get out of jail free" cards. I also don't believe in gods who issue jail.

I've been thinking a lot about getting right with *my* god lately, Anonymous Heathen.

Getting right with my god has nothing to do with asking for forgiveness on my deathbed after a life of crime, because I do not believe in a god that is made in my image. Oh, I know the Bible says that we were "made in the image of God," but it seems pretty obvious to me that since men wrote the Bible, it has to be the other way around. Judging, condemning, forgiving, punishing? Those are human behaviors, projected onto God. Once you accept that the Christian God was made in *man's* image, it makes sense that he focuses on men. And when I say he focuses on men, I do not mean the male gender (although he does that too). I mean that since he looks on the world through eyes modeled on human eyes, he focuses almost exclusively on humans, as human eyes tend to do.

Why doesn't this Christian God give animals a heaven? What happens to the people who lived before the Bible was published? Are they supposed to suck eggs? And what kind of god says, "Render to Caesar the things that are Caesar's"? A god created by man, in the image of man—that's who. Do you actually believe that the real God would create the ENTIRE UNIVERSE and also have opinions on taxes?

My god doesn't forgive people who mistreat, subjugate, steal, lie or cheat. My god does not forgive greed. My god does not forgive OR condemn. My god offers joy and shame in abundance—you get to decide which you prefer. My god is you, me, dogs, trees, foxes, deer, dirt and the atoms that make up the pigment of the colors of every person, paint hue and flower. My god is everything. My god is love.

Get right with god, Anonymous—but make sure you've got the right one.

Should I Try L.A.'s "Hot Chicken"?

. . . .

PUBLISHED JANUARY 5, 2021.

Dear Advice King,

I notice a lot of "hot chicken" places springing up around L.A., and I recently learned it's a Nashville creation. As a Nashville native, do you recommend I try one of these places, or is it just going to be "inauthentic" and disappointing?

—Hungry in Hollywood

I don't think you ALWAYS have to have an umbrella with you, Agatha. Especially if your husband is terrified of them. You make a good point when you say that weather reports are unreliable, but if it's going to break up your marriage . . .

I tried to answer the question without reading it again. I thought you were a rain-phobic woman named Agatha whose husband is scared of umbrellas.

Thanks for the question, "Hungry in Hollywood." First of all, I am not a Nashville native—I'm from Connecticut. I moved to Nashville in 2001. What food is Connecticut known for? Frozen peas? Assorted overcooked meats? In Connecticut (at least in the 1970s and '80s) the spiciest thing happening was Gulden's Mustard. Spicy foods were considered "exotic," and I got the definite vibe that people who ate them should be regarded with suspicion. Here's a short play I wrote about it, called *The Red Phone*:

THE RED PHONE

Connecticut, 1978; interior, split-level ranch

Agitated suburban father puts down his gin and tonic and tennis racket, lights cigarette, feverishly dials red rotary phone.

"Hello. Is this the FBI? May I speak to whoever is in charge of the House Un-American Activities Committee? I'm in Connecticut and I'm pretty sure I saw my neighbor eating salsa! It's CLOSED?! Who am I supposed to call? Yes, I'll hold."

The hold music is a mariachi band.

A man wearing a sombrero sneaks up behind him, and strangles him with the phone cord.

World explodes.

THE END

As I have previously mentioned, all the best plays end with the world exploding.

Hot chicken was invented in Nashville by an African American family. A long time ago. When Nashville was still segregated, and the country music industry was in its infancy.

These days, Nashville is a "destination city," with glittering hotels and skyrocketing rent. African Americans continue to be forced out of historically Black neighborhoods by developers looking for new places to put luxury condominiums and, wait for it . . . HOT CHICKEN RESTAURANTS.

Prince's Hot Chicken is the original—and authentic—hot chicken. When the Prince family invented hot chicken back in the first half of the 20th century, it wasn't intended for white people—not because the Princes were racist, but because white people had segregated them! Now it's being used as a novelty to entice wealthy whites to Nashville. (No state income tax! Hot chicken! Tomi Lahren!). And—you guessed it—the knockoff versions aren't nearly as spicy as the original.

Prince's Hot Chicken is Chuck Berry, and all the rest are John Mayer. Long live Prince's, long live economic diversity, long live heat. Fuck lukewarm luxury.

Dating a Stripper

. . . .

PUBLISHED FEBRUARY 3, 2021.

Dear Advice King,

My new girlfriend just told me she used to be a stripper. For some reason it's making me uneasy, even though I'm an open-minded guy. Is this normal, or is there something wrong with me?

Thanks!

—Sean from Albany

I'm not sure how often you have to plow your fields, Henry. It's probably on the internet somewhere. I think you might have to do it every day. Or maybe just on Mondays, and then you plant on Tuesday. And then the crops are ready Sunday, and then you plow again. I'm really not sure. One thing I do know is that if you're growing carrots, you'll need some big ladders at harvest time. Carrot trees are very tall.

Hi Sean. I tried to answer the question without reading it again. I guessed you were a novice farmer named Henry who was wondering how often he has to plow his fields.

There's definitely something wrong with you, and it's YOU HAVE COVID. Where did you find this "new" girlfriend? New Zealand?

I'm just kidding, Sean. I'm sure there's no COVID in Albany.

So your ex-stripper girlfriend is making you uneasy. Story of my life. I'm kidding again—I've never had a girlfriend.

OK, seriously? I don't care about this. This is not a problem. Are you afraid she's going to start stripping at your mom's house when you take her to meet your mom? And then your mom will think stripping is cool, and she'll want to strip too? And then your mom will leave your dad and run away with this woman and open a strip club where they both spend all day stripping? Are you afraid they'll name the strip club "Stupid Sean's"?

I've got news for you, Sean: You're a stripper. I'm a stripper, too. We're all strippers. Humans are all hustlers, working to put food on the table. Some of us work in cubicles, stripped of the sun and sky. Some earn lofty degrees, and are stripped of their youth. Some of us *actually* strip, and get to dance naked to heavy metal.

Here are the things you should really be worrying about: Is she nice? Are you nice? Does she snore? Do you snore? Do you both enjoy *Boardwalk Empire*?

Here's a poem about stripping:

STRIPPING

honesty
that's what there
isn't enough of
in this world
we have buckets
and
boatloads of fear and sanctimony
which become judgment
when we put 'em
in blenders
in our mean little
kitchens
we could be shaking
our asses
like
free naked icebergs
but we put on faces
like deck rivets
and go down with
the ship

I Don't Understand My Grandchild's Gender-Neutral Pronouns

. . . .

PUBLISHED MARCH 3, 2021.

Dear Advice King,

Back when I was growing up, a boy was a boy and a girl was a girl. Now my grandson insists we call him "they" for some reason. It's baffling—he's only one person, right?! All these new labels are silly. How can I get through to him?

—Very Confused in Philadelphia

"Back when I was growing up, a boy was a boy and a girl was a girl."

How interesting. Back when I was growing up there were no gay people. That's right, there were no gay people in my hometown. Seems impossible, right? It seems impossible because it is indeed impossible. But as far as I knew there weren't any. And do you know why? Because the gay people in my hometown probably did not feel like my hometown was a safe place to be gay. And they were right. They would have faced discrimination at best, violence at worst. So if I were an IDIOT, I could walk around saying, "Back when I was growing up, everyone was straight." But that wouldn't make it true, "Very Confused." At least you know that you are confused.

Now, why do you suppose the gay folks in my town would have faced discrimination and violence? I'll tell you why, since you are admittedly confused: religion.

Almost everyone in my tiny, all-white Connecticut hometown was a Christian. I was too. We were taught from a young age that homosexuality was a sin. We were also taught that homosexuality was a choice. Grown men (Catholic priests) told me (a child) that there were no "true" homosexuals. According to them, "homosexuals" were actually heterosexuals who chose to have gay sex "for kicks." Since I was a *child*, and *adults* were telling me this, I believed them. And it wasn't really something I had to think about much since, COINCIDENTALLY, there were "no gay people" in my hometown.

I was lucky, "Very Confused." I got out. I went to college and started dating a nice woman who was much smarter than me. She had grown up in a CITY, where she had ACTUALLY KNOWN gay people! She told me that everything I had been led to believe about gay people was incorrect. I think her exact words to me were something like, "What the fuck are you talking about?" I quickly realized that I had no idea what I was talking about, and I immediately began to question EVERYTHING I had "learned" in my tiny, all-white, "all-straight," almost-all-Christian Connecticut hometown: "Hey Linda, I just realized something . . . CHRISTOPHER COLUMBUS WAS AN ASSHOLE!"

There has never been a time when "a boy was a boy, and a girl was a girl." There have only been times when fearful, superstitious people made it unsafe for boys to be girls, and girls to be boys.

I sincerely believe that so many cisgender Christian Americans are throwing a countrywide tantrum because they're worried that they won't be allowed to bully people anymore. I also believe that cisgender Americans are pretty sure that bullying is a God-given right that is mentioned in the U.S. Constitution. I think their thought process goes something like: "Oh, so we can't be mean to people of color or women or gays because of 'cancel culture'?! Well, let's be mean to transgender people because there aren't enough of them to fight back!"

The Tennessee state senate just voted to approve a bill banning transgender athletes from competing in middle and high school sports under their gender identity. That's right, the ADULTS in the Tennessee state senate passed legislation specifically designed to ostracize CHILDREN. God's children. God makes heterosexual children, homosexual children and children who decide to transition to the genders that suit them. AND GOD LOVES THEM ALL. Less than 1 percent of United States citizens report that they are transgender. Targeting minorities is THE OPPOSITE of what Jesus preached.

FACT: The Bible says A LOT about people loving one another, and NOT A DAMN THING about sports.

Also, fuck middle and high school sports. For every success story, there are countless kids traumatized.

So your grandchild wants to be called "they." And that brings up a lot of issues for you, "Very Confused." It makes you scared that the order of "your" world is being upset. Well here's the good news, Grandpa: God's world has always been gloriously disordered, and . . . IT'S NOT YOUR WORLD ANYMORE. It is your grandchild's world. Let it, and them, evolve.

Having Fun during a Pandemic, Vol. 1

. . . .

PUBLISHED MARCH 18, 2020.

Dear Advice King,

What should we do while we're at home hiding from the coronavirus?

—Everyone

HOLY SHIT! It's my time to shine!

I've been living a quarantine-esque lifestyle for years—and I've been having a blast! This week's column will be the beginning of a series: THE ADVICE KING GUIDE TO HAVING FUN DURING A PANDEMIC™.

First of all, I feel like I should mention that right about . . . NOW, we are all *beginning to suspect* that giving 26 people half the money in the world might have been a bad idea. And it's pretty fucking funny—but really not funny at all—that the Federal Reserve can magically pull $1.5 trillion out of its ass to try to plug a hole in the stock market. $1.5 TRILLION. *TRILLION.* But we need to cut Medicare and Social Security.

"Oh, we'll be cutting."—Donald Trump

What's also pretty fucking funny—but not really funny at all—is the fact that ultra-right-wing Christians have been trying to use American foreign policy as a tool (i.e., moving the U.S. Embassy to Jerusalem) to trigger the apocalypse. "But why would anyone *want* the apocalypse?" you might ask. These maniacs hope to have all of life's big questions answered by God IN THEIR LIFETIME. OK, boomer. They want it all: Coldplay, Facebook, golf shirts, Diet Coke and then, at the end, for dessert—all the answers! Typical Christians, humble to a fault.

You also might justifiably ask why I dragged this particular group of extra-depressing Christians into this super-fun column. It's because instead of rewarding their embassy-moving and Iraq-invading with a heavenly Q&A on the nature of existence, God has gifted US ALL with COVID-19! Nice job, assholes!

One more thing before we get to the fun: In the midst of this crisis—or any crisis—be careful not to drink your own urine TOO EARLY.

There may come a time in the next few weeks when you will feel frightened and confused, and you will be tempted to engage in the time-honored emergency measure of "drinking your own urine." While this is completely understandable, make sure you're not doing it too soon! One time I got stuck in an elevator at work, and I panicked and drank my own urine. It felt like I had been trapped for days! I was just starting my second glass when the elevator door opened and my boss got on. The police report said I was only in there for 45 minutes. You live and learn.

THE ADVICE KING GUIDE TO HAVING FUN DURING A PANDEMIC™, VOL. 1

Watch New England Wildlife & More's YouTube channel.

It's a pretty misleading name for a YouTube channel, actually. The "host" mostly opens old cans of food. I haven't seen him interact with any wildlife at all, as a matter of fact. He's usually indoors. (His distraught mom's basement?) He opens old cans of food from the 1930s, '40s, '50s, '60s and '70s. He's like an oldies station, except instead of playing "Rock

Around the Clock," he sniffs (and sometimes eats!) 1950s creamed corn. An oldies DJ has a turntable, New England Wildlife & More has a can opener. Rock 'n' roll has a good beat, this guy opens bad beets. Do you like this metaphor? I do.

This is 100 percent true, by the way, and it is oddly entertaining. This man has sniffed and tasted so much expired food that, in my humble opinion, he is a national treasure.

Stay safe, everybody. We are gonna make it to the other side of this. All my love!

Having Fun during a Pandemic, Vol. 2

PUBLISHED APRIL 1, 2020.

Dear Advice King,

Should I "social distance" and self-quarantine like a responsible adult, or should I just be a complete asshole and keep going places and coughing on people because I choose to be a terrible person and not to take COVID-19 seriously?

Signed sincerely,

—Leopold in Nashville

Hi, Leopold! (Leopold is the fakest name I have ever encountered in the five years I have been in the advice business, but I understand the spirit of the question.)

I will answer your question with another question, Leopold.

What if the fire department was all lawyers?

That's right. Your house is on fire and you call the fire department, and a bunch of lawyers show up to fight the fire. Only they don't fight the fire. They stand in front of the fire and have a press conference. They say the fire isn't a big deal. And they talk about money. FOR WEEKS. They say the fire is contained. A pillow salesman steps up to the podium and tells everyone to read the Bible. And the fire burns.

The lawyers didn't bring any water, either. They say that they are not in charge of bringing water. They say it is supposed to be provided by other people, and the fire burns. They give trillions of dollars to banks and airlines, but that doesn't put out the fire. They say that maybe all the old people in America should be willing to sacrifice themselves so the fire will go out. The fire that's not even a big deal. But the fire still burns, and they realize that they can't take that thing back—that thing they said about the old people.

Then, after a month of talking to television cameras about money, they notice that the house has burned completely to the ground. So they say: "We take no responsibility because we are lawyers, real estate developers and a pillow salesman. Why did you put us in charge of a fire department?" They say 200,000 people might die because they don't know how to fight fires. They say they are doing an amazing job for amateur firefighters, though. And they say, "Who could have predicted that there would be fires, anyway?"

Yes, people should stay home. Yes, people should practice social distancing—but you would never know that from the actions of the governor of Tennessee. He's a businessman in charge of a health crisis, after all—it's not his fault. The governor of Florida is the same. A businessman in charge of a health crisis. And they're both Republicans. They, along with Donald Trump, John Cornyn, Sean Hannity and Laura Ingraham—as well as countless others—thought they could "own the libs" by making them look hysterical about this virus. But it turns out "the libs" were right, and it was the governors, the president, the senators and the pundits that got "owned."

But you know who REALLY got owned? The people who are dying from this virus. Not everything is fake news, turns out, and real life is not a game of "who owns who."

People are not "libs," or "Republicans," or "immigrants." People are just humans. Mortal humans who are in desperate need of masks, ventilators and leadership.

Take care of each other. We will get through this, and with any luck we will emerge from this more compassionate—and prepared.

Now, a little bit of fun. It's the second installment of the Advice King's Guide to Having Fun During a Pandemic!

THE ADVICE KING GUIDE TO HAVING FUN IN A PANDEMIC™, VOL. 2

Follow me on Twitter! I have been doing a thing called "The Poetry Window" almost every day. When the poetry window is open, you can submit a poem topic, and I will write it! It's a free service, and it is helping me stay sane. I hope it will bring some joy to your days in quarantine. If you don't want to actually join Twitter, you can still read the poems! Just put "@thecroftonshow" into your favorite search engine. Here are some examples:

"Bird Watching"

what kinda
bird is
that?
I don't fucking
know
it's
my
first day

It's either an eagle
or
a huge finch

"History"

the hulls
of
wooden
ships
on the bottom of
the
sea
calling
us
home

"Clear Plastic Furniture Coverings"

thank god
mom
is insane
or we would
have mustard
on the
ottoman

And one more thing: Listen to "I Love a Rainy Night" by Eddie Rabbit as often as possible.

Having Fun during a Pandemic, Vol. 3

. . . .

PUBLISHED APRIL 16, 2020.

Dear Advice King,

My elderly father is a Republican, and I cannot get him to take the coronavirus seriously. He continues to play tennis and golf, and is extremely casual about social distancing. He thinks the Democrats are exaggerating the pandemic to ruin the economy and make Trump look bad. What should I do? I'm afraid he's going to die, and I love him!

—Larissa in Miami

It wasn't that long ago that Republicans were the ones who made fun of "conspiracy theorists." I am one (a conspiracy theorist, not a Republican), so I should know.

I believe that the Loch Ness Monster was the gunman on the grassy knoll. A gut feeling tells me the Zodiac Killer was one of the members of Canadian rock band April Wine. I have "Rendlesham Forest Incident" tattooed on my, ahem, "lower back." And I still have not heard a satisfactory explanation for why Building 7 collapsed on 9/11. (The last one is real.)

In the years after 9/11, Republicans were the most aggressive in telling me to stop asking questions about it. They said, basically, that it was disrespectful to question the official narrative of a national tragedy. Building 7 fell down because it was on fire, they said. That's what the media and the government say, so you should believe them, they said.

Then, during the buildup to the doomed, unnecessary invasion of Iraq, those same Republicans told me that questioning the official narrative would be *unpatriotic*. If someone on TV says that aluminum tubes equal nuclear weapons, we should believe them, they said. The intelligence agencies would never lie, they said. Those old-time (early-2000s) Republicans were big believers in "official stories."

Those days are gone. These days, Republicans pick and choose what they believe. Intelligence agents are "deep-state operatives." Things that make them anxious are deemed to be either fake or caused by George Soros—including the coronavirus.

Why was it disrespectful, Republicans, for me to ask questions about disasters—after the fact (9/11), or before they occurred (the Iraq invasion), mind you—but it's OK for you to scream "hoax" *during* a pandemic while your fellow citizens lay dying?

I'll tell you why. Republicans—*especially* baby boomer Republicans—have a vague notion that they are invincible. They were raised on jingoistic slogans like "A Shining City Upon a Hill" and "The Greatest Generation." If you are operating under the Shining City/Greatest Generation model, abstract threats like global warming and coronavirus have GOT TO BE labeled fake, because they cannot be shot or bought. Abstract enemies scare the hell out of Republicans. They undermine the belief system that keeps them "sane"—a belief system that only works as long as there is a nameable enemy (terrorists, immigrants, liberals, etc.). You can't put diseases and temperature changes in internment camps. Republicans did not doubt the media narrative around 9/11 because it presented a situation tailored to the "Shining City" worldview—a situation that could, seemingly, be resolved through violence.

Grow up, elderly Republicans. Just because you can't shoot it, doesn't mean it's fake™.

Put down that tennis racket and put on a mask like all the other mortals.

Well, that was unpleasant. But this is fun:

THE ADVICE KING GUIDE TO HAVING FUN IN A PANDEMIC™, VOL. 3

OK, today's first tip is to listen to John Denver's album *Spirit*, and drink cold brew. That's what I'm doing right now at 3:30 a.m. on a Tuesday, 'cuz honestly, WHERE DO YOU HAVE TO BE? Warning: Skip "It Makes Me Giggle."

When you wake up at 7 p.m. because you took my dumb advice and drank cold brew at 3:30 a.m., watch 1980s Daytona 500 races in their entirety on YouTube!

Today I watched the whole 1981 Daytona 500. If you don't know who won, I won't spoil it for you, but I will tell you that the announcers talk more about how windy it is than they do about the actual race. Also, the cars are smaller than they used to be in the 1970s, and the drivers complain about it a lot. They say that the new, smaller, 1981 cars get "squirrelly"—which is a real racing term, apparently.

Stay safe! Remember, there's no such thing as Republicans or Democrats anyway—just people.

Should I Start a Home-Based Business?

PUBLISHED MAY 13, 2020.

Dear Advice King,

I know someone who is always pushing her home-based MLM business on all her friends. We thought she was crazy and caught up in a scam, but now I'm wondering: Since we're all stuck at home, isn't this really the perfect time to start a home-based business?

Thanks!

—Elizabeth in Los Angeles

Hold on while I put "MLM" into the ol' Goog. Ohhhh, multi-level marketing—pyramid schemes. HOT TIP: If you are going to join a pyramid scheme, make sure to get in near the bottom. You don't want to be the one left holding all the soap™.

Seriously, don't do a pyramid scheme, Elizabeth. I did one once, in 1972. Hypoallergenic motor oil. I ended up having to rent my friend's disused greenhouse to store the stuff. One time we got drunk and opened a couple cans. It was root beer! That's how I lost wife number two—but who's keeping count right? *Cries, pants fall down.*

I think you should start a home-based business. I started one. I'm not going outside until they find a vaccine or I'm at the wrong end of a cattle prod. They HAVEN'T CURED THE DISEASE YET. *HELLOOOOOOOOOOO.*

What business are you going to start? I started one called Poetry Mailbox™. I send custom, handwritten poems to people in the mail. I am not kidding.

I've always worked in restaurants and bars, Elizabeth. Because of the ongoing pandemic, restaurants are not a safe place to be right now. The fact that some politicians have had the gall to recommend opening restaurants while the case numbers are still climbing—while they themselves continue to work from home—is FUCKING DIABOLICAL.

Restaurants are not essential businesses. The grocery stores are open. People have stoves. A restaurant providing takeout service with a small, trusted staff makes sense. Forcing every server and bartender off of unemployment and into harm's way is UNCONSCIONABLE. Any fool who would sit down to eat in a restaurant right now is either insane or they think this virus is a hoax. And that means they haven't been practicing social distancing, which in turn means that the servers and bartenders will be justifiably terrified—and broke! The restaurants will be half-full *by law*, which means the servers will not be able to make a living. In many states, servers work almost entirely for tips. Their hourly wage is less than $3. Read that again. THEIR HOURLY WAGE IS LESS THAN $3. Half-capacity means 50 percent tips, which does *not* equal a living wage.

Why are they being forced to go to work? I'll tell you why. The restaurant workers—and the hairdressers and the tattoo artists—are the canaries in the capitalist coal mine.

The wealthy and powerful consider the workers at these businesses to be disposable. Oh, I know not all of them do. But take a look around—

many of them do. I've personally met wealthy folks who take pride (out loud) in the fact that they've never "had to" wait tables. And they take equal pride in the fact that they didn't know anybody who does (they let me know that I got a pass because I was a musician). They think that the people who *are* waiting tables are "stuck" doing so through some fault of their own. Wealthy people who were born into wealth (most of our politicians, Tucker Carlson, etc.) are even more convinced of this. To them, being a server in a restaurant is the result of a very specific personal failing: laziness. Therefore, servers deserve what they get. If that happens to be death from coronavirus, well, that's a shame—but hey, sometimes that's what you get in a capitalist society if you don't work hard enough. *Atlas—and Tucker Carlson—shrugged.*

I was at a dive bar in Nashville when a famously Republican, wealthy, Fox News-contributing country singer entered, extremely drunk. He had a bodyguard with him. He joined a table full of people, uninvited. He told them that they all looked like "worthless pieces of shit." Then he asked if any of them "had jobs." One man said yes, that he worked at a delicatessen. "That's not a job," the Fox News contributor snarled. "I mean a real job." When the man stood up to fight him, the singer's bodyguard stepped between them. The bodyguard and the country singer left the bar, got into a waiting limousine, and disappeared into the night.

It seemed to me that the drunken, famously Republican country singer had come into that bar SPECIFICALLY to insult working-class people. AND IT WAS TRUE. The bartender told me that it wasn't the first time he'd seen him do it.

Working people, protect yourselves. The people in power do not know us, they do not respect us, and in many cases, they actively DESPISE us. They are sending us out there to see if we get sick. They're trying to find out if it's safe for them. Don't be a rich person's canary. STAY HOME.

Can We Heal the Divided America?

PUBLISHED JANUARY 21, 2021.

Dear Advice King,

I keep hearing that the divisions in this country are too big to overcome, regardless of who's in charge. Do you think that's true, and if so, should I be scared or should I hold out hope that we can heal the divide?

—Denise in Alexandria, Va.

Fuck duvet covers. It's like trying to put a shirt on a ghost.

I tried to answer the question without reading it again. I thought you asked me my opinion on duvet covers.

Hi Denise! Thank you for the question. I have written on this topic before.

Here are some fresh Ruminations on Division™:

It's the oldest trick in the book. Divide and conquer.

"Let them eat conspiracies."

Get God out of it. God is not on either side. I'm not saying that there isn't a God, I'm saying that He or She is not invested in American politics. When it comes to day-to-day human civilization, God is the economy. In America, the middle class is (was) God.

Economic security is the ultimate deradicalizer.

The "gig economy" is NOT an economy. It is the next-to-bottom rung of America's informal caste system. The bottom rung is living on the street.

The "gig economy" is the crumbs crony capitalism left for those poor unfortunates who lack cronies.

The "gig economy" could just as easily be called the "errand boy" economy, and the service industry could be called the "servant industry."

When 10 percent of the country is going out to dinner every night, and the other 90 percent are servers, it's a rupture.*

More ruminating:

The "gig economy" leads to economic insecurity, which leads to loss of self-respect. Loss of self-respect leads to radicalization, ergo the "gig economy" radicalizes.

The "gig economy"—aka "the un-Christian no-benefits scam to get quickly delivered sandwiches"—is destabilizing American society. It will ultimately lead to worldwide class-based violence. Oligarchs know this, and that is why they are *literally* attempting to move to Mars.

Wealth hoarding (what we in America have been brainwashed to call "success" instead of a disorder) is inherently violent.

Hey, wealth hoarders! You better figure out a way to pass that money around, or the gig economaniacs will figure it out for you (pitchforks, torches).

Fuck the "gig economy," and fuck the focus group that decided to call it the "gig economy" instead of the much more accurate "only economy that's left when 50 people have all the money economy." And fuck duvet covers, even if you didn't ask about them.

And, finally: Empires fall. They always do.

Fun stuff!

Here's the good news: People survive. Empires fall, but people survive. And love is real. *And* love thrives in crisis. And . . . TURN OFF THE TV, MOM—IT IS SCARING YOU.

Last thing: Go listen to the Bob Dylan song "Only a Pawn in Their Game," because he says all the stuff I just said, using less words, in under four minutes.

* You may be wondering what "it's a rupture" means in this context. It means IT'S BAD. When I was in elementary school there was a song kids sang: "When you're sliding down a rail, and your balls catch on a nail, it's a RUPTURE! When you're sliding down a rope, and your balls start to smoke, it's a rupture!"

Reflecting on a Year in the Pandemic

. . . .

PUBLISHED MARCH 17, 2021.

Dear Advice King,

After a full year in lockdown, it seems like a good time to reflect on things. What do you think should be my main takeaway from this whole experience (so far)?

—George in Eugene, Ore.

Hi George! I don't know what your takeaway should be. I can only share mine. Do you want the good news or the bad news first? I'll start with the bad news.

I found out that a bunch of people FREAK OUT at the mention of death. Some of them freak out so badly that they pretend it isn't occurring. They say it's fake. They say that there is no disease. They say there are no people in the hospital. They say it's just the flu. They say it's a plot. They blame preexisting conditions. They say, "It's only the elderly," as if they themselves are not mortal, and will never be old.

I don't think these people are evil, George. I think they have been cornered, like rats, in the consumerist maze we call America. A cornered rat lashes out because it fears for its life. A cornered American lashes out because it doesn't know what to do with itself if it can't go to restaurants.

Death is dignified, consumer tantrums are not. They are disheartening. It has been deeply disappointing for me to discover that some humans are so obsessed with restaurants that they will deny death, and disrespect the dead. Death is not just "a time when you can't go to restaurants." It is something we all have to face. It's part of "God's plan," for chrissakes. We MUST do better in this area.

Now, the good news. I love nature! Before the pandemic, I had a hard time connecting with nature. If I went on a hike, it was because someone forced me. Usually, that person would be a woman, because women are smarter than men. And before you can say, "Hey, get a load of ol' Advice King, trying to score points with the ladies," consider this: When I was in college, my girlfriend had to convince me to spend a semester in Italy. I told her I didn't see why we had to travel all that way since "there was plenty of beer in Connecticut." Haha.

OK, women are smarter than *me*. How's that?

Anyway, before the pandemic, the whole time I was hiking I was thinking that I wished it would be over soon so I could sit in a coffee shop and play with my phone. I was preoccupied. I was itching to get back to the consumerist maze. I wasn't really in the woods—I was in my head.

When the pandemic hit, I couldn't go to the gym. I'm not a bodybuilder, but 30 minutes a day on the "hunting and gathering simulator" (elliptical) helps immensely with my depression. I didn't know what to do.

FUN FACT: I live in Monrovia, Calif. I live about 2,500 feet from the foothills of the San Gabriel Mountains. I had rarely even looked in their direction before the pandemic. I had always looked in the other direction—toward the coffee shops and movie theaters. For the first time in my life, I turned away from civilization. I turned toward the mountains.

I have now hiked those foothills HUNDREDS of times! I rely on them, and I love them. My new friends are bears, deer, flowers, oranges, avocados and the setting sun. I am a new man.

Death is nothing to fear. It's a sunset. And an orange. Fuck restaurants.

My Mom Is Afraid She'll Get "Canceled"

PUBLISHED MAY 12, 2021.

Dear Advice King,

My 78-year-old mother watches too much Fox News. She is extremely worried about "cancel culture." She's afraid she's going to be "canceled." My mother is retired. How do I convince my mom that she's not going to be canceled?

—Lori in San Francisco

She's gonna get canceled, all right—BY THE GRIM REAPER. That's the only cancellation she should be worried about. That's the only cancellation WE ALL should be worried about. Unless she has a podcast. If she has a podcast, she better watch her step. I'm kidding. I don't even know what that means, exactly. I'm not kidding about the Grim Reaper, though. That motherfucker is COMING. He's coming for you, me, moms, podcasts—the whole works.

The Grim Reaper is coming for Sean Hannity, Laura Ingraham, Steve Doocy and Ainsley Earhardt. He's also coming for Jake Tapper, Rachel Maddow and Joe Scarborough and Mika. Own the libs? The sun is gonna explode and OWN US ALL. The dinosaurs were famously canceled by a meteor. Cleopatra was canceled by an asp.

Metaphorically, the United States Congress is a gaggle of jabbering skeletons, yelling into skeleton cameras operated by skeleton camerapeople, beamed into skeleton televisions. The same skeleton congresspeople, televisions and cameras that will populate the windswept graveyards of our not-so-distant future.

Too much?

Elon Musk is a wealth-hoarding skeleton—one of the worst types. He recently hosted *Saturday Night Live*. *Saturday Night Live* is one of corporate America's premier skeleton showcases. It's on NBC, a network owned by Comcast. The board of directors of Comcast is populated by some of the scariest skeletons around, including the one that runs DuPont Chemical. It does not surprise me that Comcast would attempt to normalize wealth-hoarding by employing a charmless billionaire to host America's premier skeleton showcase—a comedy show, ostensibly. It's a comedy, all right—the "Upper Hell" of Dante's Divine Comedy, where the gluttonous reside.

WOW. I shouldn't have done acid that one time(s).

People reading this column might be thinking, "Why does this asshole always talk about the fact that we're all gonna die? We know that already!"

I agree! It seems as if it should not be necessary to remind mortals of their imminent deaths. But if everybody "knows this already," why are we acting like such dicks?

NEWS, not just Fox News—the whole mainstream modern information landscape—is a pornographic fear hayride designed to make people buy stuff. No one needs to know all this bad news. Bad news is a fact of our deeply flawed, unexplainable existence, and buying identity theft protection, gold, freeze-dried meals or Lamborghinis WON'T FIX IT. Guns won't fix it. Titillating yourself with dark, unlikely scenarios—MOM GOT CANCELED BY THE WOKE MOB—won't fix it.

All we can do is be kind, locally. Jesus was canceled by his own dad, and he still managed to do this. Fear is the enemy of love. Tell your mom to settle down.

CHAPTER 4

A LITTLE ABOUT ME

Buying a Used Car

. . . .

PUBLISHED OCTOBER 17, 2018.

Dear Advice King,

Do you have any tips for buying a used car? Also, should I buy a used car?

—Jordan in Butte, Mont.

One tip I have for buying a used car is DON'T BRING ME WITH YOU. I want to buy every car I see. And I don't want to haggle. I like to pay the exact price they are asking, right away. Through extensive psychotherapy, I have been able to determine why I prefer to pay full price: I am what is called a "people-pleaser." Being a people-pleaser is expensive, Jordan.

In 2003, I bought a 1986 Ford Econoline van that was in some old guy's yard with grass growing up real high around it. When the old man told me the van had been sitting there, undriven, for 10 years, I was excited! I really was. I'm not making that up. It's still not clear to me why I thought this was so great, but I'm pretty sure it had something to do with me imagining that the van would be "well-rested." Even with extensive psychotherapy, I have been unable to determine why I think cars need rest.

The man said he wanted $1,100. I climbed inside. There was wall-to-wall carpet. And a TABLE. It had a table in it. In the car. And the back seat folded down INTO A BED. The front passenger seat SWIVELED.

So I look at this, and I'm thinking, *That's like $3,000 worth of furniture.*

We took it for a test drive, and I couldn't help but notice that it stayed in first gear for much longer than most cars. The engine was really screaming when it finally dropped into second. And when I say it "dropped into second," I mean it DROPPED—it sounded like a bomb went off. I asked the man if there was something wrong with the transmission. To this day I'll never forget what that old bastard said. He said, "Not as far as I know."* That was good enough for me! I gave him $1,100 and roared away, powered by that well-rested first gear.

A couple days later I brought the van to a mechanic. (I should mention that this is another reason you shouldn't take me along when you buy a used car: I prefer to take the car to the mechanic after I buy it, rather than before.) They told me that they would tow it to a junkyard and have it crushed for me, free of charge. I was confused. "Hahaha," I said. "What do you mean?" I said. They said, "We will tow it away for you, and have it crushed." "Hahaha," I said. "What do you mean?"

This went on for a WHILE.

Everything on that van that was made of rubber was dry-rotted. Every fucking hose. Every fucking gasket. All four tires. There was a major oil leak. But I drove that thing for three years! It was the driving equivalent of cutting off your nose to spite your face. It got about six miles to the gallon. I COULD SEE THE GAS GAUGE NEEDLE MOVE AS I DROVE. I never used that goddamn table.

Jordan, I always look for used cars that cost around $1,100. The problem is, I can find a reason why ANY car is worth $1,100, so I buy it every time. I think crazy things like: "Look at all that stuff! Lights, seats, cigarette lighter, bumpers, hubcaps and a radio. And look how big it is! I bet the door handles and the horn are worth $1,100 by themselves!" Then it fails emissions and I own a bunch of valuable door handles.

Go ahead and buy a used car, Jordan, but remember: The engine is more important than the furniture™.

. . . .

* In that old man's defense, how was he supposed to respond? He's thinking, "Why is this weirdo asking me if there's something wrong with the transmission when there's CLEARLY something wrong with the transmission?" He was probably frightened of me after I asked that.

How Do I Get Over a Breakup?

. . . .

PUBLISHED OCTOBER 2, 2019.

Dear Advice King,

How do you get over a breakup? Me and my girlfriend of three years just broke up. I'm 38. I like to kayak.

—Bert in Knoxville

Wow. Bert? I don't think I've ever met a Bert. Is that your real name? I guess that's irrelevant, "Bert."

Sorry about that. Bert is a fine fake name, and I hope you and your probably fictional ex-girlfriend are doing OK. What's her name? Ophelia?

Speaking of "Ophelia," you know what I don't like, Bert? Americana songs that have wacky old-time women's names in them just to make them seem more Americana-y. I don't believe any of these modern-day banjo boys know people named "Gladys Sue."

Can you tell I'm delaying, Bert? Who the fuck knows how to get over a breakup? I'm glad you like to kayak, though. I don't know why you mentioned it in this question, but I'm glad you like it. This question is like, half question, half OkCupid bio.*

"BERT" OkCupid Bio:

"Hi, my name is Bert. I am 38. I like to kayak."

That's a pretty good bio, actually—it's much better than mine was. I joined OkCupid a couple of years ago. When you join, you have to create a "dating profile," and you have to give yourself a fake name. A good OkCupid name for you, Bert, would be "KayakKrazy."

. . . .

* For my elderly readers: "OkCupid" is a dating "app." An "app" is a service, basically. You can see pictures of the people, and read a little biography of them, just like if you were using a dating service.

I named myself "GordsGold."

Gord's Gold is the title of a 1975 Gordon Lightfoot greatest-hits album. Looking back on it, I don't think I really wanted any dates. Naming myself "GordsGold" in a 2017 dating profile was perhaps the most naked act of self-sabotage I have ever engaged in—and self-sabotage is my goddamn wheelhouse, so that's really saying something. It's the equivalent of a woman calling herself "CrazyCatLady." And it gets worse. In my bio, I said I liked "vinyl records" and "going to thrift stores." I was 47 when I wrote that bio. Do you know what a 47-year-old woman on a dating app wants to do? I'm not entirely sure, but I can guarantee you it's not "go to thrift stores" with a guy who calls himself "GordsGold." As far as I can tell, most 47-year-old women on dating apps want to "travel" and "taste wine."

I think there should be a dating app for 47-year-olds who only have $200—IGuessSoCupid™.

My real recommendation for you, 38-year-old Bert, is to kayak your ass off. Exercise helps to alleviate depression. Maybe join a kayaking club. Are there kayaking clubs? I wouldn't know. I'm too busy looking for love in the vinyl section of the Salvation Army. Sample opening line: "Do you like Gene Pitney?"*

I'm Going Bald

PUBLISHED DECEMBER 15, 2015.

Dear King,

I am the frontman in a rock band, and I am going bald. I am 28 years old. My hair is still long, but it's really thin on top, and it's getting wispy

* For my younger readers: Gene Pitney was a 1960s pop singer. His records are often found in thrift stores.

all over. Like, even the long part is not growing thick like it used to. What should I do? Is it possible it could be my diet?

—Tony in Madison

My advice to you? Throw your guitar in the garbage, because you won't be needing it anymore. You MUST have long hair to make music.

Just kidding, Tony!

Shave your head, fool. As soon as possible. You will feel relaxed for the first time in years. Even a licensed yogi couldn't meditate (at least outdoors) if he had a comb-over—the fear of a wind squall coming along and revealing his bare dome would take him out of the moment. But Allen Ginsberg had a comb-over, and I guess he meditated. I can't see how. I bet he was faking it. Although he had a huge beard. Some people like Ginsberg keep what's left of their hair on top and grow out all the other hair—beard, ear, nose, neck, chest, back, pubic, foot. That way they feel like they COULDN'T be bald.

"Me, bald? Quite the contrary, asshole. I'm a fucking hairball."—Allen Ginsberg

If you are balding and have some bullshit hair arrangement on your head, every day becomes the equivalent of a fresh ride in a speeding convertible. Each curve in the road offers a new opportunity for embarrassment. That convertible thing is supposed to be a metaphor, but sometimes people *actually ask you* to go for a ride in a convertible. So even if you have what's left of your hair carefully organized so no one knows that you are balding (even though I can guarantee you they already know), a metaphorical convertible ride—just everyday shit—could dislodge it. Or—God forbid—a *real* convertible ride could dislodge it. Either way, you will be a nervous wreck, walking around with a hair sculpture worrying about real things AND metaphors.

I started losing my hair when I was 21. I call it the "Halamo." That stands for "Hair Alamo." Fuck the regular Alamo, I will never forget the "Halamo."

I was in college, and I was already pretty sad. I was depressed. I was an alcoholic. I had a girlfriend who always said how cute I was. Like,

A LOT. She told me how cute I was so much that I started to obsess about my looks. I started to wonder if she would still like me if I got less cute. I started to wonder about that A LOT. In fact, I wondered at the kinda level that eventually gets diagnosed as Obsessive-Compulsive Disorder. IT WAS INTENSE FUCKING WONDERING. Hey, I might have been a depressed alcoholic with undiagnosed OCD, but I had thick, curly hair. At least I had my beautiful curls to run my worried fingers through, right? THANK GOD FOR MY CURLS, right? Well, guess fucking what. OCD-grade "wondering" isn't very good for your body. First I got IBS (look it up), then I got dandruff, and then, one day in the fall of 1990, I walked out of the shower and looked in the mirror to see that part of my hairline was missing. "The Halamo."*

For the next five years I was a madman. I carefully arranged my hair each morning and prayed no one would ask me to go for a ride in a convertible. I used gel. I used mousse. I used hats. I used a goose. (I didn't use a goose, I just thought it would be fun to make it rhyme.) I avoided air vents. If someone tried to touch my hair I pulled away violently, which made me look weird. My mother said, "Maybe you should get a weave." She said it as if "weaves" were inexpensive and looked great. She also said, quote: "There are a lot of men running around who could use weaves." My mother was no help.

I hate to break it to you, Tony, but it's not your diet. Every guy who starts losing his hair hopes that maybe it's his diet. It never is. Also, that thing where you get your hairline from your maternal grandfather? Bullshit. Turns out that you can inherit baldness from any fool in your whole family tree. You could be losing your hair in the same pattern as your 19th cousin Wilfred, the alchemist's assistant.

Since I finally buzzed my hair in 1995 (I don't shave it down to the skin, by the way, I leave about a quarter-inch)—and got treatment for OCD, depression and alcoholism—I have fronted a rock band and had friends and girlfriends and everything. In fact, all the women I've dated say they prefer me bald! Axl Rose should have shaved his head. He

* 9/HairLeven, if you prefer.

thought no one would like him anymore. But guess what! They would have. They would have liked bald, somewhat sane Axl a lot better than deranged, "What if someone asks me to go for a ride in a convertible?" Axl. Axl wasted half his life trying to re-seed his scalp, and his "hair" still looks like shit.

Don't live in fear of phantom convertibles, Tony. Shave your head!

Should I Roller Skate?

. . . .

PUBLISHED SEPTEMBER 27, 2018.

Dear Advice King,

Should I go roller skating? HAHAHAHAHAHA.

—Some Creep, Anytown, USA

About 250 people sent me this question, AND IT'S NOT FUCKING FUNNY.

For those of you who don't already know, I broke my hip. Apparently there's a rumor going around that I broke it roller skating. I'm here to tell you that that's grade-A horse shit. I've never roller skated in my life! Why would I start doing it now, in my late 40s? Do you think I'm an idiot? And if you do think I'm an idiot, why the fuck are you always asking me for advice? Do you think a respectable publication like the *Nashville Scene* would give an advice column to some guy who might encourage the elderly to roller skate? You do?!

Well, that's just plain insulting to all the good people who work at this fine newspaper. In fact, it shows a lack of respect for all journalists, everywhere. You should be ashamed of yourself.

OK, I broke my hip roller skating. SO WHAT! Are people over 40 supposed to just lie down and die? You think I should spend my days down at the library looking at picture books, don't you? I'll tell you what, Jack, there's a lotta gas left in this ol' dune buggy (yes, I am calling you "Jack," and referring to myself as an "ol' dune buggy"), and if I wanna roll backward into traffic on a set of sparkly roller skates that's my fucking business. I DIDN'T roll backward into traffic, but the point is that it's still a sort-of free country, and I reserve the right to hurt myself however I want to.

I bought it, I'll break it™.

But I will give you a little real advice about roller skating: DON'T FUCKING DO IT. Roller rinks are only slightly safer than active volcanoes. AND THEY SELL SLUSHIES AT ROLLER RINKS. Do you know how much sugar is in a goddamn slushie? Let's put it this way: There's a reason volcanoes don't have slushie concessions. Before I had a cherry slushie, I was skating fairly reasonably. After I had the slushie, I was skate-DANCING.

I don't even dance ON MY REGULAR FEET.

This may be an urban legend, but supposedly a group of Swiss volcano scientists had cherry slushies on their lunch break. They became so agitated that they donned Speedos and did cannonballs into the lava. They were never seen again. Obviously.

Take a peek inside the bathrooms at a roller rink—if you dare! Grown men careening around with their dongs out, peeing on the walls. They grab one another, attempting to balance themselves—still urinating! The night I was there, a man had rolled off the toilet while he was in the midst of shitting. He rolled right out of the bathroom and into the snack bar, covered in feces. He was screaming. Everyone was running. This is family fun?

Then I broke my fucking hip, and somebody turned the music off. I lay motionless on the floor. The disco ball silently spun.

I signed a piece of paper that said, essentially, that roller skating in no way contributed to my roller-skating accident.

The rink's manager knew the EMTs by name.

"Hi Randy. Hi Don." she said.

"YOU GUYS WANT A SLUSHIE?"

Should I Try Cocaine?

. . . .

PUBLISHED NOVEMBER 24, 2015.

Dear Advice King,

I am 45 years old and I have never tried cocaine. I am scared I will end up like Len Bias. Should I do it anyway? Is it worth the risk?

Thanks,

—Clem, East Nashville

Clem? Your name is Clem? Bullshit. No one's named Clem. OK, Clem. Clem Clem Clem. That's a fun name to say. Clem Clem Clem Clem Clem Clem Clem. I'm about the same age as you, Clem Clem Clem, so I remember Len Bias. His death made national headlines back in 1986. There are no national headlines now. His death would be a tweet. The space shuttle exploding would also be a tweet. Cocaine was really popular in the 1980s. And the 1970s. And the 1990s. And now. I was first offered cocaine in college, and I was afraid to try it—I was afraid because of Len Bias.

Len Bias was a famous college basketball player who died of a heart arrhythmia he got from doing cocaine. He was doing cocaine to celebrate signing an NBA contract. Len Bias's death was ESPECIALLY frightening because it was his first time trying the drug. And he was in great physical condition. If a well-conditioned athlete had an arrhythmia from doing cocaine, I figured MY heart might fall straight out of my ass.

On the other hand, Len Bias was supposedly walking around snorting it out of a coffee cup. I mean, a coffee cup? If you have enough cocaine to put in a coffee cup, then you have too much cocaine. And anyone knows better than to do *that* much cocaine. So maybe it was Len Bias's own damn fault, and as long as I don't go bonkers and snort a whole coffee cup full . . .

Then I thought about how Jim Morrison said you should "get your kicks before the whole fucking house goes up in flames," and my friends engaged in some top-notch peer-pressuring, and I snorted cocaine.

At this point I have to tell a funny story. When I was 16 I was working as a supermarket cashier, and one of my co-workers was a guy named Ernest. I think Ernest was 17. One day we went to his house on our half-hour break and drank beers out of his parents' refrigerator. While we were sitting at the kitchen table smoking Marlboro Reds, Ernest said something that I never forgot—and I forget a lot of stuff. "Cocaine is the Champagne of drugs." That's what he said. To this day I have no idea what it means. Is Champagne the cocaine of drinks? Can you christen a boat by throwing cocaine all over the bow? I was pretty sure Ernest had never done cocaine. Maybe his older brother told him that? His older brother probably also told him to call people with red hair "Howdy Doody." I got called Howdy Doody long after that show was off the air, by kids too young to have ever seen it. I can only assume that other people in their families were saying, "If you ever see someone with red hair, call them 'Howdy Doody.' It will make them sad, and making other people sad is what life is all about." I bet Dick Cheney still tells everybody he meets to remember to call red-headed people "Howdy Doody."

So I did the cocaine, Clem Clem Clem Clem Clem. Luckily, I lived to tell the tale. Cocaine is a drug that makes you feel really good for no reason. It mostly makes you feel really good about the sound of your own voice. I think if you gave a sheep cocaine it would never stop baaah-ing. You get really excited about EVERYTHING and talking feels SOOOOOOO good—but nobody needs to hear endless speeches about how much you like things. But you don't give a FUCK, because talking about how much you like everything feels so damn good.*

. . . .

*You are feeling so good because you are burning through all the endorphins your body had set aside for the next two months. The next day you will feel like a doormat that a dog barfed on. The only thing that will make you feel better is . . . MORE COCAINE! Repeat until arrhythmia or rehab.

Agreeing feels really good, too. There's nothing like cocaine to get a group of folks seriously into agreeing with each other. Making good decisions is impossible because everybody says yes to everything. For example, in the 1970s and '80s, everybody in the music industry was on cocaine. Take a look at this Steven Stills album cover from 1984.* That image tells you everything you need to know about cocaine, Clem Doggy. Steven Stills was on so much cocaine in 1984 that he bought a racing boat and started racing around in boats. *Then*, when Steven Stills was on the MOST cocaine a human can be on that isn't a whole coffee cup full, he decided he wanted his album cover to be a picture of his own racing boat flying (Sailing? Motoring?) through outer space. The guy at his record company *should* have said, "No fucking way, Steven. You need to go to a psychiatric hospital." But the guy at the record company was also on cocaine, so he said, "SURE. I AGREE. RACING BOAT IN SPACE IS A GREAT IDEA. I AGREE. I AGREE. SNORT."

Boats don't work in space. People trying to race boats in space are wasting their time. Don't try to race a boat in space, Clem. Don't do cocaine.

Should My Family Have a Confidentiality Agreement?

. . . .

PUBLISHED JULY 22, 2020.

Dear Advice King,

Mary Trump's new tell-all book has apparently violated a Trump family "confidentiality agreement." This never occurred to me! Should I implement a confidentiality agreement with my own family? I'd appreciate your input!

—Robert in Washington, D.C.

. . . .

* For those of you reading *The Advice King Anthology*, the Steven Stills album I am referring to here is *Right by You*.

I really have no idea what kind of oil is best for a 1997 Yamaha snowmobile. Also, I understand you are frustrated, but in the future please don't swear so much in the question.

I tried to answer the question without reading it again. I thought you asked me what "fucking oil" you should put in your "fucking snowmobile."

Wow. The real question is a crazy question.

The answer is no. Certainly not.

Well . . .

Now that I think about it, I wish I had a confidentiality agreement about my 1975 tee-ball season.

I didn't get a single hit. OFF A TEE. At the end of the season our lunatic coach handed us—a bunch of 6-year-olds—our batting averages on little pieces of paper. Mine said "000." A grown man actually wrote "000" down on a piece of paper and handed it to me, age 6. Yeah, it would be nice if no one knew about that.

Or that time I found a folded-up piece of paper on the street when I was 10. I opened it, and it was a picture of a naked woman! I took it to my room and hid it under the carpet. Then the problems started. I could not stop looking at it—to the point that I was beginning to have trouble living my life. All I wanted to do was LOOK AT IT. I started making stuff up—"I have to iron my hat!"—so I could go back up to my room and LOOK AT IT.

I decided to tell my father. I took the picture out from under the carpet, handed it to him, and said, "Dad, I am worried. I can't stop looking at this picture." He said, "Why?" (Nice job, Dad.) I said, "Because it gives me energy."

Nobody needs to know about that either.

Hey! I just realized that both of these stories revolve around "pieces of paper."

PSA: YOUNG PEOPLE, DON'T END UP LIKE ME! AVOID PIECES OF PAPER!

Robert, any family that is so fucked-up that it needs a confidentiality agreement is not a family—it's a biker gang. Also, after reading this column, I realize that I should sign a nondisclosure agreement with myself.

ADVICE KING PANDEMIC FUN GUIDE

Listen to the Gene Clark album *No Other*.
Watch the Les Blank documentary *A Poem Is a Naked Person*.
Send a letter to someone you love.
Go for a walk EVERY DAY.

This column is dedicated to the memory of Michael Brooks. Thank you for the information, and the inspiration. If you aren't familiar with Michael's work, please google him.

Am I Being Too Cautious about Pandemic Dating?

. . . .

PUBLISHED JULY 8, 2020.

Dear Advice King,

I met a guy online who wants to meet up, but when I told him I would only meet somewhere outside—with masks on and socially distanced—he said I'm being overly cautious and that we "can't live in fear forever." Am I being unreasonable? Thanks for your help!

—Joan in Santa Barbara, Calif.

In my experience, if the listing says the turntable "only needs a belt," it means that fixing that turntable is going to be a giant pain in the ass. If it's so easy, why haven't the people who placed the ad replaced the belt? Also, I've never heard of a "Hoover" brand turntable. There's a famous "Hoover" that makes vacuum cleaners, though. Good luck!

I tried to answer the question without reading it again. I thought you asked whether you should buy a used "Hoover" brand turntable that needs a belt.

Hi Joan! Don't ever listen to anything men say. ESPECIALLY horny men. Men "have sex" with modified flashlights.

Women have a higher life expectancy than men. Almost everyone who has gone over Niagara Falls in a barrel has been a man. Here's a sad story about a man who went over Niagara Falls in a barrel:

"The first Canadian to conquer the Falls was Karel Soucek. Karel survived the plunge, but later that year Karel was killed while recreating the drop from a platform inside the Houston Astrodome. (Karel's barrel hit the edge of the water tank.)"

That quote is taken from Niagarafallslive.com. Pay a visit for more stories about men with terrible judgment!

But I digress.

My dad went to a Catholic college in the 1950s. He said he went out with a woman named Helen for three years before they kissed. I don't know why he told me this, because it makes him sound insane—and that's how I know it must be true! My personal policy is that if you haven't kissed in the first TWO years, you might want to seriously look into whether you are, in fact, "going out." However, since Helen (if she existed, and wasn't a broom with a dress on it) and my dad waited THREE YEARS to kiss, the least this COVID cowboy—this pandemic petitioner, this bubonic beau—can do is suffer through a couple of socially distanced dates DURING A HEALTH CRISIS. And when this "flu floozy" inevitably says that his lack of access to sex is the REAL health crisis, tell him to go fuck Niagara Falls.

Now, here are a few suggestions for how to safely pass the time during this worldwide stress festival:

Take a trip down the Karel Soucek rabbit hole!

Listen to the Graham Nash album *Songs for Beginners*!

Drink cold brew coffee in the middle of the night while writing an advice column and put yourself to sleep with melatonin!

Wake up . . . confused!

Go for walks, wear masks, and lean on each other. XO.

What Should I Bring to My Company Potluck?

. . . .

PUBLISHED AUGUST 9, 2016.

Dear Advice King,

What should I bring to my company potluck?

—Jenny in Nashville

I don't know, Jenny. I don't know anything about food, because I grew up in 1970s Connecticut in the kind of family that hands down a recipe for hard-boiled eggs. On a good day, we ate stuff like "tuna casserole" and "stewed tomatoes with hamburger meat." On a bad day, we ate "Chinese Chicken."

Here is the recipe for "Chinese Chicken":

> Lightly bread a chicken breast.
> Heat a frying pan to 5000 degrees.
> Put chicken in pan.
> Cook chicken until it has nearly disappeared.
> Serve with ketchup.

When the guests begin to eat "Chinese Chicken," it is traditional for the chef to say, "It's dry, isn't it," in a tone of voice that suggests she will commit suicide if anyone says yes.

One time my friend from college called my house when we were eating "Chinese Chicken." He said, "What are you doing?" I said, "I'm eating dinner, so I'm going to have to call you back." He said, "Oh, what are you having for dinner?" I said, "Chinese Chicken." My friend said, "Chinese Chicken? What is that?"

What a wild question. Around our house we just figured Chinese people liked really fucking dry chicken. We put ketchup on it—maybe they did, too.

I told my friend to hold on. I cupped the phone and called out to my mother, "Why is it called Chinese Chicken?" She said, "I just always thought it looked like the chicken that comes in Chinese food."

Jesus. Even the stuff I *thought* I knew about food wasn't true. I didn't know much about "Chinese Chicken," but I definitely assumed there was something Chinese about it. I began to question everything my mother had told me. Were those really tomatoes in the "stewed tomatoes with hamburger meat"? How could she be so sure I didn't like green peppers without me ever tasting one? Was President Nixon really "railroaded"?

Whenever our family was invited to an event where we were supposed to bring food, my mother made "Ambrosia Salad." "Ambrosia Salad" is very similar to the stuff that leaked out of the Fukushima nuclear reactor, except it's a dessert. It has canned mandarin oranges in it, and that shredded coconut that comes in a bag. You could successfully interrogate me with either one of those things.

CREEP: Where is the treasure buried, Chris?
ME: I'll never tell!
CREEP: You want me to get the canned mandarin oranges?
ME: Ummmm . . .
CREEP: Or maybe the *COCONUT IN A BAG*?
ME: It's under the dogwood tree.

"Ambrosia Salad" has a bunch of other horrible shit in it, too—marshmallows, heavy cream—and it's pink. I bet serial killers love Ambrosia Salad.

If you don't like your boss, you should bring an "Ambrosia Salad" with extra coconut to the potluck. I strongly suggest that you wear a welding mask or an old-fashioned diving helmet while you are assembling that fruity violation of the Geneva Conventions.

At this point I would like to mention that my mother was doing her best, and that I wouldn't be alive if it weren't for her experiments in the kitchen. If my father had been in charge, we all would have been dead a long time ago. He can't even identify food. He ate potpourri once.

Real talk, Jenny? Buy something at Trader Joe's and put it in a bowl.

Making a Will

PUBLISHED FEBRUARY 9, 2016.

Dear Advice King,

When should I make my will?

—Jane in Denver

Hi Jane. Nice to hear from a Coloradoan! My old pal John Denver was from Colorado. He lived at Starwood in Aspen. I'd say you should make a will as soon as you have some good stuff to give away. I wrote my first will on the back of a shoebox lid when I was 10. I had what I thought was a pretty valuable beer can collection, and I've always been preoccupied with death. It said, "Give my beer cans to Mom, and bury me in the treehouse."

Well, I didn't die, and it turns out my beer can collection wasn't worth shit. I remember telling my grandfather that my beer cans were valuable. He said, "To whom?" I got really mad—especially because he said "whom"—but he had a point.

I had a beer can price book that told me my Duquesne Cone Top was worth $35, but what if you can't find anybody to buy it for $35? Then what's it worth? Try to pay a mortgage with beer cans. I know from experience that even if you bring the beer can price guide with you and carry the cans in a briefcase and dress real nice, they'll laugh you out of the bank. If I could do it over I would handcuff the briefcase to my wrist.

I rewrote my will in the 1990s because I had a ton of good CDs—including rare Pearl Jam and Oasis maxi singles. Upon my death, all my CDs are going to my alma mater. I'm not EXACTLY sure what an "alma mater" is, but I know it's extremely classy to leave your stuff to it.

You live in Colorado, so I'm sure you have a bong. And Chinese juggling sticks. And a shovel. That's enough for a will. I bet you have a son named "Emmanuel" or "Gorp" or "Musk Ox"—give him the bong and the juggling sticks. Leave the shovel to your alma mater.

I feel bad for kids with hippie names, because everybody knows the parents just named them "Leaf" or "Top Bun" or "Zip Line" because they liked saying it when they were baked. Names like "Gorp" and "Bath Bead" are chosen because they are simply flat-out hilarious to a stoned person—names like "Emmanuel" and "Leaf" are chosen for their soothing properties. During times when hippie parents are irritable because they're "coming down" from the goongrass they don't want to hear anything "harsh." A name like Fred, for example, is considered "harsh" because of the "loud D" at the end. I've seen many crabby hippies throw sandwich ingredients around because someone made a "loud D" sound. "Emmanuel" and "Leaf" are like E-Z listening music to the ears of a weedbeast in withdrawal.

Another reason to write a will is so you can be mean to relatives you don't like. You can say, "I'm NOT leaving my Chinese juggling sticks to Karen, because she's an asshole," and some old lawyer guy will read that right to Karen's face.

Lastly, you should make a will right away, because it's where you tell people how you want to be buried. Or not buried, or scattered, smothered, covered, whatever. I wonder if somebody who really loved Waffle House has had their ashes scattered, smothered and covered.* I'm

. . . .

* That would be human remains with melted cheese and onions.

going to have my skull covered in gold and put on the top of a 600-foot granite tower in the middle of Antarctica. The tower will have a button on the side. When somebody pushes the button my skull will scream "I KNOW THAT'S RIGHT" in my actual, recorded voice. LOUD. Real fucking loud. Like, "The Who live in concert 1976" loud.

CHAPTER 5

POLITICS

How to Speak Up about the Metro Budget

. . . .

PUBLISHED JUNE 10, 2020.

Dear Advice King,

What did Nashville's Vice Mayor Jim Shulman mean when he accused his constituents of "bad politics"? How are Vice Mayor Shulman's Nashville constituents supposed to express themselves if doing so at a public hearing is "bad politics"? Please advise me on how to successfully interact with Vice Mayor Shulman.

—Daniel in Nashville

First of all, what Daniel is referring to happened last week, at a public hearing on the proposed 2021 budget for Metro Nashville. Nashville's Vice Mayor Jim Shulman got very mad at the public for expressing their opinion, which is pretty funny since that was the whole reason for the hearing. Also, he works FOR the public, ostensibly. Sooooooo, anyway . . .

Dear God, you just made me read a budget. I designed my life so I would never have to read a budget. What a depressing experience. They put a cheerful picture of some kind of sculpture on the first page, by the way. Just proves that old adage "you can't judge a dystopia's budget by its cover sheet."

The budget I'm talking about is the proposed Metro Nashville budget for the fiscal year 2021. I also designed my life so I would never have to hear about "fiscal years." Thanks a lot for ruining my entire life's plan with this question, Daniel.

You might be thinking, "What does a life designed specifically so you never have to read a budget look like?" Well, you just don't own much stuff or have a family. And you don't have a fire pit, a roof deck or a lake house. And you don't play golf. It's fine, too. I have a lot of fun, and I've never had to read a budget—UNTIL NOW.

The first thing I noticed was that police and jails are supposed to get $290,642,200. The second thing I noticed was social services are penciled in for a hot $7,408,000.*

Since you are reading this sophisticated column in this erudite publication, I am going to assume you have been paying attention to what's been going on in the United States (and the world) in the last couple weeks. If you have, I'm sure you've heard people talking about "defunding the police." "Defund the police" does not necessarily mean, "get rid of the police." It means taking funds away from the police and putting them toward community services.

Are you aware that it is nearly IMPOSSIBLE to get timely help for a mental health emergency in this country? People who are having mental breakdowns are routinely told to "go to the emergency room." The emergency room costs money. About 28 million people in America don't have health insurance, so they tend not to go to the emergency room.** They stay home and self-medicate with alcohol and pills until they FLIP THE FUCK OUT. Then the police are called. The police are not mental health professionals—far from it, in fact. Violence often ensues. So, maybe if you broke off a few million from the "police and jails" part of the budget, and put it toward public mental health services . . .

I know, it's a CRAZY IDEA!

Since police are, ahem, "in the news" right now, people happen to be looking at budgets all of a sudden, many for the first time—like me—and they DO NOT like what they see. The "bad politics" Jim Shulman is talking about could also be described as "new politics," or

. . . .

* Editor's note: There are a lot of other things that you might categorize as social services throughout the budget. But as the Nashville People's Budget Coalition points out, this budget proposes an increase of $6 million for the criminal legal system with cuts in almost all the other categories that they classify as "public goods." That includes a cut of more than $7.1 million from Metro schools.

** American emergency rooms aren't equipped to handle mental health emergencies, either. They basically tell you to go home and make an appointment with a mental health professional. Best-case scenario, they give you sleeping pills. Worst: They put you on a 72-hour hold, and THEN they tell you to go home and make an appointment with a mental health professional. I know this from experience—I suffered from severe panic attacks in my 20s.

"politics that challenge the status quo." In case you haven't noticed, Mr. Shulman, the status quo is NOT WORKING, so people would like to CHALLENGE IT. And that's what public hearings are for, Mr. Shulman.

Your constituents aren't engaging in "bad politics," Mr. Shulman—they are engaging in good politics that you just don't want to hear about or deal with. And your response to these new, improved politics is NOT new, or improved in any way. You are attempting to use the "Silent Majority" defense. That old, discredited, Nixonian mind trick: "Most people are not this radical, but they just can't get through on the phone because all these rabble rousers are taking up too much time. There are a ton of people who think our budget is great, I just wish they were here instead of these other . . . fake people?"

Is that what they are Mr. Shulman, fake people? That's how you treated them. Those polite, composed citizens who you were caught on camera trying to intimidate. The ones patiently waiting to express their opinion at a PUBLIC HEARING ON THE BUDGET. Were those people "paid by George Soros"? Is the whole nation—and all the people of all the other nations out in the streets—paid by George Soros? Is everyone who disagrees with a budget that gives 40 times more money to police and jails than to social services crazy? No, they aren't. These are your real constituents, Mr. Shulman, and they are hurting. You cannot dismiss them as a conspiracy. The "silent majority" is the conspiracy. You—and many others like you in positions of power who are not used to being challenged—are the ones who are acting crazy.

The people who attended that hearing did everything right, Daniel. There is no reason to change your mind or your approach. It is time for those in power to change theirs.

Is It OK to Detain Children?

. . . .

PUBLISHED JUNE 20, 2018.

Dear Advice King,

Is it OK to rip children out of their parents' arms at the border and lock them up in cages like dogs by the thousands because they are desperately fleeing their homelands to try and find a better life? Somebody on TV recently used the Bible to somehow justify this . . . are they correct? Seems a little strange to me.

Sincerely,

—Worried in West Nashville

No, it is not OK. It is utter madness. Donald Trump is depraved. Mike Pence, Jeff Sessions, Stephen Miller, John Kelly, Kellyanne Conway, Kirstjen Nielsen, Nikki Haley and the immigration agents carrying this out are all depraved. DEPRAVED. I do not exaggerate. This "policy" is the textbook definition of depravity. Anybody who defends this "policy" is depraved. I put "policy" in quotes because I refuse to dignify child abuse by referring to as a "policy." It is violence against children. It is a hate crime.

Anybody in a position of power who stays silent on this "issue" is also depraved. Silence is complicity. I put "issue" in quotes because this is not an "issue," it is barbarism. Barbarism is not an "issue"—it is an emergency.

When people across the globe think of America at the moment, what do you suppose comes to their minds? I'll tell you. Meanness, materialism, racism, Kim Kardashian and violence against children. And Christianity. Christianity? If Jesus Christ returned right now, he would turn Americans into pillars of salt—and then burn the salt. Jesus would embrace every refugee. Jesus would die on the cross a thousand times before he pried a single child from the embrace of his or her mother. If a present-day white American Christian saw Mary, Joseph and that Middle Eastern baby hanging around a manger, they would call ICE. I wish I was kidding. Baby Jesus would be in an abandoned Walmart, screaming for his mom.

One more thing: A lot of politicians are saying that separating children from their parents is a "law Democrats made" and Jeff Sessions decided to enforce. This is not true. Obama *did* begin detaining families—sometimes for long periods in terrible conditions. Before Obama introduced this policy, families who crossed the border illegally (a misdemeanor, by the way; looking for a better life, by the way; sorta like the PILGRIMS WERE, you assholes) were given a court date and released.

UNACCOMPANIED minors were detained until a suitable foster home could be found for them. In April of this year, Jeff Sessions introduced a new policy in which *all* children would be separated from their parents. This policy was introduced to deter immigrants and asylum seekers. Trump advisor Stephen Miller, who came up with this disgusting plan together with John Kelly, has admitted this. Donald Trump lied repeatedly, saying that this was a pre-existing law that he had no choice but to enforce. THIS IS NOT TRUE. If you have heard *Fox and Friends*, or Sean Hannity, or Rush Limbaugh, or Mark Levin, or Tucker Carlson, or Ann Coulter say this, THEY ARE LYING. The white Trump administration is ABUSING BROWN CHILDREN for political gain, and because they are plain old racists.

If you support this, or if you harbor hate in your heart toward these poor refugees—your brothers and sisters—you can, and will, go to hell.

What Should My New Year's Resolution Be?

. . . .

PUBLISHED DECEMBER 28, 2016.

Dear Advice King,

Given the current political environment, what is a good New Year's resolution to make? I want to resolve to do something that will make a difference. What is your New Year's resolution?

—Beth in Clarksville

Great question, Beth. I know what you mean. Stuff like "I'm going to try to stop cursing so much" doesn't seem appropriate at a time like this. By the way, I think everybody should curse MORE at a time like this. Swear your head off. There's nothing that makes me madder than a politician whose policies are immoral, profane, obscene, etc., demanding decorum from the people affected by those policies. I'm sure you heard about Ivanka Trump getting yelled at on a plane. What does she expect? A hero's welcome? Her father just challenged Russia to an arms race! Here's the quote: "Let it be an arms race. We will outmatch them at every pass and outlast them all."

"Outmatch them at every pass"? What fucking "pass"? Does Donald Trump think a nuclear war would take place on the set of an old Western movie? Ivanka Trump continues to support her father even though he called for violence at his campaign rallies, suggested banning Muslims from the United States, refused to denounce white supremacist organizations and bragged about sexually assaulting women. She makes no secret of her plans to benefit financially from his presidency. Ivanka deserves to get yelled at on a plane—and everywhere else.

> New Year's Resolution No. 1: This year, I'm gonna swear more (at public figures).

New Year's Resolution No. 2: I'm going to organize a "Million Nude March" to protest Exxon CEO Rex Tillerson's secretary of state nomination.

Every problem on this whole planet is caused by oil (a slight exaggeration—but only fucking slight). So, does Trump pick a fucking foreign policy expert to be secretary of state? Nope. Does he pick a fucking human rights advocate? Nope. He picks THE FUCKING (I'm gonna swear way more for the remainder of this article on account of my first New Year's resolution.) CEO OF A FUCKING OIL COMPANY. That's right, he picked the CEO of Exxon. He could have picked ANYONE. ANY-FUCKING-ONE. He could have picked any fucking nice person. If he had his heart set on picking a fucking CEO, he could at least have picked the CEO of a company that does helpful stuff. The CEO of a cupcake company, for example. If it absolutely fucking *had* to be someone from the energy industry, why not the CEO of a solar power company? Or the CEO of a wind farm company? The fucking CEO of a dog-grooming company. ANY-FUCKING-BODY EXCEPT THE FUCKING CEO OF A GODDAMN FUCKING OIL COMPANY. The only person he could have picked that *might* be worse is Satan him-fucking-self.

OK, that's too much swearing. I have to conserve my energy in case I run into Steve Bannon or Reince Priebus or Mike Pence or Kellyanne Conway or Roger Ailes or . . .

I don't know when the Senate is having hearings on Captain Fuckface Rex Tillerson's (I'm gonna swear SOME) candidacy for secretary of state, but I think we should all be in Washington, D.C., when they happen. And we should be nude. Hear me out. First of all, I'm dead serious about going to Washington for those hearings and letting our elected officials know that the CEO of Exxon IS NOT an acceptable choice for secretary of state. I recommend that 1 million people show up because the police are well-equipped to deal with small demonstrations. They will pepper spray and hogtie some folks, and everyone else will decide to go home. The police are NOT equipped to pepper spray and hogtie

1 million people. The police are REALLY not equipped to pepper spray and hogtie 1 million nude people. The way the police usually deal with nude people is they kill them—that's how badly they don't want to touch them. The police are only supposed to kill one person at a time, because more than that causes a big scene. The police DEFINITELY aren't allowed to kill 1 million people, even if those people are nude.

WE WILL NOT DISROBE UNTIL WE HAVE TAKEN OUR PLACES IN FRONT OF THE CAPITOL. It is very difficult to travel to Washington, D.C., (or anywhere else, for that matter) if you are ALREADY nude.

See you at the MILLION NUDE MARCH.

P.S. THIS IS A REAL IDEA.

Those are my resolutions, Beth. I'm also going to quit smoking. I don't smoke very much, but I want to be in good shape if shit goes down when I'm nude on the Washington Mall.

So here are your resolutions for 2017, Beth:

1. Match profanity with profanity: Swear more at public figures who are doing horrible things.
2. Attend the Million Nude March.
3. Quit smoking.
4. If you don't smoke, start smoking, and then quit.

HAPPY NEW YEAR!!!

What Should I Do Now That I Don't Work at the White House?

. . . .

PUBLISHED AUGUST 2, 2017.

Dear Advice King,

What should I do now that I don't work at the White House? Thanks!

—Anthony Scaramucci

Oh, hi Anthony! You did a wonderful job as the White House communications director. Most people already knew that the Trump administration was disgusting, but you definitely "communicated" it again, extremely effectively—and quickly! I usually wait until I've been on the job for at least a couple months before I accuse my co-workers of "sucking their own cocks" in the press.

Best option? Join one of those Fox News round tables where everybody is an uninformed bully. Or preferably, you could jump into the mouth of an active volcano.

Sorry to be so hard on you, Anthony, but you are a shining example of the principal enemy of the mental and physical health of the human race—you are an uninformed bully.

"Uninformed bully" is redundant, actually. Bullies are defined by their lack of interest in facts. A lack of interest in facts is, in fact, the source of a bully's power. Bullies mock people who are interested in facts. The bully reframes thinking as "worrying," which implies weakness. It's a high school trick, and there's a reason it works so well in high school—everyone is terribly insecure and sort of dumb.

The scenario—interior, high school hallway, springtime:

ANTHONY SCARAMUCCI: Hey Betty, do you want to go to the prom with me?
BETTY: I'm sorry, Anthony, but I'm already going with Neil deGrasse Tyson. We're riding our bikes because of global warming.
SCARAMUCCI: More like global WORRYING. What a loser.* I'll pick you up at 8 in my monster truck.
BETTY: OK!

THE END

Fun fact: Betty got pregnant that night because condoms are for "losers"—"The Mooch" was not present for the birth.

Condoms work. Global warming is real. Scientists are not "worried," they are INFORMED.

The Iraq war was a monster truck prom night. Getting rid of Glass-Steagall was a monster truck prom night. For-profit health care, mass incarceration, offshore accounts, corporate bailouts, the Dakota Access Pipeline, Keystone, fracking—all MTPNs (monster truck prom nights).

After high school you are supposed to go to college and become smart and confident and realize that bullies are just dangerous idiots with thyroid problems. But most people can't afford college these days—and high school isn't what it used to be. And even if you GET to go to college IT isn't what it used to be either, so people remain terribly insecure and sort of dumb and end up working in human resources where they mistake bullies for leaders and thinking for weakness and animal instinct for decision-making and insults for strength.

MISFITS LIKE SCARAMUCCI SHOULD BE SHUNNED, NOT HIRED!

If you absolutely must hire a bully, have them sweep the boiler room wearing a sign that says BEWARE: ENERGETIC AMORAL DUMBASS.

Also, do not hire anybody who wears mirrored sunglasses.

* "What a loser" is the mating call of the scumbag.

Are you sad, Anthony? Good. Real advice? Go on that TV show *Dancing with the Stars*. They specialize in humanizing lunatics. If Stalin were alive he would be jitterbugging with Julianne Hough.

Who Should I Vote For?

PUBLISHED NOVEMBER 2, 2016.

Dear Advice King,

I really don't like either major-party presidential candidate. I want to vote my conscience on Election Day, but I don't feel right about Clinton or Trump. Should I vote for Gary Johnson? Jill Stein? Evan McMullin?

—Kenny in Bordeaux, Tenn.

Evan McMullin is running? The breakfast sandwich?

"Vote your conscience"? HA! No self-respecting conscience could bring itself to vote for any of these misfits. There's no room for lofty ideals in a fully realized corporatocracy, Kenny—self-preservation is the only game in town. From this dystopian point on, you will be "voting your ass"™.

"Voting your ass"™, or "voting with your ass"™, is a type of voting that becomes necessary when the choices are so horrible that making the wrong selection could, quite literally, cost one ONE'S PHYSICAL ASS. In this case, your ass better vote for Hillary Clinton.

Am I excited about a Hillary Clinton presidency? Fuck no. But my ass is very excited. See, my ass loves the status quo, because the status quo keeps the blood (and cold brew) pumping into its cheeks. My ass understands that a Donald Trump presidency could result in it (my ass) being blown clean off. My ass has no opinion about Gary Johnson or Jill Stein because my ass is a REAL thing concerned with REALITY. My ass doesn't know who the fuck Evan McMullin is.

I wish we weren't in this position, Kenny. I wish people did stuff instead of just talking about stuff, but it's too late for that now. We've known for years that we were headed up Shit Creek, but I think most people were under the impression that we still had a paddle. This election will be remembered for being the moment when we realized the paddle was gone. The pathetic thing is that we've all had a guided goddamn tour. We sat there in the metaphorical canoe reading *The New York Times* and watching the bombed-out scenery roll by like it was a fucking TV show. It was all real—the corporate wars, arms deals, torture reports, drone strikes, subsidized sports stadiums, oil spills, foreclosures, bailouts, National Defense Authorization Act, ex-Goldman-Sachs-executive treasury secretaries, private prisons, warrantless surveillance, industrial ghost towns and fracking earthquakes. Fracking really causes earthquakes. I know it sounds like a joke, but it's true. Every lost pension, every child with lead poisoning, every crowd-funded cancer treatment, every offshore account and on, and on, and on.*

An ordinary man would take this opportunity to run screaming from the creek/paddle metaphor, but I am not an ordinary man.

Until recently I think people thought, "Well, OF COURSE we're up Shit Creek, but we still have a paddle, so I'll start paddling in a minute. I'll start paddling as soon as I'm finished posting on Facebook. But wait . . . maybe posting about social issues IS paddling! If it is, then I can paddle from home!" Just FYI, paddling a canoe "from home" is a deranged idea. It also DOES NOT WORK.

Hillary won't take a meaningful position on fracking. She won't take a meaningful position on the situation at Standing Rock. She won't take a meaningful position on the waking nightmare that is the proposed AT&T/Time Warner merger. She also famously said—out loud—that she told Wall Street to "cut it out."

On the plus side, she is the ONLY CAPABLE, NON-MADMAN CANDIDATE IN THIS RACE, Kenny. That is to say, she is the only

* And Citizens United.

candidate that could possibly function as a paddle. As I, ahem, clearly established earlier in this column, we are in desperate need of a paddle. EVERY SANE PERSON MUST VOTE FOR HER.

Donald Trump couldn't take a meaningful position even if he wanted to because he is a COMPULSIVE LIAR. That is not hyperbole. He compulsively lies. He is also a racist, sexist, immoral narcissist *and* he's been accused of sexually assaulting multiple women, as well as a child. Donald Trump is a horrible, genuinely dangerous person.

In conclusion, I believe that Donald Trump is AN ACTUAL PIECE OF SHIT WEARING CLOTHES. You can make shit out of a paddle, but you can't make a paddle out of shit™.

VOTE WITH YOUR ASS. VOTE FOR A PADDLE. VOTE HILLARY.*

Who Should I Vote For?

. . . .

PUBLISHED FEBRUARY 5, 2020.

Dear Advice King,

I am an undecided voter. Who should I vote for in November?

—Fran in Moline, Ill.

I really don't recommend using a shampoo and conditioner "in one." It doesn't make any sense. They're two different things. You wouldn't use a "flashlight and orange juice in one," would you? Of course not. I don't think they make a "flashlight and orange juice." But you know what I mean, Larry.

. . . .

*But stay engaged after the election, fools.

Oh shit. I'm sorry, I just woke up from a nightmare, and I was confused, Fran. I thought your name was Larry and you wanted to know if I recommended using a "shampoo and conditioner in one."

You're probably wondering what my nightmare was, huh? I dreamt that the president of the United States awarded Rush Limbaugh the Medal of Freedom in the middle of his State of the Union address. I have to stop drinking coffee before I go to bed! It makes my dreams really, really, really, really, really dumb—and frightening. Did I mention dumb? Let me just check the news to make sure . . .

OH MY FUCKING GOD.

I also dreamt that the president wore a ton of orange makeup and his son-in-law was in charge of America's Middle East policy.

OH MY FUCKING GOD.

I also dreamt that he banned people from 11 countries from traveling to the United States, and that those countries were Muslim-majority and full of people of color. And that he called several other countries with largely non-white populations "shithole countries." And I dreamt that he said that Nigerians who come to America would "never go back to their huts."

I dreamt that he called a political opponent "Pocahontas" at a ceremony honoring the Native American code talkers of World War II. I dreamt that this man never served in the military, but said, "I like people who weren't captured," referring to a political opponent who was held as a prisoner of war and tortured.

I dreamt that he had been accused of sexual misconduct by 25 women.

I dreamt that one of his top advisers was a white supremacist.

I dreamt that he allowed Turkey to slaughter the Kurds.

I dreamt that his racist attorney general instituted a "zero tolerance" policy at the southern border of the United States, which resulted in thousands of children of color (including infants) being taken from their parents, on purpose, as a penalty for them attempting to immigrate here. And I dreamt that the United States deported the parents. And I dreamt that the United States kept the kids. And I dreamt that the

United States did not keep track of where the parents ended up. And I dreamt that the United States didn't keep track of where the children ended up. And I dreamt that the children would never be reunited with their parents. Ever.

OH MY FUCKING GOD.

And finally, I dreamt that this president's supporters did not like when people compared this president to Hitler. And I dreamt that they *really* didn't like it when people compared *them* to Hitler's supporters. This part of the nightmare was terrifying *and* confusing.

Hitler blamed Jews for Germany's problems. He said he would make Germany great again. Once the German economy started to do better, Hitler's supporters ignored the Jews in the cages.

This American president blamed immigrants for America's problems. He said he would make America great again. Once the American economy started to do better, his supporters ignored the travel ban, the stolen children, and the immigrants in the cages.

They are pretty fucking similar.

OPEN YOUR EYES.

"Blessed are the meek, for they shall inherit the earth."—God*

Vote to save the soul of America, Fran.

Vote to love thy neighbor.

Vote for human rights.

Vote for ANYONE besides Donald Trump.

I swear to do the same.

* Matthew 5:5.

Is It Too Early to Plan for Halloween?

. . . .

PUBLISHED AUGUST 30, 2017.

Dear Advice King,

Is it too early to start planning for Halloween?

—Laura W.

Vice President Mike Pence sure doesn't have to worry about planning for Halloween. Mike Pence is ready all year round in his one-of-a-kind, permanent, natural, unremovable Michael Myers mask. He even has the personality of Michael Myers! Actually, now that I think about it, Michael Myers is a lot more likeable than Pence, so the whole thing might not work.

Mike Pence also looks just like one of those crash-test dummies. His android-with-a-low-battery vibe matches those things even better than Michael Myers. He could be either, really. That guy's all set for Halloween.

Sorry, what was the question?

Oh, yes, getting ready for Halloween.

Halloween is redundant this year, Laura. The U.S. government has been scaring the fuck out of everybody since January. Donald Trump's "policies" are the metaphorical equivalent of him screaming "BOO!" at all the nice people in the world.

Nice people make greedy people feel guilty, so greedy people are mean to them. The greedy people say it is because the nice people are "liberals." They say that "liberals" aren't really nice. They say that "liberals" are faking being nice to seem "superior" to mean people—which is funny, because embedded in that premise is an admission that being nice is better than being mean.

They also do stuff like convince poor people to give up their own health care so that rich people's premiums won't go up because . . . being mean to yourself is better than being fake-nice like a liberal?

I'd take a fake-nice person over a flat-out mean person any day, because in order for someone to seem nice they have to do at least one nice thing.

The Trump cabinet is made up of guilt-ridden money addicts venting their self-loathing in the form of ghoulish executive orders. It's a shame that mean people don't go to therapy (only "liberals" go so they can seem improved/superior?), because if they did they could find out about a little thing "liberals" know about called projection.

Projection is when you blame someone else for a quality YOU have without you understanding that that is what's happening. Like, for example, a senator could buy himself a $300 bottle of wine with taxpayer money and be mad at himself and not know it and introduce a bill to cut food stamps. He'll say, "I am sponsoring this legislation because I am tired of poor people being fiscally irresponsible," and he thinks that's what he means, but what he's really doing—subconsciously—is punishing HIMSELF, by proxy, for being a greedy piece of shit.

Via *The New York Times*, Jan. 12, 2015: "The median net worth of a member of Congress was $1.03 million in 2013, compared with $56,355 for the average American household."

The United States is run by people in costume. It is run by millionaires dressed as "public servants." These are the same fuckers who allowed themselves to LEGALLY insider-trade until 2012—and then fought enforcement of their own law in 2015!

I think it would be good if we all dressed up as someone friendly for Halloween this year. My suggestion is that EVERYONE (including men) should be Princess Leia. If you insist on being scary, go as the ghost of the Environmental Protection Agency.

Beating Donald Rumsfeld at Squash

PUBLISHED JANUARY 25, 2017.

Dear Advice King,

What's the best way to beat Donald Rumsfeld at squash (played in a see-through glass court)?

—Greg in Mt. Juliet

First off, I have to say that this is the one of the best questions I've received in the nearly four decades I've been a part of this business. Thank you, Greg.

A lot of people think the whole "Advice King" thing got rolling a couple of years ago in the *Nashville Scene*. The Advice King actually started in 1978 as an Everglades-based ham radio broadcast. Most of the questions I received were unintelligible due to the crackling on my handset. The questions I could hear were mostly about those boats with the big fans on the back—how to fix them, why they were the only kind of boats around there, can they be used to make huge smoothies, etc.

Turns out the editor of the *Orlando Sentinel* was one of the people who used to call in! He was always asking stuff about alligators—how old can they get, are they always mad, etc. Anyway, he hired me to write the column. I worked at the *Sentinel* from 1980 until 2014. I won eight Pulitzer Prizes. That was back when they still had that cross-promotion going with Wurlitzer—"A Wurlitzer for the Pulitzer"—so I also have eight jukeboxes. In 2014, the *Nashville Scene* made me an offer I couldn't refuse,* and here I am!

* $10,000 per column, plus expenses. I write 26 columns a year. You do the math, ladies. Did I mention I have eight jukeboxes?

OK, down to business. You vs. Donald Rumsfeld. In a fucking glass cube. I like it. That guy's a scumbag, Greg. You ready for that? He's a scumbag, and he hates to lose. He'll pull your goggles way out off your face and snap them back. He pokes and spits. He's been known to go after opponents' ballsacks.

Something most people don't know is that Donald Rumsfeld is only 5 feet tall. When he was defense secretary, he used a children's desk—he never noticed it was a children's desk, and no one ever told him. Take advantage of his low center of gravity. He's extremely stable, but he doesn't move well. Footwork is your friend—unless you are also 5 feet tall! I didn't even consider that. If you are 5 feet tall, you'd better be ready for a street fight. Rumsfeld hates other short people because he considers them to be trespassers in his "zone." Go in there with a garbage can lid to protect your nuts and a knife in your tube sock. Maybe hollow out your racket handle and fill it with quarters.

I actually don't know the rules of squash. I think you're just supposed to wear the other guy out. Like, "Whoever collapses first has to agree to do the evil business deal." There is some kind of scoring system, but Rumsfeld, a fierce advocate for "lying one's ass off," will just say that the score is not the real score—unless he is winning, in which case he will say it IS the real score.

Can you imagine if the referees for professional sports were people like Donald "There Is No Insurgency" Rumsfeld or Kellyanne "Alternative Facts" Conway? Professional sports would go out of business, because no one would admit that anyone besides Republicans ever scored—even if you showed them the replay! Which is ironic, because in real life Republicans never score. And that's one of the main reasons they can't face facts—because one of those facts is THEY NEVER SCORE (sex).

Fuck winning. Here's what I would do, Greg:

1. Tell Rummy you have trophy for him.
2. Have him wait on court while you get it.
3. Go get garden hose instead.
4. Block door to squash box with big piece of furniture.
5. Put hose under door.
6. Turn on the water.

WE ALL WIN!

CHAPTER 6

LIFE & LOVE

Am I Selfish for Not Having Kids?

. . . .

PUBLISHED MARCH 28, 2018.

Dear Advice King,

I'm not having kids. Am I bad? Am I selfish? Thanks from a big fan!

—Cindy in Chicago

Hi Cindy! I think you are smart for not having kids. I'm not having any kids either. Everyone who has kids is always tired, and they can't stop saying how tired they are over and over. I hate being tired. And I like to talk about lots of topics, not just one.

People who have kids are mad at people who don't have kids because they are jealous of their freedom—and their robust nights of sleep. They also suspect that well-rested, childless folks are always having super-fun parties that they never get invited to. They are right.* Nobody likes to miss super-fun parties, so the people with kids try to trick everybody into having kids. These procreative sociopaths imagine that once everybody has kids they'll never have to miss another party, because there will be nobody left on earth with enough energy to throw one. They are right.

How do you "trick somebody into having kids," you ask? There are a million ways. Here are three:

THREE WAYS PEOPLE WHO HAVE KIDS
TRICK PEOPLE WHO DON'T HAVE KIDS
INTO HAVING KIDS

. . . .

*FUN FACT: When you are a parent, not only do you miss the party, but you have to watch "Thomas the Train" instead. I've never seen "Thomas the Train," but I assume it's about a train that promotes conformity.

1. They tell women that if they get pregnant, they'll "glow." Who wouldn't want to glow? Too bad it's not true. Pregnant women are sweaty from carrying around all that weight. The "glow" is actually a sheen.
2. They tell you that you won't have *really* felt love until you have felt the love that you will inevitably feel for your child. Who cares? I'll happily settle for some fair-to-middling love and plenty of free time. Also, I know parents who got some bum kids,* and I can tell that they aren't that crazy about them.
3. They will tell you that they are "actually having the best time ever," even though they "totally understand that it doesn't look that way to you." As they say this, blood runs from their eye sockets, and their pants are on backward. Their 5-year-old son is in the kitchen, quietly approaching an electrical outlet with a fork.

Misery loves company, Cindy. Have you ever seen a horror movie where the ghosts are lonely? And they rattle chains and smash plates all night long because they're mad that they're not alive and therefore can't go to parties? They're trying to communicate their pain to the living. People with kids are a lot like those ghosts. Except they are alive and their pants are on backward.

In conclusion, the fact that parents can't go to parties makes them as mad as live poltergeists, only they don't rattle chains—they rattle rattles! Baby rattles.

Have kids or don't have kids, Cindy. It's nobody's business but your own.

. . . .

*Like a "bum leg," but a child.

Should I Get Botox?

. . . .

PUBLISHED FEBRUARY 22, 2017.

Dear Advice King,

I'm in my mid-30s, and my frown lines are becoming more noticeable. Should I get Botox?

—Anita in Brooklyn

Are you frowning too much, Anita? Before you start injecting Legionnaires' disease into your face, you might want to examine your lifestyle.

Did you know Legionnaires' disease started in 1976 at an American Legion convention in Philadelphia? That is 100 percent true. Can you imagine? American Legion conventions can be a drag even if you don't catch a groundbreaking illness.

Some legionnaires suspected they got the about-to-be-named-after-themselves ailment from cottage cheese and pear salad on the buffet—"I KNEW it was too flavorful!" Others thought it was simply a Galliano hangover. The trendiest figured they must have picked something up during their ultra-fashionable (1976) "group" sex sessions back at the motor inn—"We were naked except for our name tags. Larry had a tarp in his car. I woke up with a bad cough. There was Noxzema everywhere."

Do you think group-sex people ever get real wild and "interact" with other stuff in the room like lamp bases, smooth countertops and umbrella stands? I do. Did legionnaires get invited anywhere after they invented their own disease? What is a legionnaire?

HOLY SHIT. You wanna know something crazy? I just talked forever about Legionnaire's disease FOR NO REASON because I googled it and it turns out Botox isn't made out of Legionnaire's disease! It is made out of botulism. My bad.

Botulism is a deadly disease a person can get from eating improperly canned food. In 1820, Justinus Kerner, a "German medical officer and romantic poet," realized that the botulism toxin might be useful therapeutically. Here's a real poem called "The Saw" by Justinus Kerner:

In yonder mill I rested,
And sat me down to look
Upon the wheel's quick glimmer.
And on the flowing brook.
As in a dream, before me,
The saw, with restless play,
Was cleaving through a fir-tree
Its long and steady way.
The tree through all its fibres
With living motion stirred,
And, in a dirge-like murmur,
These solemn words I heard—
Oh, thou, who wanderest hither,
A timely guest thou art!
For thee this cruel engine
Is passing through my heart.
When soon, in earth's still bosom,
Thy hours of rest begin,
This wood shall form the chamber
Whose walls shall close thee in.
Four planks—I saw and shuddered—
Dropped in that busy mill;
Then, as I tried to answer,
At once the wheel was still.

Pretty good if you like poems about mills. I like poems about the jungle. Here's a poem about the jungle that I wrote. It's called "The Jungle":

What the fuck
Is that a fucking tiger
Behind that bush
Or am I just freaking out
Because I'm in
The Jungle

I also like swearing in poems. This is a poem called "ZACK" that I wrote about Zack de la Rocha:

Look at this fucking man
No fucking doubt he has a plan
He spits fire
You fucking morons

The botulism toxin is deadly if ingested, but it can harmlessly paralyze a muscle if it is properly injected. For years, botulism injections were used to treat patients suffering from uncontrolled muscle spasms. In 2002, some plastic surgeons started using it to paralyze facial muscles to reduce the appearance of wrinkles—frown lines, specifically.

So, yeah, Anita, go ahead and paralyze your face if that's what you think is best. You'll have to re-paralyze it every few months, because that stuff wears off. And it doesn't make you look young so much as it makes you look WEIRD. But it's a free country and you can paralyze whatever you want to paralyze. If you run out of money for Botox maybe you can smooth things out by taking little bites of improperly canned food.

Don't eat moldy meat! Flatten your wrinkly face by changing your wrinkly life: What kind of soap do you use? Does it smell good? Do you keep a dream journal? Do you keep a regular journal? Do you keep a journal written from the point of view of a fictional person named Frederica? When was the last time you were in a sack race that WASN'T part of a work thing? How often do you handle clay? Weekly? Monthly? Less than that?! How often do you astrally project? In an average day, would you say you spend more time surfing the internet or bottle-feeding baby animals?

Fuck Botox, Anita. Moisturize, and try new things.

My Boyfriend Flirts at the Dog Park

PUBLISHED JANUARY 11, 2017.

Dear Advice King,

How do I stop my boyfriend from flirting with random women at the dog park?

—Beatrice in Los Angeles

Have your boyfriend neutered.

Just kidding—that's illegal! You are only supposed to neuter animals, Beatrice.

I wonder what kind of dog you have. If it's a big dog you could train it to rip the ass out of your boyfriend's pants every time you get jealous. The attack word could be "insecure." I'm assuming you and your boyfriend *have* a dog. If you do not, and this guy just hangs around dog parks, you should break up with him immediately.

Legally "neuter" him with antidepressants. One of the main side effects of antidepressants is decreased sex drive. If he isn't depressed, MAKE him depressed.

What does he talk to these women about? I went to the dog park when I was single (WITH a dog), and I could never get anything going. Here's a play I wrote about trying to flirt with women in the dog park:

"DOG PARK ON A HOT TIN ROOF"

EXTERIOR, DOG PARK—2006

ME: How old is your dog?
LADY: 8.

THE END

Does your boyfriend have a "man bun"?* If your boyfriend has a "man bun" you should not let him go ANYWHERE, including dog parks. Cut that thing off while he is sleeping (the bun, that is) because it is not a hairstyle, it is a hairy invitation. A "man bun" is the male equivalent of a lower-back tattoo—a lower-back tattoo says "NOW BOOKING SECRET SEX PARTIES." I'm surprised they don't have man bun dispensers in the bathrooms of highway gas stations.

Tell him that if he can't "keep it in his pants" he has to wait in the car.

Refer to it as the "dong park." "Are we going to the DONG park? You sure are chatty at the DONG park."

Stop going to the dog park.

Get rid of the dog.

Get rid of your boyfriend.

Get rid of the dog and your boyfriend.

Burn down the dog park.

Feed your boyfriend to the dog.

Go into the convent.

Should I Try Therapy?

PUBLISHED SEPTEMBER 4, 2019.

Dear Advice King,

I've tried everything I can think of to deal with my stress and anxiety. I can't seem to figure out a way to feel good. I have never been to a therapist, because I was raised to believe that therapy was only for weak and insane people. I'm at my wits' end! Should I try therapy?

—Crazy in Alabama

*For the benefit of my older readers, "man bun" is a modern slang term used to describe a hair bun worn by a man.

You can yell all you want, Randy, but YOU are the reason the Jet Ski doesn't work anymore. It's not Lenore's fault.

How did I do? I'm still doing that thing where I try to answer the question without reading it.

Fuck! This question has nothing to do with personal watercraft, and there's no one named Lenore in it.

I encourage you to try therapy, "Crazy." Everybody is "crazy," by the way. Human existence is a recipe for madness. In the end, we *all die*. If that doesn't make you slightly anxious, you are a moron.

Therapy is a service humans provide for other humans. One human (the therapist) listens to another human (the client) talk in exchange for money. The therapist offers advice to the client, because that's part of the service. And that's it! In case you are confused, here are some other examples of services: shoe repair, haircutting, pest control and dance lessons.

So why are people so reluctant to go to therapy, but not reluctant to get their shoes repaired? Here are a couple of reasons.

1. Parents. Parents often discourage their children from seeing therapists. It's because those parents' parents discouraged THEM from seeing a therapist. THOSE parents' parents definitely discouraged THEM from seeing a therapist, because it was like 1910, and coal mines outnumbered therapists 5 million to one. Before that, nobody encouraged anybody to see a therapist—everybody died of consumption before they could even get their shoes repaired.

   Parents hate therapy because they are pretty sure that THEY are the ones that fucked up their kids, and they are terrified that if their kids go to therapy they might figure this out and turn on them. Without therapy, they hope, the kids will blame themselves for their problems and become alcoholics or something.
2. Capitalism. Capitalism has successfully reduced all the beauty and mystery of human experience to a dreary, simplistic cycle of work and death. An essential component

> in this reductive process has been to demean introspection. "Thinking too much" was long ago branded a sign of weakness, rather than a sign of intelligence and humanity. When psychotherapy began to gain popularity in America, capitalist bullies called therapists "shrinks"—short for "headshrinkers." The intent was to associate mental health care with voodoo, i.e. something "crazy."
>
> Corporate advertising made—and makes—it perfectly clear what behaviors are acceptable and "normal" in capitalist America: working, buying shit, driving, buying shit, drinking alcohol, buying shit, dying and buying shit. Well-adjusted people spend less money.

Don't listen to your parents, and don't let yourself be bullied by the capitalists. Go to a therapist. It's fun!

One more thing. There are good therapists and bad therapists, just like there are good barbers and bad barbers. If you don't vibe with your therapist, find another one! If I talk to one more person who says they "saw a therapist once" and they "didn't like it" so they *never went again*—instead deciding to just bitch to their friends for the rest of their (and their friends', because they have to listen to them bitch) miserable lives—I WILL GO ACTUALLY CRAZY.

When you get a bad haircut, do you just cut your own hair for the rest of your life? If you don't like your therapist, TRY A DIFFERENT FUCKING THERAPIST. If you are afraid to go to a therapist because you are afraid of what you will find out . . . GO FIND IT OUT ANYWAY! WE ONLY GET ONE SHOT AT THIS.

How Do I Stop Procrastinating?

. . . .

PUBLISHED FEBRUARY 17, 2021.

Dear Advice King,

When I work on creative projects, I spend most of my time procrastinating. I used to rationalize that it was part of my "process," but it just adds more stress. How do I become more focused and efficient?

—Jennifer in Van Nuys, Calif.

I like that! "Part of the process." Hahaha. I'm gonna use that next time I'm watching a 1983 high-dive competition on YouTube instead of writing this column—"it's part of the process."

"It's part of the process," he said to himself, as he dragged a lint roller across his bald spot and googled "Dyan Cannon topless."

Lord, Jennifer, if I knew the answer to this, I wouldn't be answering this question at midnight the day before my deadline. If I knew the answer to this, I'd be an award-winning gymnast. If I knew the answer to this I'd be . . . Elon Musk? God forbid.

I believe that we all should be very afraid of people who do not procrastinate.

FAMOUS PEOPLE WHO DID NOT PROCRASTINATE:

1. The motherfuckers who tore down New York City's Penn Station.
2. The motherfuckers who launched the Iraq War.
3. The band Styx before they made the album *Kilroy Was Here*.

Procrastination is a nasty word for something very human and worthwhile: deliberation. "Procrastination" means, by definition, that you intend to do something—otherwise it wouldn't be procrastination, it would be loafing. Not that there's anything wrong with loafing. I'd take a loafer over one of these Randian "Ideal Man"-type sociopaths who this shitty global money culture has elevated ANY DAY OF THE WEEK. But since procrastination is the lead-up to an action and is a result of the healthy anxiety that should accompany the taking of an action—especially a significant one—we need more of it, not less. It is a sign of sensitivity.

Lack of "procrastination" (consideration, deliberation, YouTube, gummy worms) is what leads to terrible decisions. And WHAT'S THE RUSH?! Is the planet about to fall off its axis without another boutique hotel? Do we really need more high-end restaurants? *Now?* When people are living in cars and tents and crowdfunding medical care? Maybe we should stop and think.

Is Elon Musk a hero for making luxury cars and rockets? *Or* is he a moron for making luxury cars and rockets? Maybe if he'd procrastinated a little he would have decided to direct his obviously prodigious energy toward goals more human—and humane. He's the richest man in the world because of making gadgets. WE DON'T NEED ANY MORE GADGETS. Gadgets, diamonds, ballers, billionaires, influencers, boutique hotels, high-end this, high-end that, rockets, luxury cars and the title "the richest man in the world" are the fucking problem, not the solution.

"The second-richest man in the world," Jeff Bezos, is another celebrated non-procrastinator who is—not coincidentally—involved with gadgets. He is a "GEEEEENIUS" who figured out that an army of low-wage, micromanaged workers can get stuff delivered fast. Gadgets, mostly. Gadgets made in China by an army of low-wage, micromanaged workers. WHAT A GEEEEENIUS. The Pharaohs who "built" the pyramids and the Manifest Destiny dickheads who "built" the railroads were also geniuses, by that standard. Labor exploitation genius? Fuck that.

What was the question? Ah yes, procrastination. Did you know that Elon Musk wanted to bore giant tunnels under Los Angeles so he could get to the airport faster? We need MORE procrastination, not less.

Take your time, Jennifer—do it right.

Should I Write Poetry?

PUBLISHED SEPTEMBER 2, 2020.

Dear Advice King,

I enjoy your poetry! I would like to try writing poetry. Do you have any tips? Also, can you please write a poem about our current situation (COVID, financial uncertainty, creeping fascism)?

Thanks!

—Tracy in Canton, Ohio

There once was a woman from Canton
Who bought some land to plant on
She dropped her seeds
And pulled all the weeds
But her apples were killed by a phantom

Hi Tracy! That's not a poem—that's a limerick. I write limericks to warm up. It's like stretching before you exercise. Nothing puts me in the mood to write a good, real, classy poem like writing some rhyming trash about a man from Nantucket.

There once a man from Nantucket
Who carried his balls in a bucket
The bucket did rust

His gonads did bust
and his girlfriend departed for . . . St. Louis

Sometimes it's hard to rhyme the last line.

Speaking of rhyming, here's a funny thing: It used to be REQUIRED for poetry to rhyme, but these days most people think poetry that rhymes is corny.

Poetry Tip No. 1: The less rhymey a poem is, the fancier it is considered.

For example, one of the fanciest poems of all time is by William Carlos Williams. Here it is:

"The Red Wheelbarrow"

so much depends
upon

a red wheel
barrow

glazed with rain
water

beside the white
chickens

See, that poem doesn't rhyme. And it's not long. And it's not full of big words, or flowery descriptions. Which leads me to my second tip.

Poetry Tip No. 2: Economy of words.

When I was in college, I accidentally signed up for an advanced poetry class. I had never written poetry. The professor was a friendly hippie woman, so she allowed me to stay in the class. It was something she soon regretted.

You see, back then I thought poetry was when you took something you wanted to say in regular words, and said it in big words instead. And I thought you were supposed to add way more description than you would ever use in "regular" writing. So after this woman was nice enough to let me stay in her advanced poetry class even though I was a beginner, I handed in stuff like this:

"Shoe"

Metatarsals prostrate in
the temple of Buster Brown
The insole a meandering
moldering
mattress
for my calloused flopping flippers
Like a foot-boat in a
foot-storm
the sole is THE SOUL??
Lugubrious. Obsequious.
Navigate the engorged tributaries
and weathered wizened cobblestones
of love, you leather foot-house
with peacocks hulking in the
dappled evening
dapple

When she was done vomiting, she gave me a D- (at least it didn't rhyme), and wished she'd never gotten a job at that college.

It turns out the best poetry—in my opinion—is NOT unnecessarily descriptive. My favorite poets will only use a big word if it also happens to be the BEST word. A poet's job is to evoke, and, by evoking, to move. There should be just enough words—no extra. No fanciness for fanciness' sake. Keep editing until YOU are moved, Tracy, and the chances are that others will be moved too. And don't put too much pressure on yourself in the beginning! Have fun, write often, and if you stick with it, I bet you'll be pleasantly surprised.

Here's your poem:

"Shoe"

Put yourself in someone else's
sometime
Because this is all temporary
and empathy is
the
name of
the game

So Now What Do We Do?

. . . .

PUBLISHED NOVEMBER 16, 2016, THE WEEK AFTER DONALD TRUMP WAS ELECTED PRESIDENT.

Dear Advice King,

NOW what the F do we do?!

—Pete in Seattle

About what? JUST KIDDING

I'm listening to Survivor's *Vital Signs* with clothespins on my nipples. It seems to help. Also, I only eat Junior Mints now. FUN FACT: I'm on the roof wearing a diaper.

Become one of those traveling tinkers who wears a pot as a hat.

Start a rat farm.

Talk exclusively about "supermoons."

Instead of cereal, eat a bowl of Thorazine every morning.

Live in a pond and breathe through a reed.

Live in a bog and breathe through a reed.

Breathe through a reed for no reason.

Change your name to Reed.

Most people would tell you to build a bunker, Pete. I actually received the question, "How do I build a bunker?" I don't have any idea how to build a bunker. When I had to build a birdhouse in shop class I decided to build it around the bird to make sure it would be the right size. I got an F, and the bird was never the same from all the hammering.

I think that if your room is messy enough, you don't need a bunker. I could hide under some laundry or behind a stack of *Easyriders* in an emergency.

If you have your heart set on building a bunker then I would say buy a big sheet of plywood and spray paint "KEEP OUT" on it. Dig a hole that you can fit in. Put some snacks and soft drinks in the hole. When the trouble starts, get in the hole and pull the plywood over the top. Push up on the plywood and take little peeks to see if it's safe to come back out.

REAL ADVICE STARTS NOW

Personal (adjective): 1. of, affecting, or belonging to a particular person rather than anyone else.

Our hackneyed, unattainable-by-definition search for "personal happiness" is dividing us.

There is no such thing as "personal happiness." It is a concept that was cooked up by marketing creeps to sell cable subscriptions and anti-aging creams. The more we try to achieve "personal happiness," the more isolated, frustrated, and sad we become.

We must, as a planet, shift our concerns from the personal to the communal, and part of being effectively concerned with the community means being involved in politics. When I say "involved in politics,"

I know a lot of you are thinking, "But I already share political stuff on Facebook." Unfortunately there's a big problem with that version of "political activity," and that is that it DOESN'T DO ANYTHING. Those things you share only reach your Facebook friends, 100 percent of whom already agree with you. Also, although it may not seem like it, your Facebook friends make up .0000000000000000000000000000 00000000000000000001 percent of the world's population—and that number is probably way too big.

Your Facebook post didn't affect the political process at all. Not even a little. The fact that you eat local produce and dress like an old-time cowboy didn't do anything either. All that pot smoking and TV watching? Nope. "But what if the shows were REALLY GOOD?!"

All of the planet's most fortunate people live in bubbles—sex bubbles, food bubbles, drug and alcohol bubbles, social media bubbles, fitness bubbles, language-policing bubbles. The inside of some people's bubbles is so nice that they forgot that most of their fellow citizens' bubbles have popped. They've been popping for decades. A whole bunch popped in 2008.

So, in 2016, the people in America with no bubbles were considering voting for a madman because he was the only candidate talking to them. The Americans in nice bubbles called these people a "basket of deplorables," and told them everything was going fine. The no-bubble people voted for the madman.

It's time for us ALL to burst our bubbles, folks. It's time for empathy. It's time to get out on the street and talk to your neighbors. It's time for politics. Interact with people you disagree with. Interact with legislators. Interact! The defense budget of the United States was $598 billion in 2016. Corporations are not paying taxes. Social programs are being cut.

I hate to bring up the old "united we stand, divided we fall" line, but it's still really all we need to know. Here it is in its original context, one of Aesop's fables from the sixth century B.C.:

"THE FOUR OXEN AND THE LION"

A LION used to prowl about a field in which Four Oxen used to dwell. Many a time he tried to attack them; but whenever he came near they turned their tails to one another, so that whichever way he approached them he was met by the horns of one of them. At last, however, they fell a-quarrelling among themselves, and each went off to pasture alone in a separate corner of the field. Then the Lion attacked them one by one and soon made an end of all four.

"UNITED WE STAND, DIVIDED WE FALL."

I'm Bored, and No One Wants to Do Anything

. . . .

PUBLISHED MAY 17, 2015.

Dearest Advice King,

I'm a person who loves to do activities. I like doing all kinds of things, including going to events, making dinners and eating them with human beings, going out to different places with human beings, going on walks. The problem is that it seems others aren't interested in doing things or aren't motivated to exit their homes or workplaces. I invite folks to get a cheap ticket to the symphony, or to go on a free walk in our beautiful city, but usually the only quick "Yes" I can rely on is when I suggest going to a bar to get a beer. I love beer, but sitting and smoking and drinking it in the same bars is old news. I don't demand a fancy life, but I wish someone would say, "Hey, there's a random Beethoven opus (or whatever the hell they're called) being played in the park, grab your fuckin' quilt!" Dear Advice King, is it me? Is it Nashville?

YOLO,

—Hopeless in Hot Chicken City

Hi, "Hopeless." I feel your pain. I was born in 1969. When I was growing up, it was an "all-activity" world. I mean, we had television, but there was never anything on. There were 13 channels. I didn't have a "social network." I had one real-life friend—the kid who lived next door. His name was Eric. I didn't even like him very much. He didn't like me either, but we did activities together because we realized that if we didn't, we would die of boredom. United, we could play catch. Divided, we were stuck watching 1970s daytime television. I couldn't have watched television anyway, because whenever I asked my mom if I could turn on the TV, she would say, "No."

We had a regular phone, because that's the only kind of phone there was, and the only people I ever called on it were my grandparents. Besides them, the only person I knew was Eric, and I sure as hell didn't need to call him. He was always right there, in my face, pestering me to do activities.

"Wanna throw rocks??"

"Wanna throw rocks??"

"Wanna . . . ummm . . . throw . . . *other* rocks??"

VCRs hadn't been invented. I had a View-Master, but a kid can only look at "The Monuments of Washington D.C." so many times before he or she quite literally wants to go fly a kite. So me and Eric flew a kite (or more accurately, we ran with a kite dragging behind us . . . this column is turning into a *Family Circus* cartoon). We "flew" a kite, walked around, stood by the road holding sticks, "flew" the kite again, walked around more, and then stood. By. The. Road. Holding. Sticks. Activities!

Here's the problem, "Hopeless": None of that stuff would have happened if I'd had a smartphone. I might not have even known that there WAS a kid living next door. And if I *had* happened to look up from my phone long enough to meet Eric, and we didn't hit it off right away, I would have had no incentive to forge a friendship. Eric and I weren't a perfect match, but all the arguing and the rock-throwing got us into good physical and mental shape. It socialized us.

Today's adults didn't grow up having to rely on kites, rocks and complicated friendships for their fun—they had cable television, VCRs, Game Boys and computers to occupy them. Their primary relationship growing up was with video monitors. The "reality" they are used to is more virtual than real. Have you noticed how today's kids seem to overuse the word "awkward"? If you are used to virtual reality, REAL reality is going to feel pretty goddamn awkward. People don't obey commands like electronic devices do, which makes modern "adults" very easily frustrated. Easily frustrated people can't have serious conversations—or even games of Frisbee—without losing their temper and stomping off in a huff, so imagine one of these modern misfits trying to participate in a substantive real-life relationship! Why talk or hang out (awkward!)? Text. Why date or fall in love (awkward!)? Hook up, or even better, just masturbate to porn.

There's a reason why today's young adults seem extra-obnoxious to older people. If these young men and women can't get what they want, they don't know how to finesse the situation—they just say they want it again, except louder this time. They talk to people like they are squashing the button on a broken video game controller.

You know what makes these techno-misfits feel less awkward? Alcohol. Alcohol provides a facsimile of the warmth that is generated from human connection, but without having to navigate the minefield of an actual relationship.

Keep trying to fill that social calendar, "Hopeless"! You're the last of a dying breed. Alcohol, energy drinks, hook-ups and texting will be the sum total of human "happiness" if these virtual-people don't put down their devices and start fighting for the genuine fucking article.

Karaoke Overdose

PUBLISHED DECEMBER 16, 2014.

Dear Advice King,

My girlfriend loves karaoke. A lot. She probably goes three nights a week, and it seems like the only way I ever get to spend any time with her is when I'm accompanying her to some smoky place where people are butchering Garth Brooks' "Low Places" through a crummy P.A. I hate karaoke. Also, she's not even a very good singer. I love her, but what do I do? How do I get out of this?

—Austin in Germantown

Karaoke . . . is that the thing where you have a grill in the middle of the table and the chef guy juggles the food, or is it the thing where you jump off buildings and awnings and rain gutters like a monkey? Let me google it.

Ohhhh, *THAT* thing—the Japanese singing game for people with nothing to do. I'm glad you came to me with this.

Three nights a week? That means it's really four. Your girlfriend likes getting drunk, Austin. Karaoke is one of those things you say you are going to do when you really mean you are going to get drunk. Like camping. You know when you go "camping" because it's not acceptable to stay home and drink 20 beers? You set up the tent as fast as you can and you use the wrong stakes in the wrong holes and the thing that's supposed to go across the top ends up on the bottom, but you leave it that way and start drinking beer at 11 in the morning? And you drink for 14 hours straight, and your friend Rob almost falls in the fire? And you and Rob are doing coke sitting on an upside-down canoe and talking endlessly about how great it is to "reboot" out in nature until someone who is trying to sleep tells you to shut up, and you do for a second, but then you start getting louder without noticing and you get sad 'cause there's no more coke and that same person in the tent tells you to "SHUT THE FUCK UP!" and they're really mad this time? *That* kind of camping. That's what karaoke is. Except it's worse because I feel like people know camping is dishonest. Like fishing. Fishing was debunked as a hobby a long time ago. Everyone knows it's just addiction with a tackle box. People act like karaoke is as wholesome as knitting. Do a lot of knitters take a break from knitting to call their dealer?

Some people treat karaoke as if it were *real* show business. They have an I-can't-make-birthing-class-tonight-because-I-have-to-do-karaoke attitude. A "the show must go on" type ethic. Except it's not a real show. It's a fake show. It's a fake ethic. It's a "the drinking must go on" ethic. Karaoke has absolutely nothing to do with singing. Karaoke bars are about singing like strip clubs are about dancing. There is a REAL show business. On the outside chance your girlfriend is a talented singer who is only doing karaoke because she is unaware that there is a *real* show business, alert her immediately to its existence.

Before I went to rehab, I used to go to karaoke nights at a dive bar on Gallatin Road. There were a lot of missing teeth and prematurely wrinkled faces. Meth addicts. Meth addicts were singing "I Wanna Dance with Somebody." No one wants to dance with a meth addict. The only thing keeping these people from grinding their teeth to dust were the times they had to open their jaws during the "singing." The host had just gotten out of the hospital for a drug-related heart attack hours before the "gig." He ripped the tubes out of his arm and left the ICU because he couldn't miss the "show." He was singing the Kenny Rogers song "Lady" to a young woman with *no* teeth when he grabbed his arm and fell down. People started dead-seriously screaming to "Get him a beer!" He was taken away in an ambulance. After he was gone everybody was like, "He's a tough sonofabitch, he'll be back in the saddle in no time. They won't be able to keep him down long, I'll tell you what." Back in what saddle? The "Total Eclipse of the Heart" saddle?!? The at-the-bar-still-wearing-a-hospital-bracelet saddle?!? Terrible saddles.

Karaoke dwells at the intersection between dreams and reality, faith and doubt, longing and betrayal, real singing and fake singing. Nero fiddled while Rome burned, Americans sing "Don't Stop Believing" while EVERYTHING burns. A raisin in the sun doesn't explode—it gets drunk and does karaoke. If television is the opiate of the masses, karaoke is the Jägerbomb. The slurred lyrics of "Living on a Prayer" echo through the mausoleum that houses the corpse of The American Dream.

Also, karaoke is a lot of fun if you don't overdo it.

Do I Sleep Too Much?

PUBLISHED 1/19/2016.

Dear Advice King,

Am I missing out on life if I sleep 10 to 12 hours a day?

—Matt in Hendersonville

No. Life is horrible. The more time you spend paddling your dream canoe down Soft Ice Cream River (sleeping), the less time you will have to spend getting "permits" and hearing about ISIS. I'm listening to Carly Simon again, by the way. The people around me are all talking about ISIS, but all I hear are the sweet sounds of Carly's 1987 album *Coming Around Again*. If you have to be awake for an extended period in this concrete hellscape we call "the modern world," I recommend listening to as much Carly Simon as possible.

The world used to be covered in grass, and everyone slept very little. No one wanted to miss out on all the grassy fun. If you were hungry, you could catch a leaping salmon in a baseball glove. If you were thirsty, you could dip your cup in a pond. Everybody wore clothes made out of bark and hats made out of sunflowers. If you wanted to get laid you had to be friendly and have a nice hat.

Mean creeps didn't like this grassy world. They didn't want to take the time to craft a nice flower hat—they wanted to get laid RIGHT

AWAY, with no effort. These unpleasant people got together and started what is now known as "politics." History's first legislative body was a gang of assholes who wanted to be able to procreate without having any personality or style. Their first act was to make it illegal to have an elaborate hat without a "permit." Then they started paving everything because the green grass, flowers and flying trout were making their mean gray faces look like shit. "Asphalt" and "permits" replaced humor and hats as the sexual currencies of this new, political "civilization."

You may say, "Is anything in the above paragraph true?" It's a helluva lot truer than the fucking Nina, Pinta and Santa Maria, Matt—I can guarantee you that. My point is that legislative bodies—now, then and forever—are just gangs of gray-faced scumbags using hierarchical bureaucracy as a tool to get laid.

Monday, Tuesdays, Wednesdays? Fake. A creation of the gray-faced. "Jobs," "benefits," "hours," "weeks," "money," "success," "THE GRID"? Fake, fake, fake, fake, fake, fake and FAKE! "The grid"? Get a jackhammer and some wire cutters and that grid is history—and if the people don't tear it down, time and Mother Nature will.

"The grid" is just a name for the system of financial oppression that the gray-faced use to get sex. "Oh, you can't pay your cable bill? Shit. That's too bad. That's gonna fuck up your credit, which will affect your access to food and shelter. Tell you what—climb in bed with me and we'll forget all about it."

Fuck the grid. You can't put a goddamn grid on me, and you can't put a goddamn grid on a ball floating in space. We need to get back to the friendly, grassy, gridless world that made people want to get out of bed in the morning.

Should I Use a Neti Pot?

PUBLISHED JANUARY 4, 2018.

Dear Advice King,

Yes, I've finally been convinced to get on the neti pot train. Although I am now booger-free, it feels like I have water on the brain. Question 1: Is that normal? Question 2: Are homeopathic remedies like this the real deal—or voodoo nonsense? Should I start drinking essential oils and clearing my chakras too? I want my 2018 to go off without a hitch.

Thanks!

—Ann Marie in Jacksonville, Fla.

Hi Ann Marie! That's a lot of questions.

I should start by saying that I'm pretty sure most people don't think using a neti pot is as crazy as you obviously do.

Also, the fictional "neti pot train" you mentioned sounds disgusting. I picture an old-time locomotive that runs on mucus and the passengers are huge noses wearing top hats. They produce the train's diabolical "fuel" by using the pots. The last stop is MY DREAMS. Thanks for nothing.

For the benefit of readers who are even more sheltered than Ann Marie, readers who have never even *heard* of neti pots and are therefore incapable of being suspicious of them, I will now describe these weird devices and the exotic ceremony associated with them. BUCKLE YOUR SEATBELTS, BASIC BITCHES: They are like little teapots, except instead of tea, they are filled with warm salt water. You pour the water into one nostril, and it comes out the other. The water passes through the sinus cavities, clearing them.

I just thought of something! Are you putting the neti pot in your nose? If you are sticking it someplace else, that might explain why you think it's so "homeopathic."* I recommend googling "neti pot," "nose" and "ass," just to be on the safe side.

In response to Question 1, I get the feeling that you had water on the brain from the get-go, Ann Marie.

As for Question 2, unless you want to spend 2018 on the toilet, do not "drink" essential oil. You'll be "going off without a hitch" all right. A shit hitch. You'll be shitting.

There is a thing that Gwyneth Paltrow invented because she doesn't have a job called "oil pulling," where you SWISH essential oils around your mouth. If you think having an oily mouth will make you feel better, knock yourself out.

Chakras? If you can find 'em, clean 'em™.

My real advice is to try anything and everything, Ann Marie: neti pots, firewalking, oil pulling, oil pushing, oil painting—whatever! If it makes you feel better, do it! Healthy people are people who can help other people—and people need all the help they can get in 2018. And 1945. And 2001. And 2025. And every other difficult year in the past or future. 2017 wasn't uniquely horrible**—every year is terrible—and rewarding, and beautiful, and terrible again. These are the same imperfect years that every generation has had to help each other through. Let's all try to be healthy and kind enough to end up on the right side of history—voodoo encouraged.

* In America, the word "homeopathic" is interchangeable with the word "crazy."

** I realize social media made it feel that way—and it's not gonna stop until we stop knocking (clicking) on every door of what is essentially a haunted house.

Searching for Me Time

PUBLISHED APRIL 28, 2015.

Dear Advice King,

At the risk of sounding like a walking cliche, I feel like having a family is beginning to chip away at my personal identity. I always wanted kids, but now that I have them, I feel like I have no personal time, no privacy, and no fun. I love my kids and my husband, but how the hell am I supposed to find any "me time"?

—Gail in Goodlettsville

You could do what 1970s dads did: Say things are getting too "heavy," put your bowling shoes, bikini briefs, rings, necklaces, belt buckles and aftershave in a duffel bag and hit the road in your Ford LTD with the kids crying on the lawn. Get a job in Tulsa painting cars, hang a macrame clipper ship above the couch in your furnished room, and smoke a lot of joints. End up in jail with a Komodo dragon bite after attempting to rob a pet store with a guy named Manny.

If you don't want to "split" so you can get your "head together," I recommend . . . babysitters! Babysitters were invented for situations like this! You can get a babysitter and learn how to walk on stilts and take singing lessons and then walk around town on stilts singing. You'll have a brand-new personal identity! You won't be known as "that regular lady with kids" anymore—you'll be known as "that lady with kids who lost her goddamn mind." You can become a bush pilot or a dentist or a pastry chef, or learn how to play the bouzouki. Babysitters, my friend!

Perhaps you can't afford all the babysitting needed to live out your dream of becoming a bonded locksmith. You said you love your husband, right? Well, that must mean he is a good guy. Tell him how you are feeling and work through it together. I'm sure he'd be willing to take care of the kids on a Sunday while you are doing Kung Fu or making an ice sculpture.

Other options: Spend as much time in the bathroom as possible.

One more thing: I am living your dream, Gail. I am a single man with no kids. A big part of my "personal identity" is watching 9/11 conspiracy videos in my underwear. I also eat giant bags of Skittles and weep. Be careful what you wish for.

Should I Homeschool My Kids?

PUBLISHED AUGUST 19, 2020.

Dear Advice King,

It looks like I'll be teaching my three kids at home for the foreseeable future, but I'm a horrible teacher and my wife and I both work! Do you have any tips on how to handle this situation?

Thanks!

—Aaron in Memphis

Throw the thing in the garbage! It's not supposed to take six years to do a puzzle—especially one that's 300 pieces. And it's a picture of a rhinoceros? That shouldn't take six years. You might want to see a doctor, Edna.

I tried to answer the question without reading it again. I thought you were a woman named Edna who couldn't finish her rhinoceros puzzle.

Homeschooling! Ha! Looks like daddy has to relearn algebra.

It's a little off-topic but, just now, typing the word "algebra," it occurred to me that I didn't take advantage of the fact that "algebra" has the word "bra" in it nearly enough when I was a student. You don't know what you've got till it's gone.

"ALGEBRA SAYS 'BRA' RIGHT IN IT! THE SQUARE ROOT OF FIVE IS A BRA! BRAS BRAS BRAS! LADIES WEAR THOSE!!!"—*Me, shortly before being tased at the Department of Motor Vehicles next week.*

Actually, it's not time to teach your kids algebra. Fuck algebra—it's *Swiss Family Robinson* time. Teach your kids how to tame a jackal.

The Swiss Family Robinson is a book about a family that was shipwrecked, and they tamed a jackal. WE are shipwrecked at the moment. COVID is the reef, and we are the boat. We don't need streaming services now, we need actual streams. We don't need apps, WE NEED APPLES.

And we shouldn't be selling our children a version of success that includes hoarding resources. Lessons in compassion and self-sufficiency are what kids need. Give a child a fish, and they'll probably hit the dog with it. TEACH a child to fish, and they can feed themselves, the dog and all the families living in Walmart parking lots. Teach that child that Jesus didn't value money, and neither did Buddha or Muhammad. TEACH YOUR KIDS THAT LIFE IS A SUPPOSED TO BE A JOURNEY TOWARD ENLIGHTENMENT, NOT A GAME SHOW WITH CASH AND PRIZES.

Success, the way it's defined in America, is about "winning" and dominance—things that are NOT looked upon favorably in the Bible. And that's an extreme understatement. It's "The meek shall inherit the Earth," not "The strong shall have a five-car garage and all the health care."

Billionaires are immoral. Teach your children that. IT IS IMMORAL TO AMASS RICHES. Your fellow humans are suffering.

Racism is immoral. Teach your children that.

The rat race is over, and it has left us on a particularly desolate expanse of tundra where COVID and cancer aren't cured, but a rich 17-year-old can push a button on their phone and an 85-year-old "independent contractor" delivers them a sandwich. NOT SUSTAINABLE. If you raise your kids to believe in the false promises of the American mirage, they will never love anyone. Teach a person to consume, and they will try to consume people, too.

Teach your kids about affection and consent. Keep them off social media for as long as you can. Let them know that there's nothing "badass" or "American" about drinking alcohol. And try not to lose your temper in front of them too much—it will give them a nervous condition.

Who do we remember from the past—the "winners??"

No.

THE LOVERS.

The "Friend Zone"

. . . .

PUBLISHED FEBRUARY 10, 2015.

Dear Advice King,

I'm stuck in the friend zone. I have feelings for a girl that I've been spending a lot of time with lately, and despite how much I tell her I think she's special and beautiful and cool, she never seems to give me any signals back. I can take a hint, but every time I try to move on and forget about her, she rings me up to hang out some more. What should I do? Is she just using me for some sort of emotional fulfillment? Should I suck it up and consider myself lucky to have a cool friend? Should I stop hanging out with her altogether so I can end this torture? I'm clueless here.

—Evan in Berry Hill

The "friend zone," eh? More like the "moron zone," or the "seventh-grader zone." This "friend zone" is an imaginary area. Women do not have "zones." You are just acting like a weirdo. You are developing crazy theories about women in an attempt to avoid the pain of rejection.

You told her she was special and beautiful and cool, and you didn't get any signals back? Well you are not in the "friend zone," Evan. You are in the "shit outta luck zone." Her lack of response was a loud and clear response. She is not interested in you IN THAT WAY. If you keep hanging around after that, it's your own damn fault.

Guys talk about the "friend zone" like it's a waiting room, as if women work like the Department of Motor Vehicles. Like if you show up and sit around long enough you'll eventually be brought up to the (sex) window. And if the woman doesn't bring you up to the window in what you feel is a reasonable amount of time, then that lady is a rotten, mean Department of Motor Vehicles instead of a REGULAR PERSON who doesn't want to have sex with you. AND, if women have zones and they transfer men in and out of these zones according to time served, good behavior, et cetera, that makes women seem more like prison bureaucracies than people. Women hate being compared to penal systems and DMVs, Evan, it's dehumanizing.

Do you use salad dressing, Evan? Do you think someone babbling about zones could ever make you eat a salad dressing you didn't like?

As far as her bloody "ringing you up," my lonesome little squire, it's like this: Imagine you applied for a job. You fill out an application. You don't get any, ahem, "signals back." Now what a normal person does is he finds another place to apply. What you do is start hanging around the place that isn't hiring, batting your eyelashes. Next thing you know, you are fixing the roof. For free.

Is "friend zone" a play on "end zone"? Like the man just "received the kickoff" (met the woman), and now he has to try to get a "lovedown"? Well, you're not going to move the ball saying she's "special and beautiful." That sounds just like the shit her dad said to her when she graduated from high school. Fifteen-yard penalty. I will now be exiting this metaphor.

Listen up, Evan: Women are not multi-zoned mechanisms designed to give, or deny, pleasure to men. They are people, and as such are entitled to their personal tastes. You and only you are responsible for your own happiness. You will not be ready for a relationship until you embrace these realities.

My Husband's Mind Games

. . . .

PUBLISHED MARCH 3, 2015.

Dear Advice King,

My husband frequently asks me for my preference on a variety of matters. However, when I answer, he always wants to go with the option I did not choose. I have even tried the pre-emptory tactic of going with the opposite of my original inclination, but it never matters! It's as if he isn't sure what he wants until he knows what I want—then he knows he does not want that. Is there a technique you can provide for me to have things my way once in a while?

—Carol in Inglewood

Carol, your husband is an asshole. It's not enough for him to control things—he wants to hurt your feelings too!

If he were simply controlling, he would say, "We are going to the zoo, Carol," and you would think to yourself, "My husband is a jerk. He never asks me where I'd like to go." Instead, he says, "Would you like to go to the zoo or go hiking?" and you say, "I would like to go hiking, Robert." (I'm going to call your husband Robert.) Robert says, "OK, the zoo it is!" That is a Mean Routine™. And it's not just mean—Robert is fucking with your head. He creates the illusion of valuing your opinion, which makes you think he is a caring partner, which keeps you with him while simultaneously making you feel like your opinions are stupid, which hurts your self-esteem, which also keeps you with him. This is sinister stuff, Carol. Have you ever heard of Project Artichoke?

You want a technique that will help you get your way? Call him on his bullshit. Next time he says, "Would you like to go see *The Fast and Furious 9* or that documentary about beans?" and you say, "I love documentaries about beans," and he says, "Buckle up for *Fast and Furious 9*,

Carol," *you* say, "WHAT THE FUCK WAS THAT??" If I know Robert like I think I know Robert, he will accuse you of remembering things wrong and ask if you are on your period and say that he thinks maybe you are GOING CRAZY. It's all designed to undermine your confidence.

A lot of people don't know this, but shortly before Lizzy Borden gave her father 40 whacks, her father asked her if she wanted to go to the zoo or go hiking. She wanted to go to the zoo.

In the 19th century, women in America had their opinions ignored even more than they do now. On top of that, they didn't get to have orgasms. The combination of controlling husbands and sexual frustration made women feel horrible. There were very few female doctors back then, and no good advice columns. If a woman dared, she could visit a local male physician, who was probably friends with her husband. When she said, "Winthrop keeps asking me trick questions to make me feel bad!" the doctor would tell her she had "the vapors," and that she was "hysterical." He would tell her that she was lucky she had a class act like Winthrop for a husband, that not many men would be classy enough to put up with her crazy ass. He would recommend that she massage Winthrop's calves to calm her nerves.

Luckily for you, Carol, it is not the 19th century, and you do not have the vapors. I'm here to tell you that your husband is insecure and manipulative. He thinks that if he starts letting you have your way you will eventually leave him. What if you go to the bean documentary and you meet some handsome guy who knows a lot about beans in the lobby? What if the real reason you want to go hiking is because you are in love with the park ranger?

Maybe when your husband was young he was the last guy picked for the kickball team. Maybe his mom did the same thing to him that he's doing to you. Maybe he was cross-eyed and had a hump. I don't care. That kind of stuff could *explain* his behavior, but it does not excuse it. You need to let Robert know that he is being mean and weird, and that it has to stop.

Connecting with Your Tech-Addicted Kids

PUBLISHED DECEMBER 9, 2014.

Dear Advice King,

At the risk of sounding like a square old guy, how do I get my kids to stop playing video games and texting and Snapchatting all the time? Every time I tell them to put down the devices and spend some time with their family in the real world, they just laugh and text each other jokes about me. This sucks. What is Kik? They're apparently using Kik all the time.

—Mad Dad in Nashville

Dear Square Old Guy,

Chat's outta the bag. Just because all you had was Stoopsitting, don't be jelly of Snapchatting. Jelly: It's the modern dimwit abbreviation of jealous. (Snapchatting is just, like, Morse code with finger snaps, by the way.) If kids today want to Ass Chat or play Corpsegrinder VIII or sext at your mom's funeral, there's ultimately nothing you can do. Did you supervise them? At all? How did they get this equipment? These machines are extremely potent! My co-worker Vicki once left her phone on the coffee table for 10 minutes while she went to the bathroom. When she came back, her 8-year-old son was printing his boarding pass for a flight to Somalia. First class. My friend's 5-year-old played Grand Theft Auto at a sleepover, and now she wants to be a "motherfucker" when she grows up.

I looked up Kik and read what it is, and I still don't understand what it is. Another way to "chat," but I don't know what makes it different from the other 9 billion ways to "chat" that already exist. There is no C in Kik, because if you remove or add letters to words it makes kids like them more. Here is a sentence your ultra-modern children would love: "Wavves, SMDH."

What is the content of these "jokes" they make? Are they good jokes? Like, proper jokes with punch lines? I am a professional comedian. Here is an example of a good joke about a dad: "Why does Dad like going to the dump? Because Mom is never at the dump." If your kids' jokes are anywhere near that good, you should encourage them to become professional comedy writers. If they are more along the lines of, "Dad's bald spot looks like an old pancake," then you should send them to military school.

I'll tell you one thing: This "real world" you're pitching better be pretty damn exciting. Exciting enough to RIVAL THE INTERNET! You might want to get a falcon or two, along with those big gloves they sit on. I bet if you built a half-pipe and grew a soul patch they'd put down those phones.

Seriously, are you at least trying to be cool? Every generation has its version of texting and video games. Metaphorically speaking, you are the teacher and they are your students passing notes. I bet that while your dad was in the garage restoring a chair you were holed up in your room blasting Twisted Sister and talking on the landline to your friend Onion. Same stuff. All you can do is try to learn from your parents' mistakes. Generally speaking, kids are not interested in restoring chairs, but they also aren't only interested in flash mobs. Find a happy medium. Take them to the movies. Take them to see a band THEY LIKE. Dragging them to see Gov't Mule with your friend Doug DOES NOT COUNT. Trying not to dress like a member of the John Birch Society helps, also. Have some rules—no phone at dinner, no phone or games in the hour before bed. Most importantly, DO NOT BE A HYPOCRITE. If you spend all your time on Pinterest adding shit to your "obsolete industrial equipment" board, your kids will never listen to anything you say about this stuff. Good luck, crankypants!

What Should I Buy for My Niece and Nephew?

. . . .

PUBLISHED AUGUST 16, 2017.

Dear Advice King,

My niece and nephew love Lego sets, but that shit's expensive! Exactly how much am I supposed to spend on these kids? Can I get them books instead?

Thanks!

—Least-Favorite Aunt

Fuck Legos. Have you ever stepped on a Lego with your bare foot?

Get them a goat. A live, real goat. I think goats are pretty cheap. Let me see . . .

Goats cost "$75–$300," according to the internet. I'm sure you can find a $40 goat. How much are Legos?

I'm sorry, this is nonsense. Don't get your niece and nephew a goat. A goat will eat their socks. Donald Trump expressed his support for white supremacists yesterday, and I'm all fucked up. I wish a goat would eat Donald Trump.

If you're not that crazy about these kids, mail them a couple of those "No. 1 Niece/Nephew" cards with $2 bills in them. Two-dollar bills are annoying as shit, so it's an American tradition to unload them on one's most underwhelming relatives.

If you really like these little freaks, here's some real advice: Go with your instincts, Least-Favorite Aunt—you should give them books! Books about real shit! And—and this is *very* important—take the time to get them excited about those books! It's 2017—you can't just hand a kid a book and expect them to read it. You have to PITCH that thing—books can't compete with the goddamn internet. Hand a young person a copy of Aldous Huxley's *Brave New World* or Richard Wright's *Native*

*Son** without explaining why it's cool and you may as well be handing them a hairbrush. They'll be on Snapchat faster than you can say "sext."

When I was in grade school in Connecticut, I was forced to play an instrument. It was required. "Pick an instrument," said the adults. I picked the saxophone, for no particular reason. I was told to practice my saxophone, and I was told what songs to learn. As far as I could tell, based on the information I was given about saxophones, they were invented for the sole purpose of playing at school assemblies. After school was over you were supposed to throw your saxophone in the garbage and become a stockbroker—which made perfect sense, since there were no assemblies in real life. Not one adult said anything about Charlie Parker or John Coltrane—no one even mentioned jazz! No one mentioned that there were such things as professional musicians, and no one mentioned that music, at its best, functions as a universal language of peace and love.

Without context or encouragement, playing music can be made to feel about as exciting as climbing a rope in gym class. Without context or encouragement, reading a challenging book can feel the same way. Add the perspective of a loving adult, and both can be transcendent.

Give your niece and nephew good books—and a little of your time and wisdom, Least-Liked Aunt!

. . . .

* Those are probably too advanced for a niece and nephew who want Legos, but you get the idea. *James and the Giant Peach*? *Are You There God? It's Me, Margaret*? *Manufacturing Consent*?

Should I Scream into the Void?

PUBLISHED APRIL 30, 2020.

Dear Advice King,

Will screaming into the void ever bring satisfaction, or will it leave me feeling empty, and give me a sore throat?

—Amy in South Dakota

Hi, Amy! Have you tried screaming at Mount Rushmore? Mount Rushmore is in South Dakota, in case any of my lesser-informed readers are wondering why I said that. Screaming at Mount Rushmore would feel better than screaming into "the void." At least you can locate Mount Rushmore on a map, and go there. Where exactly is "the void"? I think some people call South Dakota "The Void." Like, Missouri is the "Show Me State," and South Dakota is "The Void." Anyway, I recommend yelling at Mount Rushmore.

AMY'S TRIP TO MOUNT RUSHMORE, A SHORT PLAY BY CHRIS CROFTON

Amy wakes up in her bed in South Dakota. She brushes the tumbleweeds off of her face and heads into the kitchen.*

AMY: This pandemic has really got me down. I have an idea. I'm gonna go scream at Mount Rushmore! It's in South Dakota, after all.

Amy gets in her 2002 Chevrolet Venture and heads for the Black Hills. She arrives at Mount Rushmore, and when she opens the car door

* South Dakota's No. 1 export is tumbleweeds. The South Dakota state bird is a tumbleweed. Do not fact-check these things.

a comical number of tumbleweeds fall out. Amy walks to the base of the mountain.

AMY [SCREAMING]: YOU GUYS ARE A BUNCH OF DICKS! ROOSEVELT? MORE LIKE DICK DICKERSON THE DICKFACE! WHAT ARE YOU GONNA DO ABOUT IT YOU PATRIARCHAL DOPES? That's what I thought.

Amy smiles and lights a cigarette as she walks back to her car. She collects a bunch of tumbleweeds and puts them in the front seat. The sun is setting as she drives away. She switches on the car radio. The song "Life Is a Highway" by Tom Cochrane is playing. She turns up the volume. Up on Mount Rushmore, Teddy Roosevelt's eye twitches.

THE END

Wow. What a great play. Please excuse me for a moment while I get a tissue.

I've gotten quite a few questions about "the void" lately: Should I scream into it, how can I fill it, will we ever get out of it, etc. The truth is that we live in a void—the void between birth and death. The little gap in space and time where our "existence" happens. How we choose to behave inside the void is our choice. You can fight it. You can spend your time being angry about the fact that the gap closes too soon. You can spend your time praying to a god, hoping that she, he or it will give you extra time in the void—which you would presumably spend praying for even more time. You can eat M&Ms and watch the 1981 Daytona 500 in its entirety on YouTube, like I do.

Or you can strut around like an ass, and pretend the rules of the void don't apply to you.

The void is all we get! Let's be kind to each other inside it. Let's be honest with ourselves about the eventuality of death. Gracefully making our way through this crazy space/time gap is the only assignment that we can be sure we have been given—let's do our best! Youth is dazzling, but fleeting. Real beauty exists in experience, wisdom, perseverance and love.

Also, listen to "Say You, Say Me" by Lionel Richie as often as possible.

Living with Your Parents in Your 30s

. . . .

PUBLISHED DECEMBER 30, 2014.

Dear Advice King,

My little sister is in her 30s, and she still lives with our aging parents. She hasn't had a job in years, and she relies on them for nearly everything. My parents don't seem to realize that they're enabling her. I just want them to have some peace and quiet in their autumn years, but no matter how much I talk to my sister about it, she just blows me off, acts resentful, and keeps using their credit cards and eating their food. How the hell do I get her out of there? I'm not sure I can convince my parents to cut her off.

—Phil in Bellevue

I really am the wrong person to ask about this, because I'm not convinced that you are the sane one in this scenario, Phil. Who wants to leave the house? Leaving the house was the biggest mistake I ever made. From the moment in 1987 when I walked out the door with my duffel bag and immediately fell down the front steps, life has been a waking nightmare. Alcoholism, panic attacks, overdraft fees. Your parents are enabling her, all right—enabling her to be happy.

What are you doing with your life that's so great, King Arthur? Are you having epic relationships? Participating in high-stakes geopolitical cat-and-mouse games? Are you mapping genomes? Are you a TV chef / base jumper? I bet you are either a blogger or a barista or you work at Walmart. How do I know that? Because those are the only jobs left in this desolate country. Unless you are a venture capitalist, but I don't think venture capitalists write to advice columns or give a shit about how their parents feel about anything. At night, while you eat frozen pizza and watch Redbox movies, you get mad about the great life your sister has. My advice: Stop putting pressure on yourself to achieve and move back in with your parents!

When I was a kid my dad taught me something very valuable. He said, "Son, there's not much point to doing anything, because we, and whatever we do, will ultimately be forgotten. It will be swallowed by the sands of time." I said, "What about the guy who invented VapoRub?" Dad told me that guy died of a heart attack yelling at the man who ran the conveyor belt at the VapoRub factory and that eventually the conveyor belt guy died, too. "See?" he said. I said, "People still use VapoRub though, so isn't it good that he made it?" He said I wasn't looking at the big picture, and that eventually human beings would evolve and not even have skin to put VapoRub *on*, so ultimately the VapoRub guy was wasting his time. My dad didn't say what I was supposed to do with my life, though. I mean, I was still alive, so I had to figure out some way to spend the days. I decided to watch him and see what he did. I figured out that the best way to spend your time on earth is to sleep late and eat ice cream and candy. If your sister is buying ice cream and candy with those credit cards then she, according to everything I've been taught, is living life to the fullest.

The 20th century was for leaving home, the 21st century will be all about staying home. Have you been outside lately, Phil? Horatio Alger jumped off the roof of the iPhone factory. No jobs, everybody's head jammed up their own asses on social media while the government trashes the First and Fourth Amendments, an olde-timey culture designed to block it all out. It's depressing and dangerous. Only the very strongest will venture from the nest, and they will end up in either cubicles or indefinite detention. I think these are the End Times. At least the end of the "with-skin-VapoRub" times. Certainly as great a time to live with your parents as there has ever been. Your sister may be a 20th-century loser, but she is a 21st-century success, because to succeed in the 21st century is to survive and not lose your mind—by any means necessary.

Do your folks need a groundskeeper by any chance?

Envying the Super-Talented

PUBLISHED MARCH 17, 2015.

Dear Advice King,

Everyone I know is so super-talented and I love them, but I burn with envy. When do I get to be awesome?

—Christy in Nashville

Here's the good news, Christy: You already are awesome! The bad news: You and your friends—like me, my friends and everybody else's friends in 2015—are not all "super-talented." We are all just "thirsty"* fools who have gone mad pimping ourselves out for approval on social media.

A long time ago, if you needed to chop some wood to make a cabin you just chopped it. You chopped some, your friends chopped some, their friends chopped some. Maybe some people chopped better than others. Maybe some people were "super-talented" choppers. Who knew, old-timey chopping person? Who cared? You got your cabin built and you had some shelter, and then you cooked some soup and had terrible sex and that's all that mattered, right? Right. But then one Saturday some asshole starts chopping wood in the middle of the town

* The Urban Dictionary defines the slang term "thirsty" as "1. Too eager to get something, desperate 2. Craving attention." For example: "I am so sick of Rhonda talking about that damn jewelry she makes. She is so thirsty."

square and she's doing trick chops and she hands out leaflets with a picture of herself in a fancy hat. Now, at first the old-timey axwomen said to themselves, "That has got to be the *thirstiest* wood-chopper I have ever seen." But then they think, "Some people clapped for her," and, "I saw Cecil the Bachelor say he liked her picture," and they all start working on their trick chopping and sit for pictures wearing fancy hats and holding shiny axes. Pretty soon no one knows how to chop wood properly anymore because everyone can only do trick chopping and the cabins are falling down and everyone is broke (except Julius Hobart, the town photographer), because they spent all their money on daguerreotypes and fancy hats and ax polish.

That is a true story. It happened in Worcester, Mass., and the woman who started the public wood-chopping/picture-taking was my super-talented great-great-aunt Lavinia Crofton. Eventually she and her super-talented photographer pal Julius were tarred and feathered, and the town returned to normal. Now the whole planet has gone Worcester, and it is impossible to tar and feather the Internet. If Lavinia were alive today, she would be making Vine videos of herself twerking.

Don't mistake your thirsty modern friend's self-promoting Instagram account for evidence of her "talent." She is just modern-day Lavinia, filming herself chopping wood. It doesn't matter how you chop that wood, as long as it gets chopped, Christy. You split an extra log while she was setting up her camera™.

This world is a challenging place. Do you have people you love and who love you? Do you have a roof over your head? Do you have soup or sex? If you answered "yes" to any of the above, consider yourself "super-talented."

How Do I Return to Normal Life?

. . . .

PUBLISHED MARCH 31, 2021.

Dear Advice King,

Now that the pandemic is possibly beginning to wind down, I'm feeling pressure to return to "normal life." But I'm not sure I WANT to return to normal life. What should I do?

—Arthur in San Francisco

Follow your heart. I'm not too enthused about "normal life" anymore either. What was it again? Chasing money? Chasing Starbucks? Facebook arguing? Fuck that. That's not life, that's a version of life—and a shitty one at that.

Real life is all around us, Arthur, and it ain't us. It's birds. And trees. And they're nude.

We are an aberration. We drive around in circles, clothed, scrolling desperately through pictures. We spend our days running from death—and the thought of death—and then die after all.

Real life is in the hills outside of town. It's deer, chewing on grass. Did you know that deer sit down? I didn't. But I've seen them! When I hike the trails at twilight, I pass them—sitting! Whole families of deer, sitting in groups, doing NOTHING. Resting. In a field, enjoying the twilight. Nude. If it weren't for this pandemic, I would never have known that deer sit around enjoying themselves.

Oh, you can say, "Chris, how can you be sure those deer aren't hiding, or exhausted?" I'll tell you why: Because I can tell. It is clear. They are having a good time. Sometimes things are exactly how they seem.

You know who's not having a good time? Humans. I can tell that too. And it's not because Hillary Clinton is eating babies, and it's not because immigrants are stealing our jobs, and it's not because of China.

It's because our way of life sucks.

AMERICAN DREAM:

1. Move far away from your home and loved ones to pursue "success."
2. Get "success."
3. Watch TV. (Level of "success" can be measured by size of TV.)
4. Decide that since you are "successful," and still unhappy, it must be because you don't have "HBO Max."
5. Get "HBO Max."
6. Decide that since you now have "HBO Max" and you are still unhappy, it must be because Democrats are eating babies.
7. Get sick, far from home.
8. Find out that even your "gold standard" insurance will attempt to deny you care.
9. Crowdfund your MRIs.
10. Die.

You may notice that nowhere in that scenario do you get to sit nude in a field with your loved ones at dusk.

You may also notice that nowhere in that scenario do you help anyone else. And I'm not talking about adding a wing to a museum!

I'm not talking about the American Dream where you get rich and spend your whole life drinking wine and then at the last minute you donate a wing to your favorite museum and get a trophy, and pay lip service to Jesus on your deathbed. I'm not talking about THAT American Dream, because that's not a dream—it's a sweaty, empty, self-seeking, unenlightened nightmare.

Fun fact: Ayn Rand died alone. Ironically, she was collecting Social Security, and enrolled in Medicare.

After this pandemic, I'm going to make my way back home. I'm going to write, I'm going to hike, and I'm going to try to be of service.

And I'm going to sit in a field at twilight, with my friends. I'll wear pants at first, because I'm still not fully evolved. I'm hoping to be nude as a deer by the time I have to crowdfund my MRIs.

War is over! If you want it.

Our Species Might Be Doomed—How Do I Laugh about It?

. . . .

PUBLISHED MARCH 20, 2019.

Dear Advice King,

I've recently felt an inability to delight in the absurdity of world events, mostly because I'm starting to think our species might be doomed. And what's more, I suspect we kinda deserve it. How do I get back to laughing about our foibles and pratfalls? Asking for a friend lol.

—Andy in Cleveland

King Tutankhamun was an ancient Egyptian pharaoh, and he is dead, Andy. He died when he was about 19 years old. He was 5-foot-6. He had a severe overbite, and a deformed left foot. His two children were stillborn.

Think about how King Tut must feel, Andy. On top of all that stuff I just mentioned, he's a ratty old mummy—and I can guarantee he's *still* in a better mood than you or me.

Modern humans need to get into The Mummy Mindset™.

The Mummy Mindset™—also known as the "Skull-in-a-Stack-in-the-Catacombs Mentality," or the "15th-Century-Peasant-with-a-Hump Outlook"—is a state of being in which a person (or skull, or mummy) understands and accepts the facts of their particular predicament, and is happier because of it. The "particular predicament" that you, the peasant with the hump, King Tut and the skull share is *mortality*—the nonnegotiable fact that life sucks, and then you die. Obviously it's easier to accept your predicament when you're already dead than it is while you're alive and on Twitter. But the sooner you lower your expectations, Andy, the happier you will be. You'll be as happy as a skull in a stack™.

You know who has a lot in common with King Tut? The daughter of that lady from the show *Full House*. You know the one. Everything was going her way. The lady from *Full House* bribed somebody to get her daughter into a fancy college. She was hanging out on a big yacht instead of studying. She was living just like a boy king. Except she has normal feet, and no overbite, so she was *really* feeling invincible.

The *Full House* lady's daughter was publicly humiliated,* but she is still alive. King Tut broke his femur, got malaria and died. So I guess they don't have *that* much in common, but anyway, I bet that *Full House* lady's daughter feels worse about her public humiliation than King Tut did about his death.

You, faithful reader, are probably thinking, "Advice King, why would that *Full House* person's daughter be more upset about public humiliation than malaria?"

It's because the *Full House* daughter had false hopes. You have false hopes, Andy. I have false hopes, too. WE ALL HAVE FALSE HOPES. We are postwar Americans, raised on promises (thanks Tom Petty). Around the time of the advent of television, some smart asshole realized that a population that has never come to terms with its own mortality is more likely to buy stuff. They will buy shiny junk when they're young and certain that they'll live forever, and they'll scramble to buy any product that claims to fend off death as soon as they realize that it's actually going to happen. "They" is us. We have been taught to fear death, so we LOSE OUR SHIT when anything goes wrong.

The Egyptians were excited about death. They packed for it. King Tut had The Mummy Mindset™. He knew shit was going to go wrong—all

. . . .

* Her mom got arrested.

he had to do was look in the mirror to be reminded that life is hard and unpredictable.

Laugh it up, Andy—in the end we're all pharaohs!

Should I Eat More Fruit?

PUBLISHED NOVEMBER 8, 2017.

Dear Advice King,

I'd like to live as long as possible. Should I eat more fruit?

—Bill in Poughkeepsie, NY

Hey Bill! How's Poughkeepsie treating you? The WWF (now WWE) used to tape their 1980s Saturday morning wrestling program in your town. That show changed my life—but that's a story better suited to a different column. One called "How Saturday Morning Wrestling Changed My Life."

I'm 100 percent positive you should eat more fruit, Bill. We should all be eating more fruit. According to the Food Czar—or the "Fruit General" or whoever—we're supposed to eat like 50 servings of fruit per day. And 28 servings of vegetables, and 40 servings of grains, and 200 servings of lima beans. How are you supposed to pay for all this food, by the way? You can't interview for a job with five servings of "grains" falling out of your mouth.

Couple things, Bill.

First thing: Are you old enough to remember the "Five Food Groups"? In the 1970s everybody in America knew about the "Five Food Groups." I never heard a damn thing about contraception, but I heard all about those goddamn groups. Guess what. Agricultural lobbyists put that list together. That's a true fucking story, Bill. I drank about 650,000 glasses of whole milk between 1975 and 1984 because of politics, not science. Thank goodness Exxon didn't get involved—we would've been pouring crude oil on our pancakes.

The other thing: There's always some American health nut who gets kale colonics twice a week and has a heart attack at 50, while some 102 year old lady in Sumatra is happily eating nougat and smoking rum-soaked cigars like she has every day since she was 8.

There's a guy in Fiji who's 131 and his neighbor says she's never seen him eat ANYTHING. The neighbor only eats sardines and she's 112.

Turtles live to be 300 years old. I don't think they eat any fruit. What do turtles eat? I'm not gonna look it up. I bet they eat muck. And grubs. I recommend eating whatever turtles eat, Bill—you'll live to be 300! You'll be mute, and in a shell, but you'll be alive! The fact that there's a turtle still walking around now who saw people sign the Declaration of Independence blows my mind every time I smoke weed.

FUN FACT: My dad has only ever eaten caramel corn as far as I can tell, and he's 76.

Are you constipated, Bill? Fruit is supposed to help with that. But I only eat about three servings of fruit per YEAR, and I shit like a wild animal.

After the past two hours of careful study, I have concluded that location has more to do with longevity than fruit servings. People who live the longest seem to live in remote or rural locations. I believe that the less contact one has with laundry detergent and Wi-Fi, the longer one will live—whether one is gluten-free or eats carpet tacks.

But what do I know, I'm not a lobbyist.

What Should I Bring to Burning Man?

PUBLISHED AUGUST 21, 2019.

Dear Advice King,

I am so excited! I am going to the Burning Man festival for the first time! What should I bring?

—Britton in Los Angeles

You might want to try using less yeast. I think that's why the buns are getting so big.

I'm continuing the new feature where I try to answer the question without reading it. How did I do?

Crap! This question has nothing to do with oversized buns!

"Burning Man," eh? Is that the thing with the juggalos?

I just looked it up. I was thinking of "Gathering of the Juggalos." They *are* similar. Both are multi-day "arts" festivals that have a ton of people with gauged ears at them. Burning Man is more like "Gathering of the Rich Juggalos." Gathering of the Juggalos is poor people who are so bored that they gauged their ears, and Burning Man is rich people who are so dumb that they gauged their ears. Is that right?

At Burning Man they burn a huge wooden statue of a man—at Gathering of the Juggalos they burn each other™.

Anyhoo, bring water, because Burning Man is in the desert. You should also bring things to trade for water. Burning Man attendees—"Burners"—are told to barter for what they need, because Burning Man is intended to be a "commodity-free" zone. There is a document, the "Ten Principles of Burning Man," that is supposed to explain this. I read it, and I have no idea what they are talking about. It encourages "radical self-expression," which sounds a lot like regular self-expression, and it says you're not supposed to litter. "The Ten Principles" are basically a list of things that nice, normal people do all year long, but for some reason these "Burner" people only do them for nine days a year. If you know someone who never lets anyone express themselves and is always littering, he or she is probably an off-duty "Burner."

So bring water, and a six-CD changer to trade for more water, and a sarong. I looked at the Burning Man website, and it really said to bring, as far as suggested clothing, a sarong. And a jacket for nighttime, because it gets cold on "the playa." People who go to Burning Man can't stop saying "the playa" (pronounced PLIE-ah). "Playa" is a fancy word for a "flat area." If you are on drugs it's impossible to stop saying it.

Oh yeah, bring drugs. Drugs, water, a six-CD changer, a sarong and a jacket—in that order.

Burning Man is mostly about doing drugs. Drugs that make it fun to say "the playa," and make gauged ears look attractive. I think those drugs are LSD and mushrooms, mainly—although I bet I would fuck someone with gauged ears if I was on meth, so maybe meth too. And a tent.

"The Ten Principles of Burning Man" have one principle that is especially confusing in the context of the other nine: No. 4, "Radical Self-Reliance."

No. 6 is "Communal Effort."

How do these two principles function together? The answer is, they don't. "Radical Self-reliance" is code for, "I don't want to pay taxes," and has no place on the manifesto of an art festival. Bring a set of earplugs in case you run into a libertarian* who wants to tell you about how Burning Man could be a model for a new society.

* Republican.

What Do I Buy at Whole Foods?

. . . .

PUBLISHED MARCH 14, 2018.

Dear Advice King,

When I go to fancy grocery stores like Whole Foods I have no idea what to buy. I'm not familiar with any of the brands, and I honestly don't recognize a lot of the products. My new boyfriend shops at these stores. How can I pretend to know what I'm doing?

—Lost in the Supermarket, Nashville

I'm right there with you, "Lost in the Supermarket." I grew up in the 1970s and '80s, when the main food groups were meat, cigarettes and divorce—two of those aren't even food!

Eating was just something you did to "get something in your stomach" so you wouldn't be doing other stuff "on an empty stomach." Nobody cared what food it was.

"Eat this pickled egg, Larry. You don't want to get divorced on an empty stomach."

We were more comfortable with our own mortality back then too. I think part of the reason was that TV only had 13 channels—and they went off the air at a certain point every night. Experiencing a time when there was literally "nothing on TV" left previous generations better prepared for death. Each night the TV said, "FUN'S OVER, GO TO BED." People were unconsciously prepared for the end of their own metaphorical "programming day," when they would have to "go to bed," forever.* Now that TV never goes off the air, people never wanna go off the air either™.

. . . .

* Johnny Carson is the Grim Reaper in this scenario.

What does this have to do with food, you ask? Fair question. People who are OK with dying will eat WHATEVER. They will eat meat made into LOAVES. These modern folks, who are planning to watch *CSI* until the sun explodes, are extremely particular about what they "put in their bodies." Whole Foods is designed for them.

Now that I have scientifically proven that your boyfriend wants to live forever—mostly so he can watch television—I will tell you how to shop with him.

HOW TO SHOP AT WHOLE FOODS IF YOU DON'T KNOW WHAT YOU'RE DOING

1. Wear a shirt that says "WHISKEY AND YOGA."*
2. Pick up every item in the store and say, "It's LOADED with sugar," really loud, before putting it back on the shelf.
3. Say "quinoa" a lot. Make sure to pronounce it correctly (KEEN-wah), or you'll have to move out of the state.
4. It is good if coffee is "fair trade." It is good if fish are "wild-caught." It is good if beef is "grass-fed." It is good if chicken is "free-range." It is not good if you mix these terms up. I asked a Whole Foods guy if the coffee was "grass-fed" and got MAJOR attitude. I called him a "wild-caught fuckhead," some displays got knocked over, and I was tased.
5. POWER MOVE: Buy a large vegetable that you don't recognize.**

. . . .

* FUN FACT: Anybody who wears a "Whiskey and Yoga" shirt has never had any "whiskey" besides Fireball.

** It is jicama.

How to Connect Sexually in the Time of COVID

. . . .

PUBLISHED SEPTEMBER 30, 2020.

Dear Advice King,

What are some fun ways to connect sexually, even from a distance?

—Horny in Gloucester, Mass.

Uh oh! X-rated advice column alert! I've been waiting a long time to write one of these.

#NUDE #NUDITY #NUDISM #SEX #BARE #BARENESS #COVID #KLEENEX

Let's kick things off with a steaming hot sex poem:

SEX

nude folks
who refuse to not be nude
doing nude things
with
exciting
nude
results

No. 1: Sexting. "Sexting," for the uninitiated, is "sexy texting." It's completely COVID-safe, since it requires no physical contact. Here's an example:

ME: Hi Sally. I wish I was with you and we were having sex. That would rule.

SALLY: Oh boy. You rascal. I have a bed where I am, and we could use it.

**ME AND SALLY BOTH ORGASM*

I'm not very good at sexting. I'm too embarrassed to write anything explicit because I don't want the NSA to know that I'm a dirty bird.

Perhaps you are like me. You want to text someone the unspeakable, consensual, extremely nude things you'd like to do with them, but you don't want creeps like Michael Hayden and General Paul M. Nakasone to be able to follow along. I found a way to do it: CODE.

I sent the code to my long-distance girlfriend Rhonda in a letter. Here it is:

VAGINA: Susan B. Anthony
PENIS: The Washington Monument
BREASTS: Groupons
BUTT CHEEKS: Car loans
FLUID: Ducks
MOTOR OIL: Motor oil

Now Rhonda and I can really let loose, and no one's the wiser!

ME: How's Susan B. Anthony? Is she covered in ducks?
RHONDA: Yes. And my Groupons are gigantic, as you are well aware.
ME: I wish I could put motor oil on your car loans.
RHONDA: I know you do. Is the Washington Monument standing?

**Mops brow* Is it hot in here?*

No. 2: Role playing. For those people who don't mind the NSA knowing how sex-crazed they are, I recommend role-playing on a video phone call. Me and Desiree—another of my pandemic "girlfriends" who I've never actually touched—use Skype. Our favorite game is called "Midnight Express," based on the 1978 film of the same name. The movie is about an American man serving a life sentence in a Turkish prison for smuggling hash. In one famous scene, his girlfriend presses her bare

Groupons up against the glass separating them in the prison visiting room while he tried to rip the roof off the Washington Monument.

Reenacting this scene at home is not difficult. First, get the video call going. Next, allow COVID to set the mood. Let's face it, our current situation is more *like* a Turkish prison than it is *unlike* a Turkish prison, so it shouldn't be too hard to get into character. When you're both equal parts horny and miserable, all you have to do is decide who's going to be the prisoner and who's going to be the visitor! Have fun pressing "stuff" up against your laptop screens!

Pro tip: Cover your computer with plastic wrap so you don't get "ducks" all over it.

No. 3: Pole with a rubber glove on it. If you STILL aren't satisfied, meet your partner at a clearing in the woods. Bring a boombox. Put a buttered rubber glove on the end of a six-foot pole. Press play on an Incubus CD, and get #NUDE.

How Should I Plan for Retirement?

. . . .

PUBLISHED OCTOBER 30, 2019.

Dear Advice King,

I am trying to save for my retirement. What stocks should I invest in? I have about $5,000 to spend.

Thanks!

—Leslie in Palm Springs

You have $5,000? Why do you need to invest? That's plenty of money for retirement. Just live in the woods and eat bananas and peanuts. Drink rainwater out of an old paint can. Carve poems into the trees.

RETIREMENT POEM

Me and my bananas
My bananas and me
Rainwater from a paint can
Is all that I need

Oh, I see. That's not good enough for you. You want a fancy retirement. You probably want to prance around the Mall of America every morning in a velour tracksuit, and live in a HOUSE.

If I had $5,000, I'd start a small business—"Milk 'n' Magazines." People could sit and drink different size glasses of whole milk and read old *National Geographic*s. No Wi-Fi, just a police scanner turned up pretty loud. Bathrooms.

FULL DISCLOSURE: I don't actually know how much money you need to do anything. I also don't understand the stock market.

Here's how I think the stock market works: Companies need money to buy goods (milk, in the case of "Milk 'n' Magazines"), so they can sell them. To raise money to buy the goods, they sell "shares" of the company. Once they start selling a lot of the goods (a shit ton of milk), they give the shareholders a cut of the profits. If they don't sell a lot of goods, they close, and everybody is fucked except the CEO, who gets $1 billion.

It's all about goods, Leslie. And services. Goods, services, widgets, tax breaks and cronies.

OK, stock tips.

ADVICE KING 2019 STOCK TIPS

1. Apple—I've had my eye on this company for a while, Leslie. They make iPhones.
2. Google—Another little stock I like. This is the outfit that makes the famous "Google" search engine. I have a feeling that at some point they will start making real, regular

engines. If these regular engines run even half as smoothly as their search engine, every car will have one, and the stock price will soar.

3. Amazon—I see this name on packages pretty often; look into it.
4. Whatever company makes bird cages. Birds are popular pets.
5. Borders, Compaq, Toys R Us, Pan Am
6. Halliburton—Oil and war will never go out of style!
7. IPO—This company is always in the news. It makes "initial public offerings." I don't know what they are, but people are crazy about them.
8. Coldplay—The band. Buy 100 shares of Coldplay.
9. Milk 'n' Magazines™
10. Hollywood Video

I hope this helps, Leslie. You can also send me the money and I'll invest it for you.

Should I Play Pokémon Go?

. . . .

PUBLISHED JUNE 12, 2016.

Dear Advice King,

Should I join Pokémon Go*? Or play* Pokémon Go*? What is it? I don't want to feel left out.*

—Nancy in Smyrna

You're asking the wrong guy, Nancy. I don't even really know what a Pokémon is. I am pretty sure Pokémons are Japanese "anime" characters. "Anime" is what the Japanese call animation. I think Pokémons are the Japanese equivalent of Smurfs. Even if that is true—and there is a very good chance it isn't—it won't help us much, because I don't know anything about Smurfs either. Here are the only things I know for certain about Smurfs:

1. They are extremely small.
2. They are blue.
3. There is a "Papa Smurf."
4. They throw barrels at the Mario Brothers.

Pokémons aren't as small as Smurfs. Pokémons are about the size of a fire hydrant. Pokémons only eat sour cream.

Pokémon Go is a phone game. Grown people use their "smartphones" to hunt for invisible Pokémons in real public places. They hold up their "smartphones" to "see" and then "capture" the Pokémons.

There you go, Nancy. That's all I (may) know. At the end of this column I will use Google to find out if I am correct.* Or maybe I won't, because I don't actually give a flying fuck about *Pokémon Go*. I'm actually worried that I may be permanently mentally diminished from just *thinking* this much about Pokémons. I can't even imagine the level of brain damage a person who actually "hunted" them—IN PUBLIC—would suffer.

If you don't value your brain, perhaps you value your limbs. Turns out hunting imaginary shit in public is just as dangerous as hunting real shit in public. People have been killed while attempting to "capture" Pokémons they've "seen" in zoo cages, sitting on top of table saws, on thin ice, etc. A lady from my mom's book club fell into an active volcano last Saturday. Her last words were, "Look at that rascal up on the hill!"

Imagine a eulogy for one of these fools.

* I'm wrong. Pokémons are characters from a '90s Nintendo game, not anime. In the '90s I was not playing video games. I was out on the streets, living.

EULOGY FOR A POKÉMON FOOL

> "Larry was a great guy. He was honest and reliable and nice. We were all really surprised when we heard he smashed the window of a commercial airliner with a fire extinguisher and walked out on the wing to catch a cartoon."

Thank God for Steve Jobs, right? Homo sapiens would never have been able to stick their heads up their asses nearly as deep without the help of Steve Jobs' magic phones. Is a genius still a genius if his big idea works, but his big idea results in the whole human race hunting Pokémons and being tracked by the government? Are the guys who built the nuclear bomb geniuses?

Fuck apps. Fall in love, Nancy. Love leads to everything, Pokémons lead to nothing. EVERYBODY FALL IN LOVE and throw your phone in a lake and support Black Lives Matter.

CHAPTER 7

TV & MOVIES

Oscar Precap

PUBLISHED MARCH 2, 2018.

Dear Advice King,

Any chance you could tell me what's gonna happen on the Oscars before they happen? Trying to decide if I should watch.

—Violet in La Crosse, Wisc.

Thanks for the question, Violet. You must have seen my recent Grammy recap. For those of you who missed it, I recapped the Grammys without watching them. Recapping something that hasn't even happened (precapping?) is uncharted territory for me, but they don't call me "Uncharted Territory" Crofton for nothing.

Before I begin the Oscar Precap™, allow me to tell you a little about some of my experiences at the movies this year. I went to see *Phantom Thread* thinking it was the new *Star Wars* movie. It turns out I was thinking of *Phantom Menace*. I saw the poster and realized right away that it was not a *Star Wars* movie, but I like to imagine that I never figured it out. I really haven't seen a single *Star Wars* movie since *Return of the Jedi*, so I could have easily been like: "I can't believe Han Solo retired from the *Millennium Falcon* and became the world's angriest dressmaker. Maybe he's so angry because he misses all the lasers and stuff. Where's the Wookiee? I should have seen some of those prequels because I am LOST."

It turns out that the new *Star Wars* movie is actually an emo fan-fiction thing called *Are You There God? It's Me, Luke.*

I saw *Three Billboards Outside Ebbing, Missouri*. Yep, I saw that. I wished I was Three Miles Outside That, Theater.

I liked *The Shape of Water* a lot, but I thought there should have been more dongs in it. The woman who was in love with that fish had to be naked about 10 times, but no men had to be naked at all. I really don't think it's fair. Not only were people who like dongs denied any male nudity, but the male lead is a fish, so the dong crowd knew they had nothing to look forward to from the get-go. "Nudity anticipation" is a little-acknowledged but extremely important aspect of the moviegoing experience.

FUN FACT: Years ago, I saw Guillermo del Toro's movie *Pan's Labyrinth*. I liked it. The other day I was trying to remember what it was called. I guessed *Secrets of the Scarlet Forest*.

I forget almost everything about most movies right after I see them. Remember that movie where Tom Hanks lived in the airport? I don't.

THE ADVICE KING 2018 OSCAR PRECAP™

WARNING: This is gonna be some unprecedented horseshit.

Comedian Lionel Bonedaddy hosted the Oscars for the 27th consecutive year. His jokes are always good, and this year was no exception. Some were really, really good. Then it was time for some awards.

Daphne Pheen, who won Best Supporting Actress last year for her role as the hot-blooded crossing guard in Tom Addison's thriller *The Belfry*, was up first, presenting the Oscar for Best Costume Design. Radley Rinker won for the period drama *John Hancock: Homebody*—another movie directed by Tom Addison.

Next, Swedish leading man Yorf Yardley gave out the little golden gentleman (Oscar) for Best Documentary. *The Devil's Utensils*—Fern Falp's hard-hitting exposé on the silverware industry—took home the bald glittering dwarf (Oscar.) Best Screenplay went to (no surprise) Tom Addison for *John Hancock: Homebody*. Now it was time for the main categories.

Lionel Bonedaddy came out and sang "The Oscar Song," like he always does. "What would you saaaaay, little gold mannnnn, if yooouuu could talk to meeeee, little gold man . . ."

Fonda LaRocka, who won Best Actor last year for his portrayal of a moody, singing dock worker in Tom Addison's first musical, *Dock Worker*, revealed this year's Best Actress winner. Effie Broochley won for playing John Hancock's wife Dorothy in *John Hancock: Homebody*.

Wilma Feath—who was Princess Leia in last year's *Star Wars 50: The Force Has Had It*—presented Best Actor to rugged Arrow Stonely. Stonely—a 5-foot-3 former Mouseketeer—was John Hancock in *John Hancock: Homebody*.

Best Picture was presented by the Tupac hologram, like it always is. I bet you think that fucking John Hancock movie won. It did! Tom Addison shook out his ponytail and said he was "over the moon."

Lionel Bonedaddy closed out the night with "Goodnight Oscar," like he always does. "Goooooodniiiiight Oscarrrrr . . . I willlll dream of yoooooooooooouuu . . . wiiiiiiiiillllllll yooooooooouuuuu dreeeeeeaaaaam oooooffffffff MEEEEEEEEEEEEEEEEEEE."

I Don't Wanna Watch Old Movies

. . . .

PUBLISHED OCTOBER 12, 2017.

Dear Advice King,

My boyfriend loves old movies—REALLY old movies. Like, 1930s movies. He even likes silent movies! I'm trying to be a good sport and watch them with him, but I actually think they are really boring. I don't want to ruin our relationship. What should I do? Thanks!

—Kathy in Woodland Hills, Calif.

I'm with you, Kathy—really old movies suck. I have a fairly strict no-movies-made-before-1960 policy. I say fairly strict because sometimes I fuck up and think to myself, "Maybe I haven't given really old movies a fair shot." For example, I've tried to watch *Battleship Potemkin* about six times. Film snobs act like you're a philistine* if you don't like *Battleship Potemkin*. FUN FACT: They don't like it either. They pretend to like it to make other people feel dumb for not liking it.**

If you ever have insomnia, Kathy, throw *Battleship Potemkin* in the VCR. It's an IMPORTANT Soviet silent film (no such thing, I'd argue) that is known for a scene where a baby carriage gets loose and goes down a staircase. I guess watching a baby carriage rolling down some stairs was the 1925 equivalent of Luke Skywalker blowing up the Death Star, so everybody is like, "You gotta see *Battleship Potemkin* because it was the *Star Wars* of 1925 Soviet silent films!" (A dubious distinction.) But it's 2017 and I can sit at home in my underwear smoking bath salts and watching fatal-car-crash compilations on YouTube, soooo . . .***

Has your boyfriend ever made you watch the original *Dracula* (1931)? I had the misfortune of seeing it. I thought it was at least 50 hours long, but when I got out of the theater it was still the same day so I guess it wasn't. It's pretty good if you've always thought that vampire movies didn't have nearly enough talking. And if you are tired of vampire movies that have fangs and biting in them.

My advice? You should break up with your boyfriend and go out with someone who likes new movies. Here's a list of modern, exciting movies you should see:

ADVICE KING MOVIE GUIDE 2017

Sex Men: A group of superheroes with huge private parts have sex with whole cities to save them from not having sex with superheroes with huge private parts.

Lego A Clockwork Orange

. . . .

*One cannot be a philistine if one knows what the word philistine means.

** I don't think anybody actually likes opera, ballet, classical music or museums either.

*** I do not do this. I do not recommend doing this. I am simply pointing out that runaway baby carriages register pretty low on the 21st-century stimuli spectrum.

American Gun Volcano: A huge volcano in the middle of America spews guns 24/7 and no one can stop it.
Sex-Toy Story: a Dixar™ film.
Lego Deer Hunter
Lego Lady Batman
Lady Bulman: Starring Samantha Bee.
The Susan B. Anthony Story: Starring Jared Leto.
Short Batman
Fat Batman
Fat Batman 2
Lego Fat Batman
Lego Fat Batman 2
Vegan Batman
Lego Vegan Batman
Man Wonderwoman
Lady Bat Wonderwoman 2
Fast and the Furious 250,000: The popular franchise returns! Singer "Pitbull" steals and fucks sports cars.

What Should I Binge-Watch?

. . . .

PUBLISHED DECEMBER 29, 2015.

Dear Advice King,

What should I binge-watch next?

—Jenny in Nashville

Happy holidays, Jenny! Thanks for writing. I'm listening to Billy Joel's *Songs in the Attic*, by the way. It is a GREAT fucking record. It's 2:13 a.m., and I'm sitting on the floor of my room drinking French press coffee. Did you know there is an exercise called a "French press"? Neither did I. Don't try it when you're drunk. Speaking of exercising, "Los Angelenos" from *Songs in the Attic* is a great song to do push-ups to.

What was the question? Oh yeah. "Binge-watching." I wish I didn't know what that meant. I wish I could say, "I'm sorry, Jenny, but I only answer questions about things normal people know about. You will need to send this question to another column—a column that is exclusively devoted to advising huge losers." Unfortunately, I know damn well what "binge-watching" is. "Binge-watching" has replaced sex as modern humanity's favorite pastime.

2015 UNITED NATIONS ANNUAL LIST OF THE MAIN ACTIVITIES OF HUMANS

1. "Binge-watching" television programs
2. Sex
3. Making GoPro videos

Sex was No. 1 for the last billion years, until this year. No. 2 was "getting a haircut" until 1974.*

However, if you INSIST . . .

I recommend "binge-watching" *Cowboys in a Bad Mood*. It's about a bunch of cowboys who are always in a bad mood. No matter what happens, there's a big shootout at the end of every show. You *knew* it was coming, because these guys all have personal problems, but it's fun to see what sets them off. David Schwimmer stars as the cattle rustler Candy J. Horn. His character is mainly in a bad mood because his name is Candy. *Cowboys in a Bad Mood* debuted in 2011, and it's already in its 88th season. Jessica Alba has won 14 Golden Globes for her portrayal of the sassy brothel owner, Peach Nettles. Jesse Ventura plays the sheriff of Deadstone, Bowie Sheath. My personal opinion is

* In 1974, "partying" became No. 2. "Getting a haircut" was No. 3.

that his character would probably be in a decent mood if it weren't for everybody else in town being in such a bad mood.

I was listening to Billy Joel on YouTube. When *Songs in the Attic* ended, YouTube switched automatically to Carly Simon, and I just listened to the song "Like a River." I'd never heard it before. It's about her mother's death, and it made me cry. It made me cry A LOT.

Before you listen:

WARNING 1: It is schmaltzy as fuck.
WARNING 2: Carly awkwardly references BENJAMIN FRANKLIN at one point, BUT STICK WITH IT—it's really a very pretty song.

If "Like a River" makes you too sad, listen to ANOTHER Carly Simon song about a river—"Let the River Run"—immediately. I guarantee it will turn that frown upside-down. "Let the River Run" makes me feel so good I wanna start a nonprofit every time I hear it.

My real advice is to turn off the damn TV, Jenny. You only get one chance at this life. If you waste your youth watching television, that's it—you wasted your youth watching television.

YOU DON'T GET ANOTHER YOUTH. YOU DON'T GET ANOTHER TELEVISION.

You actually *can* get another television, but I like the way that looks on the page.

What TV and Films Should I Watch?

PUBLISHED OCTOBER 14, 2020.

Dear Advice King,

I just subscribed to The Criterion Channel. I thought it was going to be like Netflix, but I don't recognize any of the movies! Wedding Crashers isn't even on there! What should I watch?

—Mike in Crystal River, Fla.

Hi Mike! Are you aware the world is ending? I'm kidding, the world isn't ending. It's pretty much just the United States that's ending. But seriously, have you turned on the news in the past few months? If you haven't, you are in for a surprise! If you have, why the fuck do you want to watch *Wedding Crashers*?

The days of wacky pals having entitled adventures are behind us (Americans). I could understand if you were in New Zealand, where the COVID case numbers are low enough that crashing weddings and having friends might still be viable activities—but you want to watch that shit in America? Now?! That's like watching *Leave It to Beaver* at the Spahn Ranch in 1969. The Criterion Channel has the PERFECT films for the dreary, dangerous American autumn of 2020.

I'm being a bit of a jerk, Mike. A little escapist fun can be helpful during times of crisis. I bet a bunch of Manson family members really were watching *Leave It to Beaver*, pretending the murder rampage happening around them was just a bad dream. BUT NOT ME. I mean, "not me" metaphorically, of course. I wasn't at the Spahn Ranch in 1969, although I feel like the vibe was probably very similar to, say . . . now. I mean, "not me" in the sense that, during stressful times, I often engage with art that fits my mood, rather than stuff that cuts against it—like listening to sad songs after a breakup. "Now" in America feels like the aftermath of a horrendous breakup. America hasn't broken up with a romantic partner, obviously, but it has had to face the end of its long, destructive, delusional relationship with the idea of "American exceptionalism."

It turns out that we CAN'T do anything we want and have everything turn out all right. It turns out that even in MAGIC AMERICA, if you don't enforce antitrust laws, allow unlimited money in politics, stand by as the police are given heavy military equipment, get drunk, watch sports and never vote, that even MAGIC AMERICA falls apart.

When my girlfriend leaves, I listen to "All by Myself" by Eric Carmen. When America is a pandemic-stricken oligarchy, I watch the movie *Stalker* by Andrei Tarkovsky. It's on The Criterion Channel, Mike.

Human beings like their lives to follow storylines.* When Tarkovsky made *Stalker*, the Soviet Union was collapsing, and the unifying "storyline" of communism was collapsing along with it. The "ideals" (loyalty to the revolution, working toward a classless society) that had provided a narrative underpinning for the lives of generations of Soviet citizens were revealed to be lies. The Soviet Union had become an oligarchy. Now the same thing is happening to America.

With *Stalker*, Tarkovsky considers how humans can find the will to live when the narrative has dropped away. SPOILER ALERT: We do! And crashing weddings has almost nothing to do with it.

Hang in there, Mike! Check out Redbox, I think you'll like it!

* For more on this, see the song "Storyline Fever" by Purple Mountains (David Berman), and the film *HyperNormalisation* by Adam Curtis.

How Do I Write an X-Men Movie?

. . . .

PUBLISHED OCTOBER 13, 2015.

Dear Advice King,

I know you are in show business. How do I get a chance to write an X-Men movie?

—Eric Fernandez, Pasadena

Hi Eric!

Who are the X-Men again? Do they turn into cars? Or are they the ones with the guy made out of rocks? Is Darth Vader an X-Man? What about Jughead? The only X-Man I know for certain is Wolverine. In the movies Wolverine is played by Jack Hugeman and he turns into a wolf at night. During the day he is a personal trainer. I like that. I like wolf-human hybrids a lot. Me and my friends do a fantasy football league where we are allowed to put three Wolverines on our teams. (Not three Wolverines on every team, obviously. Three Wolverines in your whole league. Your friends don't know which teams have the Wolverines. "My" Cleveland Browns won the Super Bowl last year because Wolverine, posing as a free safety, came off the bench and ate everybody.) If I was writing a script about the X-People, I'd make it where Darth Vader and the guy made out of rocks ride Wolverines. I would give Wolverine powers to duplicate himself so a bunch of people could ride him, and he also would never have to eat or drink. I'd have a guy who could turn into a building so his friends could hide in him when Lex Luthor or Boba Fett came. I would call him "Buildo." Also, Wolverine could be a boat whenever he wanted.

What the shit! I'm going to take a shot at writing an X-Men script right now:

THE X-MEN VS. MOBY DICK

Aquaman pops out of the drain in the shower of X-Men headquarters—a Knights of Columbus hall in Buffalo, NY. The man made of rocks, Bilbo Baggins, Wolverine, Batman, Darth Vader and Jughead are playing cards in the bar.

AQUAMAN: We have a problem, guys. Moby Dick is still alive, and he's being mean to all the other animals in the ocean.

JUGHEAD: Animals? I think you mean fish.

Aquaman tries to attack Jughead but is held back by Darth Vader.

AQUAMAN: Why do we have a 1940s teenager in this gang again? CAN ANYONE FUCKING TELL ME?!

DARTH VADER: His mom makes us lasagne.

Wolverine turns into a boat.

Batman has a fishing rod in his belt.

They put Bilbo Baggins on the hook and catch Moby Dick.

Vader uses the force to make Dick spit out Baggins.

The man made of rocks punches Moby Dick into outer space.

The whole gang is eating lasagne at Jughead's house.

MAN MADE OF ROCKS: . . . and then I punched his ass into space.

JUGHEAD'S MOM: Watch your mouth, Rocky! Or I'll punch *you* into space!

Everybody laughs.

Aquaman wipes his mouth, says it was great to see everybody and dives into the bathroom toilet.

THE END

Not bad for a first draft.

Eric, I have no fucking idea how you get to write an X-Men movie. I guess the first thing you should do is write an X-Men movie. Next, find out Steven Spielberg's email address. Before I moved to Los Angeles, I bought what I *thought* was Spielberg's email address from an auction. I wanted to send him some Web series ideas. It cost me $2,500. I got worried as soon as I opened the envelope, because it was a Hotmail account. Mistaspielberg@hotmail.com is NOT Steven Spielberg's real email address. It belongs to someone named "Mailer Daemon."

Another option is to do something worthwhile with your life.

How Do I Avoid Spoilers?

PUBLISHED MAY 2, 2019.

Dear Advice King,

I haven't been able to see Avengers: Endgame yet, and I'm concerned about spoilers. How do I avoid them? My neighbor already ruined the latest episode of Game of Thrones for me! Help!

—Donna in Detroit

Hi, Donna! Have you considered moving to the woods? My friend Larry recently moved to the woods to avoid spoilers. He made a T-shirt that says, "SQUIRRELS DON'T WATCH *GAME OF THRONES*." He made it with a Sharpie.

If you don't want to move to the woods, I think you are fucked. Everyone on earth watches these things, and it's all they talk about.

You could hang around with me. I don't watch *Game of Thrones*, and I'm not entirely clear on who "The Avengers" are. Do "The Avengers" have the guy made out of rocks? I think they do. I'm pretty sure "The Avengers" are the guy made out of rocks, Snow White and the Seven Dwarfs, Toecutter, Optimus Prime, Olive Oyl and Harry Connick Jr.

Game of Thrones is about a bunch of dramatically lit white people with grunge facial hair who are always having adventures in olden times. There is a girl who can tell dragons what to do, and everyone thinks she is cool. But some mean people get pretty mad, too. Here is how I picture an episode:

ADVICE KING GAME OF THRONES, EPISODE 1

Interior, hut. A BIG MAN and a PRETTY LADY are talking. They are both wearing ANIMAL SKINS.

BIG MAN: We are in deep shit, and it's also a long time ago.
PRETTY LADY: What about the thrones?
BIG MAN: They have been vacant since the Warlocks took the chalice. We have to get the chalice back from the Warlocks so all the thrones will be full again.
PRETTY LADY: I think I am pregnant.
BIG MAN: I have to go away for years on a big horsie to find the chalice.
PRETTY LADY: Good luck.
BIG MAN: You better not hang out with that stable boy who dabbles in magic when I'm gone, because I know you like him.
PRETTY LADY: He is a rascal. What if you fall in love with a Warlock?
BIG MAN: They're not my type.

Both laugh.

PRETTY LADY: I have a feeling our baby is going to be a really important plot device.

BIG MAN rides away on horsie.

THE END

I hope I didn't spoil anything.

Another option besides moving to the woods is to STOP WATCHING THE SAME SHIT THAT EVERYBODY ELSE WATCHES. I have never seen the 1981 German submarine film *Das Boot*, and no one in the last

38 years has told me the ending. When I was working at an AutoZone in Fargo, N.D., from 1988 to 2004, I *asked* all my coworkers and all the customers what the ending of *Das Boot* was—just as a test—and no one was able to spoil it. A lot of people said: "Whose boot?" And some people called me a communist.

I hope that helps! Just for fun, here's what I think *Avengers: Endgame* is about.

ADVICE KING'S AVENGERS: ENDGAME

SNOW WHITE and HARRY CONNICK JR. are at the Avengers Headquarters in the basement of a Staples store in Terre Haute, Ind., watching the crime monitor. The GUY MADE OUT OF ROCKS, OPTIMUS PRIME, OLIVE OYL and TOECUTTER walk in. TOECUTTER is carrying an OLD COTTON-CANDY MACHINE.

TOECUTTER: Look what I got off Craigslist!
GUY MADE OUT OF ROCKS: Yeah, now that we've cleaned up Gotham City we can eat cotton candy all day.
SNOW WHITE: Not so fast, Rocky, Vin Diesel has a bunch of hackers working in a warehouse down on the waterfront. They are stealing bitcoin from the Peace Federation.
OLIVE OYL: Does Terre Haute have a waterfront?

EVERYONE laughs. THE SEVEN DWARFS walk into the room, wearing MATCHING TRACKSUITS.

THE SEVEN DWARFS: Hey, Harry Connick Jr., do you wanna play bumper pool? If you lose, we shave your fucking head.

HARRY CONNICK JR. gets in the karate pose from the movie The Karate Kid and hops toward the DWARFS. The DWARFS attack CONNICK.

GUY MADE OUT OF ROCKS: Break it up! We have a crime to solve.

OPTIMUS PRIME has turned into a CLOCK RADIO and is on VIN DIESEL's BEDSIDE TABLE. OLIVE OYL and TOECUTTER are having sex back at Avengers Headquarters. SNOW WHITE, THE SEVEN DWARFS, the GUY MADE OUT OF ROCKS, and HARRY CONNICK JR. have a table set up outside VIN DIESEL's hacking warehouse. They are disguised as a youth basketball team raising money by selling cotton candy. VIN DIESEL emerges from the warehouse and approaches the TABLE. He looks at the DWARFS.

VIN DIESEL: You guys look a little short for basketball players, but it is hot out and me and my hackers would sure like to cool off with some cotton candy. I want 10 orders. Do you take bitcoin?

Inside the warehouse, OPTIMUS PRIME converts from a CLOCK RADIO to a huge VACUUM CLEANER. He vacuums up the HACKERS. THE SEVEN DWARFS get on each other's shoulders, put on a big overcoat, and dribble VIN DIESEL around the parking lot like a basketball while the Harlem Globetrotters theme song plays, finally depositing him in a DUMPSTER. The HACKERS are kicking and squirming inside OPTIMUS PRIME's VACUUM BAG.

SEVEN DWARFS: Nothing but net.

THE AVENGERS are at TOECUTTER and OLIVE OYL's wedding. They are all eating cotton candy. HARRY CONNICK JR. has a shaved head. THE SEVEN DWARFS wink.

THE END

What Movies Should I See?

. . . .

PUBLISHED DECEMBER 1, 2015.

Hey Advice King!

I love this time of year! I especially love it because of all the movies that come out. Which movies do you think I should see this year? Happy Holidays!

—Tammy in Franklin

Great question. I'm a big fan of movies. I've seen at least 100 movies (probably more!) in my life, just to give you some idea of how nuts I am about movies.

Star Wars: The Force, of Course! is one movie I'm super excited about this year. I'm really surprised they're doing a musical this time (Harrison Ford is a fucking SOPRANO!), but I trust James Cameron. Cameron is best known for the famous movie musical *Titanic.*

Remember Kate Winslet's barrelhouse number "Water's A-Risin' Boys" when she played percussion on all the engine room parts with her hatpins? I get a chill just thinking about it. And when Leonardo DiCaprio did that cover of Paul Simon's "Slip Slidin' Away" while he was falling off the raft? He's a soprano too! Winslet sang the bass parts in that one, and played spoons. I'm still a little surprised he sang the WHOLE SONG. He should have used all that energy to hold onto the raft. It's also weird because the lyrics to "Slip Slidin' Away" talk about someone named "Dolores" who isn't in the movie as far as I can tell. I watched it like 10 times looking for a character named "Dolores," and I'm 98 percent sure there isn't one.

The usual crowd is back in *The Force, of Course!* Luke, Princess Leia (who will sing first-wave feminist anthem "Anything You Can Do I Can Do Better" to Hank Solo), Hank Solo and his famous ape friend ChewingTobacco, Oboe wan Kenobi and his famous oboe and, of course, the two robots ColecoVision and Atari 2600. Darth Vader is going to be played by the guy who was the kid journalist in *Almost Famous*, which has some fans nervous, but I heard that guy can SING. Everybody's favorite, Jar Jar Binks, returns with a HUGE plotline this time. One more thing (SPOILER ALERT): James Cameron is a big fan of those old-time synchronized swimming movies, so I have a feeling some stormtroopers might be getting wet!! I am pumped, Tammy.

Other stuff . . . I think I speak for everyone when I say that I can't wait to see Jim Carrey in Ron Howard's *The Grinch*. Carrey and Howard are red-hot right now. *The Grinch* comes on the heels of Howard's Best Director Oscar win for *Meet Joe Black* and Carrey's Best Actor Oscar for his work as Geraldo Rivera in *Al Capone's Vault: The Movie*. *The Grinch*—based on the popular children's book by Doctor Suess—is billed as a "Depression-era drama," which only makes me more intrigued.

Jackie Chan and Chris Tucker are back for another romp through the future in *Men in Black VIII*. I was lucky enough to see an advance screening of this one, and IT IS GREAT. *The Fast and the Furious* and *The Matrix* joined forces for *The Fast Matrix*. They couldn't get the original cast of *The Matrix* to do it, so Jonah Hill is Neo and Katherine Heigl is Morpheus. *The Fast and Furious* regulars are all on board for this sci-fi car-theft thriller. SPOILER ALERT: It turns out the whole first Matrix movie was a dream that a cat had. The cat was sleeping in Vin Diesel's wheel well.

I saved the best for last, Tammy. Mel Gibson is directing himself as Santa Claus in *The War on Christmas*. His elves are played by Glenn Beck, Bill O' Reilly, Michelle Malkin, Anne Coulter, Sean Hannity, Megyn Kelly and Rush Limbaugh. None of those people are short enough to be elves, so Gibson is—according to the press release—DIGITALLY SHRINKING them and "altering their voices to be like elf voices." (Actual wording.) In interviews, Gibson has said that "his" Santa was inspired by George C. Scott's performance in *Patton*. Should be a lot of fun!

Happy Holidays!

What TV Show Should I Watch?

. . . .

PUBLISHED JULY 6, 2017.

Dear Advice King,

What TV shows should I watch? There are so many good ones.
Thanks,

—Tracy in Los Angeles

There sure are, Tracy—there sure as hell are. In fact, if I ever get in a bad mood or stub my toe or something, I remember how lucky I am to be alive at a time when there's so many good, good, good, good, good, good, good TV shows, and I feel better immediately. I get down on my knees every night and thank Jesus for these good shows. TV. TV! T-fucking-V.

Too much?

ADVICE KING'S ANNUAL TV ROUNDUP™

House Tippers—A bunch of people push over a house at night while everyone is inside it. *House Tippers* is loosely based on a show called *House Flippers*, which sounds great but turns out to be about remodeling. My favorite episode of *House Tippers* is the one where the teenage son falls out the bathroom window into the fish pond while he's masturbating. [Reality]

Driver's Ed—A comedy about a loveable misfit named Ed (David Schwimmer) who teaches driver's ed. He has the students drive to Mexico, where he loads the car with drugs. Every episode there's a mishap with the drugs where they shoot out of the car's exhaust pipe or something, and Ed throws his hat. Ed has a pet goat named after his ex-wife that eats the asses out of all his pants. When he sees what the goat did to his pants, he throws his hat. [Scripted]

Bottom Chef—Regular people make peanut-butter-and-jelly sandwiches, scrambled eggs, rice, etc. Celebrity judges: The Judds. [Reality]

Rambo Weekly—A weekly series based on the popular *Rambo* movie franchise. David Schwimmer stars as John Rambo, a Vietnam veteran who is pursued by a small-town sheriff played by Queen Latifah. I love the different hiding spots Rambo uses. In one episode he pops out of the baked beans at a police barbecue! FUN FACT: Schwimmer was badly burned during the filming of the bean scene—he insisted on using hot beans, and they did 22 takes.

Queen Latifah raps the theme song, which she wrote:

RAMBO, IT'S TOO LATE!

AS I'M ABOUT TO DEMONSTRATE! (repeat)

Bonus: Latifah and Schwimmer actually hate each other in real life because Latifah outbid Schwimmer on a shrubbery assortment at a charity auction. [Scripted]

All the King's Horses—This show is a *Game of Thrones*-type drama—except it's about the horses. Not animated, surprisingly. Warning: Adult language, horse dicks. [Scripted]

Flaming Balls—Andy Garcia and Al Pacino star as the patriarchs of feuding fireworks dynasties. Described by critics (favorably) as "*The Godfather* meets YouTube," *Flaming Balls* has something for everybody: sex fireworks, violence fireworks, suspense fireworks and regular fireworks. David Schwimmer plays Blammo, Garcia's single-fingered "powder man." [Scripted]

Kitchen Nightmares—Not the one with Gordon Ramsay. I pick this up via satellite from Estonia. Some guy named Valdo Sokk goes to a different failing restaurant each week—just like on the Ramsay show. First he berates the chef—just like on the Ramsay show—but this guy goes a step further and actually kills the chef. A new, presumably better, chef is hired. Sokk comes back to check on HIM a year later. Interestingly, it is never made clear whether Sokk himself has any cooking experience. [Reality]

Cake Boss—Another Estonian spin-off. Some lady bosses around a cake. The cake is always making the lady mad because it won't listen, because it's a cake. [Reality]

Ghost Hunters: Chicken Division—About a group of paranormal investigators who can only locate the ghosts of chickens. Includes recordings of pecking when there aren't any chickens around, grainy pictures of things that look like they could be a chicken, the "phantom feed" phenomenon, etc. [Reality]

Happy viewing, Tracy!

How Should I Prepare for the Zombie Apocalypse?

PUBLISHED MAY 17, 2016.

Dear Advice King,

I am interested in getting my home "Zombie Apocalypse-ready." What would you suggest I do? What do I need to stockpile?

—Afraid in Franklin

WARNING: THIS QUESTION MAKES ME MAD.*

Oh boy. You've been watching TV. You've been watching those good shows, haven't you? Those good, good shows. They're all so GOOOOD. SO GOOD GOOD GOODY GOOD. They are really good. SO FUCKING GOOD! SOOOOOOOOO GOOOOOOOOOOAAAAAAAAARR-RRRRRRGGGGHHHHHHHHHHHHHH! AHHHHHHHH! AHH-HHHHHHHHHHHHH! HELP!!!!! HEEEEEEEE . . . *World explodes.*

I am so tired of hearing about television shows, "Afraid in Franklin."

Here's the bad news: The zombies are already *in your house*. They're the ones watching TV. The zombies are YOU! You and all the other "binge-watchers" we nostalgically refer to as "Americans." The government is corrupt. George Orwell's *1984* has completely happened and nobody did anything to stop it. We are in the midst of an endless undeclared war against EVERYONE, most of the United States is a boarded-up wasteland full of pill addicts, meth addicts, neglected children, stray dogs—I'm not fucking exaggerating. So, do the educated few use their privileged position to help people? Nope. They stick their well-fed fingers in their ears and go "LA LA LA LA LA LA LA LA LA," and they watch "good" television shows. Like somehow that makes it better, the fact that the shows are "good." Like if the show you watch is "good" enough maybe watching it constitutes some kind of "activism." As if the person watching *Fox and Friends* is part of the problem, and the person watching *Veep* is part of the solution. I've got some more bad news, "Afraid in Franklin": BOTH OF THOSE PEOPLE ARE PART OF THE FUCKING PROBLEM. BOTH OF THEM ARE SITTING ON THEIR ASSES WHILE THE DRONES FLY. Both of them have been effectively removed from the equation. They have also been spayed, neutered, toasted, buttered, bought, paid for, shipped, received and a ton of other stuff that is metaphorically shitty.

FUN FACT: The privileged few don't waste ALL of their time watching GOOD-ASS television shows and then jabbering about them—

. . . .

* For best results, listen to "Bulls on Parade" by Rage Against the Machine while reading this column.

they also waste a bunch of it MAKING fucking television shows. I suppose it would be more accurate to say that they TRY to make fucking television shows—most of the time they are "working on scripts." I can guarantee you all these scripts suck. Everyone who is reading this, STOP WORKING ON YOUR SCRIPT, IT'S TERRIBLE. Join the Peace Corps. Is there a Peace Corps anymore? Probably not. Everyone who is supposed to be in the Peace Corps is "working on a script." The person who was supposed to CURE CANCER is working on a fucking script. YO MAMA is (probably) working on a script.

Are you sorry you asked this question yet, "Afraid"?*

There's a "Zombie Apocalypse" happening in the United States, all right. How else can you explain the way we behave? We are in the midst of our nation's longest war. The "Hope and Change" president has sentenced whistleblowers to 31 times the jail time of all previous Presidents COMBINED. Half the people in jail haven't been convicted of ANYTHING and are only there because they can't pay their bail. The state of Michigan KNOWINGLY poisoned a whole community. Our response to all of this? We watch *Game of Thrones*.

You wanna kill a zombie? KILL YOUR TV.

* At this point, if "Bulls on Parade" has ended, play it again.

CHAPTER 8

HOLIDAZE

The True Story of the First Thanksgiving

. . . .

PUBLISHED NOVEMBER 17, 2015.

Dear Advice King,

I know the story of Thanksgiving is more complicated than the version in the Social Studies textbooks of our youth. I'm a mother now, and I want my kids to know the truth about this holiday. What is the real story?

—Erin

The Pilgrims sailed to "America" on a boat called The Mayflower. They landed at "Plymouth Rock." Before the Pilgrims named it "Plymouth Rock," the Indians called it "That Rock over There." The "Indians" were the people who already lived in America. They had lived there for a few thousand years, in fact. They had been labeled "Indians" about 100 years earlier by some confused white people who thought "America" was "India." Before the white people came, the "Indians" were called "People." They called "America" "Home." White people love renaming shit. It gives them the opportunity to have ribbon-cutting ceremonies and shake hands with each other vigorously. The Pilgrims had a ribbon-cutting ceremony for "Plymouth Rock." They drank corn martinis and chatted about what sort of savages would leave a rock unnamed.

The Pilgrims and the Indians were friends at first. The Pilgrims were starving when they arrived, and an Indian man named Squanto helped them. Once the Pilgrims were healthy, they invited all their Indian friends over for a big dinner to say, "Thanks." Thanksgiving dinner. Erin, if you want to tell your kids a nice story about the white people coming to "America," stop the story HERE. Don't forget to mention how cute the Pilgrims' outfits were.

The Pilgrims were super, super religious Christians. Even religious people in England thought they were weird. They left England so they could be weirdly super religious in peace. The problem with super religious people is that they think they're the only ones doing religion correctly. They think that God notices how well they are doing religion, and rewards them by giving them stuff. Sometimes God gives them OTHER people's stuff, which is a really weird thing for God to do. They explain this by saying, "Too bad those people lost their stuff, but it's their own fault because they aren't doing religion right." This "We get stuff because we are 'blessed,' and other people lose stuff because they're 'not blessed'" mentality becomes a big problem for the Indians.

The Pilgrims were fundamentalist Christians. All fundamentalist Christians are real estate developers. They call their real estate business "missionary work." "Missionary work" is just holy-rolling gentrification. Once the Pilgrims were settled and healthy, they started telling the Indians that they should accept the Lord Jesus Christ as their personal savior. The Indians were like, "What do we have to do? We just saved your ass!" But it says in the Bible that Christians are never supposed to stop telling people that. It seems to me that Christians having "religious freedom" really means having the freedom to bother everybody about whether they've accepted the Lord Jesus Christ as their personal savior. Ironically, that ends up infringing on OTHER people's religious freedom. Fundamentalist Christians also like to judge things as either "godly" or "ungodly." "Godly" things include: brick buildings with pillars, stainless-steel appliances, roof decks, yoga. "Ungodly" things include: teepees, other religions besides Christianity, messy yards that bring down property values, being poor.

The Pilgrims sent word back to other fundamentalists in England that "America" ruled.

Here's the Pilgrims' actual telegram, never before published:

10 NOVEMBER 1621 PLYMOUTH, MASS.

Hello religious zealots STOP
Tons of "Indians" around for Jesus Christ personal savior rigmarole STOP

Tons of land that is all messy and needs Christians to clean it up STOP
Tons of ungodly teepees and almost no godly buildings STOP
Need more shoe buckles STOP

So the Pilgrims started telling the Indians that they were living in an ungodly manner. They said their yards were dirty and were bringing down property values and that they weren't accepting Jesus Christ and that their teepees looked like shit. They told them that they should live in luxury condominiums with roof decks and go to wine tastings and do yoga like a good Christian. They renamed the area around Plymouth Rock "Plymouth Hills" and made a YouTube video of some white people "blessed" with good credit ratings enjoying some Christian luxury living. The Indians were like, "FUCK OFF. We were here first, and we already have a religion." The Indians didn't even have credit cards. They were screwed. The Pilgrims were like, "Well, we gave these people the chance to be 'blessed,' but they didn't take it. Now they're mad at us?! All we tried to do was use our freedom of religion to make them reject their shitty religion so our God would like them, and this is the thanks we get? Good thing we are 'blessed' with guns."

So the Pilgrims and their friends killed the Indians and stole (I mean, um, were blessed with) their land, and all the white Christians with a good credit score lived happily ever after. THE END

And THAT, Erin, is the real story of Thanksgiving.

Christmas Gifts and Christmas Parties

. . . .

PUBLISHED DECEMBER 6, 2017.

Dear Advice King,

What should I get my wife for Christmas?

—Justin in Rancho Cucamonga, Calif.

Rancho Cucamonga! The best-named town there is! One time I had a nervous breakdown and was in a straitjacket screaming "Rancho Cucamonga!" for eight weeks straight.

I'm all better now! *WINK.*

Hmmm, what to get a wife for Christmas in 2017. I've never been married, so I don't know much about this. My mom is a wife. My dad gets my mom nightgowns, and she always seems pretty happy. She might want something different than a nightgown, but at this point she probably wouldn't even know it because she's only experienced getting nightgowns for the past 40 years. You can't miss what you don't know about. So you could get your wife a nightgown, Justin.

I think it's funny to give someone a gift that is really, obviously, for you—and then give them the real gift after they're very mad. So you could give your wife a duck blind, and right when she's about to blow a gasket, hand her a nightgown. She'll get a big kick out of that. And you'll have a duck blind.

Another funny idea is to give someone a gift that forces them to rearrange their whole life. Get your wife six llamas.

Trips are good! Book a trip. If you do decide to take a trip, don't go to the Australian Outback. I've been listening to a lot of true-crime podcasts lately, so just take my word for it. You'll both end up "on the barbie."

Dance lessons. A turntable. A bicycle. A pickling kit. A fancy coffee maker. Final Cut Pro. A bowling ball. One of those services that delivers meal ingredients to your house. A gift certificate for massages. Did I already say nightgown?

Dear Advice King,

What should I do if I show up to the wrong Christmas party? It just happened to a friend of mine, so it's a real thing!

—Christina in Koreatown, Los Angeles

For some reason this question reminds me of the Steve Martin joke where he says if you are ever invited to a fancy dinner party, a fun gag is to arrive late and throw all the food on the floor.

If you go to the wrong Christmas party in Los Angeles, no one will notice because everybody looks the same and is working on a script. Just say you are working on a script. Actually, say you are "*pitching* a script," because that makes it sound like you already finished a script. Also, tell everybody at the party that you want to collaborate with them on a bunch of stuff that everyone knows will never happen, because you will never see each other again, which is what happens when you show up to the RIGHT party in Los Angeles, too.

Then smoke pot and talk to a bunch of sociopathic Midwestern dudes with trimmed beards about streaming services. Uber home and eat a whole pint of dairy-free dessert.

MERRY CHRISTMAS!!!

What Should I Do with My Thanksgiving Leftovers?

PUBLISHED DECEMBER 1, 2016.

Dear Advice King,

What should I do with my Thanksgiving leftovers? Thanks!

—Ray in Connecticut

Hi Ray! I hope you had a nice Thanksgiving and nobody was murdered at the table because they tried to talk about politics. 350,000 people were killed during Thanksgiving dinner this year, up from six last year. Not to mention all the people who were scalded with gravy, hit with turkey legs, blinded by steaming yams, force-fed ambrosia, jabbed with forks, etc. Traditionally, Thanksgiving violence is related to wishbone-pull disputes, but this year the police reports are strikingly similar: Somebody's "nephew" had a "large-format energy drink" and started calling everybody a "cuck"* and saying it was "Trumptime." This "nephew" then tried to choke his great aunt/uncle, smashed the "good" plates, and slapped everybody with hot sliced meat—all while screaming, "I'm tired of being politically correct."

What to do with leftovers, eh? I don't know. Put foil on them, I think. Put foil on them and put them in the refrigerator.

So now you're like, "Put foil on them? Everybody knows that! I thought this column was supposed to be wild and crazy! What gives?" Settle down, Ray. How's Connecticut, by the way? I grew up there. Everybody still playing lacrosse like their life depends on it?

All right, Ray, here's a zany idea: Use the leftovers in bed! Personally, I think bodily fluids ruin food, but I know from some movies I've seen on the internet that not everybody agrees with me.

Smear them all over your loved one and scream, "DINNER IS SERVED!"

Pour gravy on each other's butt cheeks.

"Baste" the "casserole."

Suck the "rolls."

Put the "corncob" in the "garbage disposal."

It's a law in Connecticut that everybody has to have a golden retriever named "Baxter," so you could feed Baxter the leftovers.

I just remembered something important. People in Connecticut don't have sex. And if people in Connecticut *are* having sex, you can be damn sure there aren't going to be any foodstuffs—or female orgasms—involved. I picture a short-lived missionary pump job with both participants reading *The Wall Street Journal*. I hope this isn't the case with you, Ray. I hope you and your partner destroy the whole house when you fuck. I'm sure you do.

One thing people in Connecticut DO do a lot is play golf. Golf golf golf. Golf Golf Golf Golf Golf. They love getting out on the "links." Why do they call it "the links"? Google it, son, 'cuz I don't give a shit. Practicing your putt is the biggest thing going up there in Connecticut.

. . . .

* "Cuck" is a made-up word that angry, impotent men use to describe people who know how to read. It rhymes with the word "schmuck," which describes THEM.

SHORT PLAY ABOUT CONNECTICUT

Interior—well-appointed colonial. A golden retriever named Baxter can be heard barking in the distance.

SALLY: Where's Dad, Mom?
SALLY'S MOTHER: Practicing his putt, Sally.
SALLY: I hate Dad.
SALLY'S MOTHER: Me too, Sally.

THE END

If you are a creep who cares more about your putt than your family, you should try putting your goddamn leftovers. If you can figure out how to get cranberry sauce in a hole, I'm sure your stupid ball would be no problem.

HAPPY HOLIDAYS!!! –AK

New Year's Resolutions

. . . .

PUBLISHED JANUARY 22, 2020.

Dear Advice King,

Did you make a New Year's resolution? I know I'm a little late on this, but I'd still like to do one! Any suggestions?

—Sally in Santa Fe

My New Year's resolution is to attend more 12-step meetings. You could do that one. You could also resolve to attend less 12-step meetings—maybe you go to too many.

Do you have any bad habits? I know you can't answer me. How about resolving to give more information to advice columnists?

Oh! I have a great idea. You should do that thing where you throw away everything that doesn't bring you joy. It's called "The Keto Diet."

Some rich lady who was drowning in knickknacks wrote a book about how the secret to happiness is throwing stuff away. Her house was probably full of broken salad shooters and copies of that book *The Corrections*. Remember that fucking book? I never read it. How am I still alive? Back in the early 2000s it was practically illegal to not read *The Corrections*.

I'm only guessing that the lady who invented this particular "joy" system is rich, but you gotta figure that poor people aren't sad because they are surrounded by old Soloflexes and superfluous vases.

For your New Year's resolution, go through your house and pick stuff up. When you are holding each thing, ask yourself if it "brings you joy." Do those Mason jars you bought during the 20 minutes in 2011 when you were gonna learn how to pickle stuff bring you joy? No? How about the lamp that has needed "rewiring" since 1988? No? They go in the garbage! Feels good, right? Keep going!

Throw away those bald tires. Throw away that archery trophy. Throw away that slide projector. Throw away those Matchbox 20 CDs. Throw away all those weird shampoos in the bathroom closet. Throw away that hat. Throw away those shoes. Throw away your car registration. Throw away your sleep-apnea machine.

Hold it . . .

Don't throw away your car registration or your sleep-apnea machine, Sally.

This is the problem with The Keto Diet. Just because something doesn't "bring you joy" doesn't mean you don't need it. My friend Josh threw away all his hangers. Hangers may not bring you joy, but having your clothes all over the floor will actually remove joy. He then had to purchase new hangers. Buying new hangers right after you just threw away a bunch of perfectly good hangers is not a big joybuilder.

My uncle tore the chimney off his house because he couldn't pinpoint any joy coming from it. He said, "I looked at it, and I felt nothing." A couple of days later he put a log in the fireplace, and burned the house down. None of this brought my aunt any joy, and she left him.

HAPPY NEW YEAR!!!

Holiday Gift Guide

PUBLISHED DECEMBER 14, 2016.

Dear Advice King,

'Tis the season! What are some good holiday gift ideas for 2016? I love your column! Thanks!

—Alex in Austin

Thanks, Alex! I love my column, too. It's the best column going, IMHO. "IMHO" means "in my humble opinion," in case you don't know anything—"ICYDKA."

Just kidding around, Alex. IGYLTC. (I'm glad you like the column.)

Full disclosure: Alex didn't have the line "I love your column" in his question. I added it.

ADVICE KING™ HOLIDAY GIFT GUIDE

This "Cordless LED Salt or Pepper Mill" is a great gift idea. How many times have you found yourself wishing some household thing that hasn't ever historically needed batteries could NEED batteries instead? This battery-powered salt shaker solves that problem. It has a light on it! I'm so tired of seasoning stuff in the dark. One time I thought I was putting salt on some food but I was putting it all over the cat!

OK, here's the bad news: I just noticed that the Sharper Image website says they are sold out of cordless salt-and-pepper mills. Of course they are. They were only $49.99! Here's the good news: I looked at the bottom of the page and it says that people who bought the nighttime pepper grinder also bought the "Digital BBQ Fork." The digital fork is IN STOCK! It has a light on it!

I wish someone would make a comb with a light on it.

LETTER TO SHARPER IMAGE

Dear Sharper Image,

Please make more things with lights on them. I had a pretty good summer. How was your summer? Well, I guess I better go.

—Chris Crofton

Hammacher Schlemmer has good gifts, too. How about a "Tranquility Pod"? It's a big plastic egg that plays music and has a bed in it! I'm going to get these for everybody! Oh, wait, no I'm not—THEY COST $30,000. That's bullshit. I could convert my 1996 Jetta into a "tranquility pod" for about 20 bucks—incense, bubble wrap, sleep mask, wind chimes, Enya CD, lotion, Kleenexes. Fuck Hammacher Schlemmer.

If you have kids, especially teens, fracking equipment makes a wonderful gift. Not only is fracking a great way to make a little extra money (they call fracking "the modern paper route"), but imagine the look on Junior's face when he causes his first earthquake!

Freeze-dried meals and a huge machine gun. I don't know if you've noticed, Alex, but the world is ending. Whenever the world ends, the supermarkets run out of food. When the supermarkets run out of food, everyone will lose their minds. Pretty quickly, too. The average American will resort to cannibalism about 45 minutes after Trader Joe's closes.

Rosetta Stone—Russian. Sometimes it takes longer for the world to end than you'd think. In case we manage to hang on for another couple centuries, it would probably be a good idea to learn the language of our new masters.

The best gifts? Gifts that can't be bought, but can be taught: Love, respect and empathy.

ON EARTH PEACE, GOODWILL TOWARD MEN —*Peanuts*

Visiting Racist Relatives over Thanksgiving

PUBLISHED NOVEMBER 25, 2014.

Dear Advice King,

Like a lot of Southerners, I have a racist uncle. At every holiday gathering, without fail, he says something shitty about black people, or Native Americans, or Jewish people. You name it, he's got something awful to say about them. So what should I do when he inevitably says something racist over Thanksgiving dinner? Should I politely ignore it and change the subject, like my family always does? Or should I shut him down? He tends to make a big scene whenever given the opportunity, and I don't want to upset my grandmother.

—David P., Gallatin

Dear David,

So your uncle is a racist? And he talks at Thanksgiving about the people he doesn't like? Well, let him talk, because it's the perfect occasion. Being a racist asshole is what Thanksgiving is all about. I bet your aunt is a racist too, btw. There's no way your uncle's feelings about race didn't come up during their courtship:

1950S DRUGSTORE, YOUR UNCLE AND AUNT'S FIRST DATE:

AUNT: "This milkshake is delicious!"
UNCLE: "That's how you can tell a Jew didn't make it."

The Pilgrims were racist assholes. There's nothing more American than racism. George Washington's racist Thanksgiving diatribes were legendary. He would drink too much blush and scream about property values. Also, "Thanksgiving" was invented in 1710 by Silas Beake as a way to sell placemats. The real Thanksgiving was when some white people traded a turkey dinner for the entire eastern half of the United States. The trick was they said it in ENGLISH, and the Indians didn't speak English. They also said it while they were passing the potatoes, in the tone of someone saying, "Would you like some potatoes?" except they were really saying, "If you take any of these potatoes I will interpret it to mean you agree to give me the eastern half of the North America." Your uncle woulda fit right in with those immoral moralists.

Who is this grandmother? Is she your uncle's mom? You can bet she's a racist. The apple doesn't fall far from the racist. I bet if your uncle came back in the house from playing with a skinned knee she would say, "Did a black do this to you? They're always going around skinning people's knees." It's not just Southern uncles and meemaws spewing hate on a holiday ostensibly about racial harmony. I grew up in the suburbs of New York City, and people up there have some pretty hilarious ideas about race, too. The only difference is that people up there think they're not racist, because they have never experienced any in-person racial conflict that might bring it out. It makes a lot of sense that there is less racial conflict in that area, because there is only one fucking race. Take a Northeastern white liberal "non-racist" from Greenwich, Conn., to Memphis, Tenn., and they would shit their pants / call the police / mace everybody.

Now, as far as what to do with your uncle at Thanksgiving. Invite Cornel West? Give your uncle turkey with a lot of bones in it and cross your fingers? Send him to the basement to get more cranberry sauce and lock the door? Hot foot? I think what you should really do is let him fucking have it. He needs to know that you disagree with him. This is a job for Churchill, not Chamberlain. Your grandma will live. If the Dust Bowl didn't kill her, I seriously doubt some yelling will. Even if the story of Thanksgiving is probably bullshit, the message of love and cooperation is a genuinely great one—especially for kids. Your uncle can say this shit at the bar, the track, the Moose lodge or wherever poisonous misfits like him congregate, but NOT IN FRONT OF KIDS. Send a strong message to the children in attendance that this kind of talk is not normal or acceptable. Tell your uncle that he is not invited to Thanksgiving anymore if he can't control himself, and that if he is invited, you won't be there. Maybe Bill O'Reilly or Ann Coulter or Joni Ernst or Rick Perry or the Westboro Baptist Church will have him over.

Topeka Valentine

. . . .

PUBLISHED FEBRUARY 14, 2018.

Dear Advice King,

What is a good idea for a Valentine's Day date? Also, I might ask my girlfriend Karen to marry me! How should I do it?

—Rod in Topeka, Kan.

Two words: pedal boat. Once you're out in the middle of the lake, pull the engagement ring out of a duck's mouth. Don't actually put the ring in a duck's mouth—*unless* you or a friend have a trained "ring" duck. Pretend to pull the ring out of a duck's mouth. Say something like, "Oh my god, Karen, that duck is fucking choking! Something is stuck in its fucking mouth! I got it! Oh my fucking god, it's a ring and *will you marry me*?!?"

I'm kidding, Rod! That's a terrible idea. The duck part, I mean. Renting a pedal boat is one of the most romantic things a couple can do together besides have a baby.

I just realized that it's probably too cold in February for pedal boating in Topeka, Kan. Is there such a thing as indoor pedal boating? I'm not even going to look. It wouldn't be the same indoors.

Gimme a second to see what kind of romantic shit is available in Topeka in February.

Googling Topeka.

OK, whoever is in charge of promoting Topeka is asleep at the wheel. There's no way Topeka is as boring as it seems on my Google Machine™. I'd be surprised if Topeka has any pedal boats at all, no matter what season it is. As far as I can tell, the most romantic thing you could do for your girlfriend on Valentine's Day is move her out of town. Don't tell anybody I wrote this stuff about Topeka, Rod, because I don't want to get hate mail. Although it's probably impossible to get hate mail from Topeka because I bet there's no post office.

The only thing that sounds remotely interesting in Topeka besides the gas company and Cracker Barrel is an old locomotive they have on display at the Kansas Museum of History. It's from the 1880s. You could take Karen to see it, and read her a poem you wrote that clumsily compares your relationship to a train.

"Locomotive Lover," by Rod from Topeka

Karen you are like an old locomotive
But not old, obviously
And much smaller
But you pull me all over the place
And I need to go places because I just do
And so do you!
Blow your smoke (love) all over me
Forever
Locomotive lover
I want to kiss your caboose.

Pull the ring out from under the engineer's cap you have on. If she says no, get in the locomotive and drive it through the wall of the museum.

Real advice: Stay home. Valentine's Day is a scam, Rod. The Koch brothers invented it in 1983 to distract people from global warming. Wait until the summer and ask Karen to marry you on a Ferris wheel like a normal person.

What Should I Be for Halloween?

PUBLISHED OCTOBER 18, 2016.

Dear Advice King,

What should I be for Halloween?

—Dana in Clarksville

Hi Dana! I'm writing to you from a cheap motel room in Memphis. It has an average guest rating of 2.7 out of a possible 5 stars. That is WAY too high, in my opinion. Here's a customer review (typos included): "The sheets had burn holes in them.The pillows where hard The wall had a hole in it. The pool was nice tho and the bathroom shower is awesome.The TOLIET CAME UP OFF THE FLOOR WHEN U STOOD UP AFTER USING IT." This person gave the motel 3 stars! If it's me, and the toilet comes off the floor when I stand up, I won't go higher than 1.5 stars—no matter how nice the burn holes are.

Here's another 100-percent real review, just for fun: "Very horrible very loud very nasty extremely disgusting rooms towels not clean nasty beds horrible horrible horrible horrible horrible horrible."*

* One more actual review of the motel I am staying in because I love them: "I found my room and when I got in the room it was late, so I was ready to lay down but when I got

What a fun question! Due to the gruesome nature of the presidential campaign and about 250,000 celebrity deaths, 2016 has already been like a nonstop Halloween. If you really want to scare anybody this year, your costume will need to be truly horrifying.

ADVICE KING'S 2016 HALLOWEEN COSTUME IDEAS

1. MY MOTEL ROOM
   INSTRUCTIONS: Get a bedspread from 1978. Cover bedspread in pubic hair from a convicted felon. Make a toga out of the hairy bedspread. Glue a room number to your forehead.
2. THE GUY IN THE MOTEL PARKING LOT who has been sitting inside a running pickup truck for the past five hours, staring straight ahead at nothing.
   INSTRUCTIONS: Sit in a running pickup truck outside a Halloween party for five hours. Wear a trucker hat and a denim vest and smoke and don't say anything. Keep your upper lip moist.
3. A COCKROACH FROM THIS MOTEL. I bet the cockroaches in this motel have had to see a lot of people peeing on each other.
   INSTRUCTIONS: Buy a cockroach costume. Put it on. Hang a sign around your neck that says I WATCH PEOPLE PEE ON EACH OTHER.
4. MIKE PENCE. I bet Mike Pence rents VHS tapes of people peeing on each other.
   INSTRUCTIONS: Buy a Mike Pence costume. Put it on. Hang a sign around your neck that says I WATCH PEOPLE PEE ON EACH OTHER.

. . . .

in the bed the blankets had blood stains on it. When I explained it and showed the front desk clerk the photo the next morning, she says, 'it doesnt surprise me and with all the construction going on it doesnt surprise me.'"

5. Farm-to-table chef
6. Zika baby
7. Los Angeles open-mic comedian
8. Monsanto executive
9. Mike Pompeo
10. Your mom

HAPPY HALLOWEEN!!!!

The King's Christmas Guide

. . . .

PUBLISHED DECEMBER 11, 2019.

Dear Advice King,

This is a two-parter. First, I am not going home for Christmas this year for the first time ever. How can I make the most of a Christmas alone? Also, any ideas for cheap Christmas gifts? I am on a serious budget.

—Patty in Los Alamos, N.M.

Fuck. I just looked up Los Alamos—12,000 residents; 86 percent white. "Where discoveries are made." That's the slogan on the Los Alamos city website. Aside from the atomic bomb, I bet the main discovery being made is that the town's only sushi place sucks. And I can GUARANTEE the sushi rolls are named stuff like "Atomic Roll" and "Meltdown Roll"—"OUR SUSHI IS THE BOMB," etc. I wonder if they have a "Stop, Drop and Roll Roll." Probably not, but it's a great idea. You are welcome to it, Los Alamos Mass-Casualty Sushi Bunker.

Just kidding. I'm sure Los Alamos is a lot of fun. From the looks of things you can either invent weapons or hike. If I were you, I would go to a bar. I'm a recovering alcoholic so I can't go with you. There should be a "Spend Christmas with the Advice King" contest. Every year I pick one lonely person and I fly to their town and go to the movies with them all day. Airfare, movie tickets and unlimited popcorn would be provided by the *Nashville Scene*, so I have a feeling this idea is a nonstarter.

Bake! Everybody loves cookies and pies and stuff like that. Bake all day on Christmas Eve and then go around town giving baked goods to all the evil scientists and their families on Christmas Day! If you don't have one, get a record player. A vinyl record player. Go to a thrift store in Los Alamos and buy some scratched-up Christmas records. In a town that's 86 percent white you'll probably end up with mostly Perry Como. Who cares? Perry Como is good! Make some eggnog. Don't make it TOO strong, because you're going to be drinking it all day while you bake. Spin those records, drink that eggnog, and have a contest against yourself to see how many cookies you can make. Talk to yourself! Say stuff like, "I bet you think I'm too drunk to make cookies, huh? Well I'm NOT, asshole."

Even if you don't smoke, smoke a bunch of cigarettes! Treat yourself—it's Christmas Eve for God's sake! I recommend menthols—my stepdad Randy told me that those are what Santa smokes. Speaking of smoke, make sure your smoke alarm has fresh batteries in it in case you pass out with the oven on. My weird aunt Carly burnt down four houses during her legendary nog-fueled bake-a-thons of the 1970s. She ended up on the TV show *That's Incredible!* (that's her being airlifted out of the MGM Grand). She didn't care, either. On Christmas morning she'd shake off the ashes and hand out burnt baked goods all over her hometown of Provo, Utah. There's a statue of Carly in Provo. She's covered in soot, weeping and holding what's left of a pie.

OK, so that takes care of what to do on Christmas, AND cheap gifts. Just for fun, here's a few more cheap gift ideas, Patty:

1. Goldfish—Real goldfish, in a bag of water. Do not pay more than a dollar. If you can't find a goldfish for less than a dollar in your area, send me a self-addressed stamped envelope, and I'll point you in the right direction.

2. Old shoes—"I hope these fit! I found them!"
3. Hug voucher—"Good for one hug!" Make sure the writing is neat.
4. Spaghetti dinner voucher—"Good for one spaghetti dinner cooked by me!" FUN FACT: You don't have to actually ever make the dinner.
5. Cat—Give someone your own cat.

MERRY CHRISTMAS!!!

What Should I Do for Thanksgiving?

PUBLISHED NOVEMBER 25, 2020.

Dear Advice King,

Every Thanksgiving, I attend a large family gathering where we all play games with the kids, listen to Alice's Restaurant and enjoy a delicious potluck feast in the afternoon. It's my favorite holiday! But this year, COVID scrapped all our plans, so I will be by myself. What should I do instead that will be equally festive?

Thanks!

—James in Burbank, Calif.

If you really can't get the lid off the pickles, some pickle companies have centers where you can bring the jars and have them opened professionally. They're called "unscrewing centers." I'm googling it now and I can't seem to find any. I might be losing my mind. Good luck!

I tried to answer the question without reading it again.

Growing up, I never liked Thanksgiving. The adults wanted to drink and smoke, so they sent the kids to the basement. The basement was not a fun basement. It had an old couch in it, and some board games with most of the pieces missing. We would be down there for about three hours. Then we ate dinner at a little card table and everyone spilled their milk at once.

What kind of family do you have? A functional one? My family regarded—and still regards—potlucks with suspicion. Occasionally my mother succumbed to the pressure and agreed to be involved in a potluck. Her contribution was always "ambrosia salad." Hot tip: If you are ever interrogating me, threaten to serve me ambrosia salad.

AMBROSIA SALAD RECIPE, 1978

3 cups ham
4 cups mini marshmallows
4 cups mayonnaise
2 cups rainbow sprinkles
1 bag shredded coconut

1 quart beef stock

Mix the ingredients in a huge bowl with a concerned look on your face while "You Light Up My Life" by Debbie Boone plays on the radio. Serve.

I'm genuinely sorry that you're missing your favorite holiday, but it's for the good of humanity, James. There are SO MANY fun things you can do instead! You can eat cranberry sauce out of a can and watch porn! You can split a turkey sandwich with a rat!

I'm kidding! Go for a walk. Watch a movie. Get drunk on a Zoom call! Drink nonalcoholic beer and play records. Look at the moon. Write a love letter. Write a song. Paint a picture. Watch the 1982 Daytona 500 on YouTube.

We have so much to be thankful for! We are getting through this. Love is rising up against hate! Just remember that often, the people we disagree with are not as lucky as we are. They have been given bad information. Give them the good information, and try to give it to them in a reasonable tone of voice. HAPPY THANKSGIVING!!!

CHAPTER 9

ODDS & END(S)

I Saw a UFO

PUBLISHED AUGUST 11, 2015.

Advice King,

All right, I know this is gonna sound crazy . . . but a few weeks back I saw a UFO land in the field behind my house. Now I want to tell my friends, the authorities and the whole world, but I know I'm just going to come off as crazy. How do I convince everybody without any proof?

—Name withheld, but yes I am from the rural South

Hmmmm. "How do I convince everybody without any proof?" Didn't Patrick Henry say that? Let me look . . . nope. He said, "Give me liberty or give me death." Among other things, I'm sure. I bet after that catch phrase caught on he said stuff like, "Give me breakfast or give me death," to his wife. And he probably did promotional appearances where he was like, "Give me Johnson's Horse Feed or give me death." I wonder if he ever saw a UFO. If he did, he would definitely have kept it to himself. If he told people he saw, "Liketh, a hugeth, flying pewter plateth. Biggereth than Revere's biggest platter, and zooming abouteth!"* he would have been kicked off the Declaration of Independence committee. "Did you heareth that Patrick hath losteth it? Perhapseth his powderedeth wiggeth is too tighteth! *HAHAHAHAHAHAHA!*" That's how they talked back then.

"How do I convince everybody without any proof?" You don't have a damn thing? No burn marks on the grass? No grainy video? Not even a blurry photograph? Here is my favorite UFO photo of all time, in case you were wondering: [photo redacted]. It was taken in 1950 by

* Paul Revere was a silversmith. Millennials: Google "Paul Revere, silversmith, Declaration of Independence, Revolutionary War, horse, lantern."

this guy: [photo redacted]. I first saw that picture when I was about 10 years old. It blew my mind. Most people now think it's a fake. "They" say it's a truck mirror attached to a power line with string. While I concede that it is *possible* that it *could be* a picture of a truck mirror, and while I will admit that that guy looks like someone who might dangle a truck mirror from a power line for personal gain, I still think it's a real UFO. I'm easy, "Name Withheld." I WANT to believe, and even though you haven't provided a shred of evidence, I believe you. But you see, I believe in Bigfoot, ghosts, ESP, astral projection and the Lost Treasure of Oak Island. I also believe that Henry Kissinger and Dick Cheney are serial-killer lizards from another dimension. Not everybody is as forward-thinking as me, "Name Withheld." Most people believe that we were put on this amazing, mysterious planet to work 40 hours a week in "buildings" wearing "pants" and then "die." Your story will frighten them, make them question the things they are sure of—things they MUST be sure of, otherwise they might realize that a drab, oppressive "order" has been imposed upon a beautifully chaotic world due to FEAR, and then they would have to re-evaluate everything they think they "know."

You don't need to convince anyone else that you saw something, least of all "the authorities." "The authorities" are unimaginative and fearful people who work to preserve the stifling bureaucracy that we call "modern life." They don't want anybody thinking that there is anything more interesting in this universe than full dental coverage. They will ridicule and attempt to discredit you.

The UFO sighting is its own reward, "Name Withheld." You now know for certain that there is more to this existence than we have been programmed to believe. Let that knowledge guide your actions from this day forward. Live wildly and differently! Encourage those around you to do the same!

Garbage, Soccer and More

PUBLISHED JUNE 18, 2018.

Dear Advice King,

What should we do with all the garbage? Send it into space?

—Don in Melbourne, Australia

Australia? Stuff it in kangaroo pouches and watch it hop over the horizon. Just kidding! It's probably illegal to put garbage in kangaroo pouches. I guess shooting it into space seems like a fine idea. The only problem I foresee is the telescope industry will collapse—nobody wants to gaze up at banana peels and cigarette butts.

"Daddy, is that the North Star?"

"No, it's a bunch of old toilets."

Dear Advice King,

Should I care about soccer?

—Maria in Middleton, Wisc.

Sure. I think it's fine. I wish they would make the field smaller though. If I were a soccer player I'd have to call a cab and the driver would be like, "Where to, Mac?" And I'd be like, "Follow that ball!"

And when I say I wish the field were smaller, I mean WAY smaller. And there wouldn't be a ball, or goals, or a referee. I'd like to see a bunch of guys in speedos fight for a greased watermelon inside a dimly lit broom closet. A small surveillance camera would capture all the action. I suppose some purists would probably say that that's not "soccer." What was the question?

Dear Advice King,

I'm in my 30s and my body still hurts from the punk show I went to three days ago. Should I take the hint?

—Pete in Orlando, Fla.

What punk band was it? Blink-182? Phoenix? When I was your age I went to see the Jesus Lizard six times a week—on acid. After the shows me and my friend Onion would stay up all night doing shots of furniture polish. In the morning I walked 20 miles uphill to the salt mine where I worked as an ore car. I have been struck by lightning six times. In 1982, while in the Merchant Marines, I was pulled overboard by a giant squid. She held me captive in her underwater cave for two weeks until I was able to develop a rudimentary man-to-squid sign language and convince the (ultimately gentle) beast to return me to the surface. I dried myself off and went to see Minor Threat. In conclusion: Get the fuck out of my yard.

Dear Advice King,

I read somewhere that medieval peasants got more vacation time than present-day Americans. Should I be jealous?

—Jared in Syracuse, N.Y.

"Vacation time"?! What are you picturing? Pool noodles in the moat?

Medieval peasants had, like, one pair of underwear for LIFE—and it was made of "wearable wood." They were kicked by donkeys 24/7. Kids were bullied if they DIDN'T have lice. As far as entertainment, a juggler came to town once every leap year for 5 minutes. The only sport was a contest to see who had the most burrs stuck to their balls after a mushroom hunt. The "lucky" winner got a double serving of salty rat that night at dinner. Also, every person, including women, was named Fred.

I bet you eat microwave popcorn and check Facebook 200 times a day, Jared. Count your blessings.

Mohawks, Tarot Cards and Back-Up Cameras

. . . .

PUBLISHED AUGUST 22, 2018.

Dear Advice King,

How old is "too old" to rock a mohawk?

—Ben in San Diego

This is one of the most disturbing questions I have ever received. "Rock a mohawk"? "ROCK A MOHAWK"??

No. Not on my watch. No one waltzes into MY advice column talking about "rocking mohawks." WE ARE CLOSED.

Dear Advice King,

I want to become a tarot card reader. How do you do it? Do I need to go to school?

—Frank in New Jersey

A tarot card reader named Frank. I've never heard of that. I don't think there's any rule that the tarot card person has to be a woman, but let me check.

It's fine. I looked it up. Most tarot readers are women, but there are some men too.

I think you should change your name though. Frank is one of the least mystical names around. "Francis" is much better. And make up a good last name, like . . . "Stroganoff." And say you are Belgian. "Francis Stroganoff, the Belgian Tarot Master." Speak in an accent. It does not need to be a Belgian accent. If you want to be taken *really* seriously, live in a hollow tree and wear eyeliner and a cloak. Do all your readings through a knothole. I'm kind of kidding around, Frank, but theatrics are an important part of any successful tarot operation—maybe just wear an absurd amount of necklaces. You don't need to go to school. I don't know if there even is a school. If there is a school, it's in a tree.

The main thing you need to know about tarot reading is that nobody wants to hear bad news. Nobody wants to hear bad news from any kind of fortune teller. Tell everyone they are "going to have a new boat."

Here are examples of some tarot cards and how they should be interpreted:

THE MAGICIAN—you are going to have a new boat
THE HIGH PRIESTESS—you are going to have a new boat
THE CHARIOT—you are going to have a new boat
THE MOON—you are going to have a new boat
DEATH—you are going to have a new boat

When a customer asks how the "DEATH" card could possibly mean that they are going to have a new boat, calmly light some nag champa and say, "It represents zee death of you NOT having a new boat," and shut your knothole.

Dear Advice King,

Should I be worried that my older car doesn't have a back-up camera? Will I end up with neck problems?

—Karen in Nashville

Fuck back-up cameras. I've been successfully backing up cars since 1985, Karen. It never once crossed my mind to strap a camera to the bumper. You wanna know why? BECAUSE IT'S NOT HARD TO BACK UP A CAR.

What's next? Digital wrenches? Invisible windshield wipers?!

Also, neck problems are as American as apple pie.

Being Struck by Lightning and Naming Your Metal Band

. . . .

PUBLISHED DECEMBER 20, 2017.

Dear Advice King,

Should I be worried about being struck by lightning? What's the best way to avoid it?

—Gabe in Seattle

Great question, Gabe. And you picked the right person to ask. I've been struck by lightning a bunch of times—and you should be very worried about it. A lot of people are surprised to hear that lightning is responsible for more deaths in America than board games and mime COMBINED.

FIVE WAYS TO AVOID BEING STRUCK BY LIGHTNING (THAT I'VE LEARNED THE HARD WAY)

1. DO NOT WANDER AROUND THE PARK NUDE HOLDING YOUR BRONZED BABY SHOES DURING

A THUNDERSTORM. I'm not going to tell the whole sordid story, but take my word for it. I ended up two miles away in a bird's nest. Upside: I never had to wax my balls again.

2. If you are a submarine captain, DO NOT PUT YOUR PERISCOPE UP DURING A THUNDERSTORM. I was a submarine captain from 1978 until 1983. We ended up two miles away in a bird's nest.
3. DO NOT GO UP ON THE ROOF DURING A THUNDERSTORM WITH A PLUMBER'S WRENCH TO "ADJUST THE TV AERIAL." Just as I remembered that in 2014 nobody has aerials, I got blasted. I ended up two miles away in a bird's nest.
4. DO NOT PERFORM DENTISTRY OUTSIDE DURING A THUNDERSTORM. Seems obvious, right? Hindsight is 20/20. Bird's nest.
5. DO NOT PRACTICE THROWING JAVELINS DURING A THUNDERSTORM. You live and you learn. I went straight through the football uprights, and now everybody calls me "Three Point Charlie," which I hate.

I'm not a scientist, Gabe, but I have developed a couple of theories that I'd like to share with you: I think lightning may have some kind of special relationship with metal, and I suspect that lightning is more likely to occur during thunderstorms.

Best advice? Never go outside.

Dear Advice King,

Is Wizard a good name for my metal band? If you don't think it is, what is a good name for a metal band?

—Josh in Fort Collins, Colo.

Are you insane?! There are already about 5 million metal bands called "Wizard." Or "Wizard" plus some adjective—"Stone Wizard," "Green Wizard," etc. I bet five metal bands decided to call themselves "Wizard" while I was just typing the word "Wizard." Then somebody said, "I think there's already a band called 'Wizard,' so maybe we should be called 'Stone Wizard.'"

So now there's five new bands called "Stone Wizard."

Metal musicians are obsessed with wizards because metal musicians smoke a lot of weed, and the smoke reminds them of fog, and fog makes them think of wizards because there was a lot of fog in J.R.R. Tolkien books.

Here are some great metal band names that don't have anything to do with *The Hobbit*. You're welcome.

BIGFOOT FARTZ
EXPLOSION
CRIME BLOOD
ASS KING FOR A FIEND
TABLE SAW
MEAT LABYRINTH
NIGHT LEATHER
JOCKSTRAP GAS MASK

Shoveling Snow, Pet Outfits and More

. . . .

PUBLISHED JANUARY 17, 2018.

Dear Advice King,

I'm tired of using my shovel to pile up all this snow. Plus I feel like I might have a heart attack doing all that work. Should I buy a snowblower?

—Ken in Lancaster, Pa.

I think you might want to consider leaving the snow where it is. It'll melt eventually. If not, do you have a lawnmower? A lawnmower might work just as well as a snowblower—they seem pretty similar.

Helicopters are a lot like snowblowers too. Do you know anybody who has a helicopter? I bet if a helicopter flew real low above your house that snow would be gone in a jiffy.

My old neighbor Randy used dynamite to clear his driveway until he got arrested in 1982. Good luck!

Dear Advice King,

What're the best outfits a pet can wear? Are there any types of pets that should abstain from wearing outfits?

—Jamie in Baltimore

What do you mean "wear"? Pets can't "wear" anything. They can only "have stuff put on them." If you come home from work and your dog has successfully donned a tuxedo, go back outside and call the police.

This is off topic, but did you know Maryland's official state beverage is milk? The state sport is jousting! What a crazy state! Don't drink too much milk before you joust, Jamie, you freak.

Do animals ever need clothes? Does a dog need a hat, or does the dog's owner just want to see a dog in a hat? I honestly don't know. What I *do* know is that I'm currently playing poker against a chimp dressed as a matador. He's winning.

Full disclosure: The chimp isn't actually a matador. I put that outfit on him. I also have three parakeets that I dress up as Boyz II Men. I call them "Parakeetz II Men."

As long as you're not hurting them, I think it's fine to clothe your pet. Any pet. My weasel wears a purple helmet™.

Dear Advice King,

Why is the game "cornhole" so popular? Should I play "cornhole"?

—Sue in Los Angeles

FYI, California's state beverage is wine.

Why is "cornhole" so popular? White people figure if they spend every waking hour throwing bean bags and babbling about craft beer they won't have any time left to think about the Muslim ban, DACA, the destruction of the EPA, what's happening in Syria, etc. Eva Braun would have loved cornhole. I don't think you should play cornhole, Sue.

Dear Advice King,

Should I call my ex-girlfriend?

—Martin in Boston

Massachusetts' state beverage is cranberry juice.

No. Whatever reason you made up to justify why it TOTALLY MAKES SENSE to call your ex-girlfriend is complete bullshit. Take a deep breath, put down the phone, and go to the gym. When you get home, watch metal-detecting videos on YouTube.

Demons, Babies and Vitamins

. . . .

PUBLISHED MAY 22, 2018.

Dear Advice King,

Do you believe in demons? Like, actual demon possession? I sincerely believe I may have been contacted by one last week, and I'm now feeling extra protective of my soul. Her name is Annaliese Michel and I am freaked. How might one go about becoming totally unappealing to demons?

Signed,

—Demon Candy

I don't believe in demons, which is weird, because I'll believe almost anything. I even believe in the Loch Ness Monster. But if I tune in to the *Coast to Coast AM* radio show and it's about demons, I change the channel immediately. Some hungover-sounding guy will call in and say, "My 1992 Ford Tempo keeps breaking down, and I think it might be a demon. I put a bunch of oil in it, and it was gone really fast. Like, EXTRA fast. Also, I think a demon is giving me headaches in the morning after I drink." And the host, George Noory (who is a dope, in my opinion—Art Bell forever!), will act really interested: "That's fascinating, Randy. How much oil did you put in, and when? By the way, one time a demon stole my poodle."

Basically, I believe feeble-minded people blame demons for stuff that is their own fault. When there's nobody left to blame but yourself, blame a demon™.

When you say "contacted," what do you mean? Were you using a Ouija board? Did the demon spell out that long-ass name? What makes you sure it was a "demon" and not a ghost? I believe in ghosts. Ghosts are usually nice, but not always. I think you are dealing with an angry ghost. Your Vitamix is probably sitting right on the spot where some 17th-century grandma is buried. Vitamixes are loud. Move your Vitamix.

Dear Advice King,

Gonna have a baby soon. Anything I should know ahead of time? Thanks!

—Sean in Boston

Babies. Everybody's having babies. I'm thinking about having a baby so I have someone to play cards with. Also, I prefer to play cards with babies because you can cheat like crazy. Raise 'em, call 'em, take the pot every time—whatever—they don't know what any of it means! You don't even have to have a deck of cards, honestly. Deal them some lettuce leaves or candy bar wrappers.

You should know a bunch of stuff before you have a baby, I'm sure, but I don't know any of it. I'm a rolling stone, Sean. I think it was Shakespeare who said "A rolling stone gathers no babies," and he was right.

STUFF A CRAZY UNCLE (ME) THINKS YOU NEED FOR BABIES

1. Money
2. House
3. Food
4. A bed that looks like a race car
5. Blog

I hope this has been helpful!

Dear Advice King,

Do I REALLY need to take vitamins? I feel it's bullshit.

—Ashley in Nashville

I don't think you need to take vitamins. Lots of people who don't take vitamins live a long time. The people you read about who live to be over 100 years old never mention vitamins. They usually say they ate weird stuff—like twine.

Eugenia Lattimore, 164: "I ate small portions of heavily salted, boiled twine 15 times every day, and I did one sit-up at sunset. Every night I drank a quart of 10W-30 motor oil. The day after Lincoln was shot I ate nougat to console myself, but I never had it again."

I take vitamins occasionally. Have you had a bad experience with them? You seem pretty angry. Did you take some that turned out to be sawdust capsules? Sometimes I wonder if vitamins are made of sawdust. Who is checking? The FDA? I doubt it. I bet Trump appointed some guy who made his fortune selling sawdust vitamins to be the head of the FDA. Trump is 71 and he only eats Kentucky Fried Chicken and gold furniture.

Finishes plate of twine, wipes mouth, shuts laptop.

My Co-Worker Stinks

PUBLISHED JANUARY 16, 2015.

Dear Advice King,

I have this coworker. Let's call him Gary. Gary stinks. Bad breath, body odor, the whole nine yards. He sits in the cubicle next to me and I can barely stand it. Is it human resources' job to tell this guy to clean up his act? Our boss? Should I do it?

—Janice in Mt. Juliet

The whole nine yards, eh? Did you know that no one knows the origin of the expression "the whole nine yards"? I found that out on Wikipedia. Your question is so boring that I googled the origin of the expression "the whole nine yards."

Do you have a landline with voicemail at your office? Call Putrid Pete, disguise your voice as Louis Armstrong and say, "Mr. X thinks you stink!" Or, "Mr. X says take a shower or else!" Call one time and just say, "Mr. X!" and hang up.

Have one of those rear-view mirror fir tree air fresheners dangling off your glasses when you talk to Fetid Fred. If you don't wear glasses you should start wearing them so you can do this.

Shit exclusively in paint cans and keep them all in your cubicle. I can guarantee you won't smell Musty Mel anymore.

Get a job as a surveyor. I had a physics teacher in high school who told the class on more than one occasion how he envied the life of a surveyor—making your own hours, never working in the same place, being outdoors. He was a very strange man, and I'm pretty sure he was confusing surveyors with cowboys—but they *do* work outside, and it seems to me they usually work across the street from one another. So even if you were working with a Rancid Ron, you probably wouldn't smell him because he'd be across the street.

I once had a job with a co-worker who had over 100 cats in his APARTMENT. He talked about finding surprise litters of kittens in "nests" in his living room. Everything in our office was covered in cat hair and kitty litter. It was a union job, however. If your pungent pal is protected by a union, you might as well forget it. We tried to force Catbox Carl to buy a lint brush, but some union officials wearing stained undershirts and smoking nickel cigars ruled that coming to work covered in cat feces was protected under the "workplace jewelry" codes of 1966.

In some lines of work Odorous Ollies go with the territory. Are you a gravedigger? An exterminator? I remember reading about a fish cannery that went out of business and left hundreds of pallets of fish rotting inside their old warehouse. Rats ate that fish for months and became as big as small dogs. When the rats ran out of fish to eat they started eating each other. I can only imagine the Savory Sam who volunteered to go in and mop up that mess. If a guy is willing to enter a hell-house to fight dog-rats, his hygiene (or lack thereof) is not relevant. Also, to successfully sneak up on a rat, it helps if you smell like another rat. Do rat-fighters have cubicles?

Perhaps you work on the Large Hadron Collider, but I doubt they have an office in Mt. Juliet. If this guy is one of the world's top nuclear scientists and he refuses to brush his teeth, there's not much human resources can do. Those eggheads are irreplaceable. Most of the top guys on the Manhattan Project reeked. Does the Large Hadron Collider even have a human resources department? What the fuck am I talking about?

In conclusion, based on your description and my experience as a professional advice columnist, I am almost certain that "Gary" is the notoriously ripe Dick Cheney. Dick Cheney is a dangerous war criminal, Janice. Under no circumstances should you call him stinky to his face.

IF YOU SMELL SOMETHING, SAY SOMETHING. Contact Homeland Security.

Autocorrect Faux Pas; My 35th Birthday

PUBLISHED JUNE 15, 2016.

Dear Advice King,

Fuck my stupid phone! My wife and I were going to my in-laws' house for dinner, and I accidentally texted my mother-in-law about having "butt sex" instead of "baked beans"! What's your most embarrassing autocorrect mistake, and how did you recover? How can I recover from this?!

—John in Hillsboro Village

Why is your mother-in-law so uptight? Is your mother-in-law an aristocrat? Aristocrats don't like stuff that's "crass." Aristocrats do all kinds of crass stuff, but they have a bunch of rules about how you're supposed to talk about it. If you don't know how to talk about it right, they will accuse you of having "no class." They might be having *actual* butt sex 24/7 with pool boys, riding instructors and friends' spouses, but then someone accidentally *texts* them "butt sex" and they act like they've been gravely injured. If your mother-in-law is an aristocrat, the best way to recover is have somebody on horseback deliver her a fruitcake.

I doubt your mother-in-law is an aristocrat since you were trying to send her a text about baked beans. Aristocrats hate hearing about baked beans. Your mother-in-law is probably a Baptist. Baptists talk almost exclusively about baked beans.

TEXT EXCHANGE BETWEEN JOHN AND HIS BAPTIST MOTHER-IN-LAW:

BAPTIST MOTHER-IN-LAW: Hi John! We can't wait to see you and Clara at the church potluck tomorrow! What are you bringing? We are bringing baked beans.

JOHN: Can't wait! I love butt sex! Clara loves butt sex, too! We are bringing mild salsa.

BAPTIST MOTHER-IN-LAW:

Clara's phone rings.

The best way for you to recover in this scenario is tell the Baptist lady that the devil must have put "butt sex" in the text.

Relevant question: Why would your autocorrect make "baked beans" into "butt sex"? If anything it should make "butt sex" into "baked beans."

I'm listening to Charlie Rich's *Greatest Hits* as I write this. So fucking good.

My most embarrassing autocorrect mistake was the time I was messaging my girlfriend Rhonda about how I was thinking about teaching harp lessons, and she got a text saying I was thinking that it would "teach her a lesson if she got herpes." I sued the phone company and won $3,500, but I never recovered. Rhonda moved away and married a dentist. I spent the $3,500 on a subwoofer.

Dear Advice King,

What should I do for my 35th birthday?

—Lynn in Brooklyn

Drink 35 beers. Adopt 35 cats. Bury 35 dollars in your yard. Eat 35 pickles. Hold your breath for 35 minutes. Get a baseball jersey with the number 35 on it. Hop around the block 35 times on a pogo stick. Insist to anyone who will listen that there are only 35 inches in a yard.

I hate to break it to you, Lynn, but 35 isn't exactly a milestone birthday. I suggest you do something normal like go to a restaurant where you grill your own meat at the table. Get one of those molten chocolate cakes. Or pump a wineskin full of Rumple Minze and play Skee-Ball down at the pier.

I'm listening to the Bertie Higgins song "Key Largo" right now, Lynn. Ol' Bertie only had one hit, but if you're only gonna have one hit, "Key Largo" isn't a bad one to have. The video is even better than the song! Here it is.* It's my present to you. I hope you have as much fun

* If you are reading this in *The Advice King Anthology*, do yourself a favor and track down this music video.

on your birthday as the woman in that video has with Bertie Higgins! Happy 35th!

Pot, New Nashville, Carpet Remnants

. . . .

PUBLISHED MAY 9, 2018.

Dear Advice King,

Now that marijuana is practically legal, what should I do? I know you live in California now—what is your experience with modern pot? Do you use it? Does it make your life better?

—Ken in Baton Rouge, La.

I've been sober for six years, Ken, so I don't smoke pot. I used to smoke pot, though—I smoked a lot of pot. I started smoking it in 1986, when it was still a sensible drug. What do I mean when I say it was "sensible"? I mean it didn't make you feel like a radioactive coconut crab from another galaxy—it just made you like the Dire Straits song "Telegraph Road" more than you probably would normally. So you could hang out, extra-dig Dire Straits for a couple of hours, and have a calzone. Then you could get dressed in normal clothes, and go out to a party.

Have you seen what this current-day super-weed has done to young people? They can't look you in the eye. They listen to instrumental music because "talking music" frightens them. THEY WEAR PAJAMAS ON AIRPLANES.

If you ask them why, at 28 years old, they are listening to day-spa jams on leaf blower headphones and carrying a backpack filled with gummy bears, they'll tell you it's because they have "social anxiety."

YOU EVER THINK THIS "ANXIETY" MIGHT BE LINKED TO THAT LOW-GRADE PCP PACIFIER YOU'RE HONKING ON,

CHIEF? Also: WHICH CAME FIRST, THE CHICKEN OR THE PANIC ATTACK?

Sorry I got so upset, Ken. Truth be told, I'm hamming it up a bit to add excitement to the column. I tried the "new" weed before I got sober. Sometimes it worked out, sometimes it didn't. When it did? Laser Floyd and a calzone. When it didn't? Ambulance! Be careful, Bob Marley!

Dear Advice King,

Any good places in town to pick up carpet remnants for a decent price?

—Clancy

Thanks for the question, Clancy. I would say the answer is definitely "yes," but I need to know where you live.

Dear Advice King,

My rent tripled. A "pedal tavern" ran over my foot. A bachelorette barfed on my dog. Someone painted a mural on me while I was asleep. I'm sick of this "It City" bullshit. Where should I move? What should I do when I get there?

—Over "It" in Nashville

I wonder what the subject matter of the mural was. A hot chicken deejaying?

That sucks about the bachelorette. Bachelorettes barf—that's what they do. They go "WOOOOOOOO" for about nine hours, and then they get really crabby and start barfing. A bachelorette barfed on the Pope just recently. It was OK because she was super-apologetic. She said "my bad" and everything.

DON'T GET ME STARTED ON PEDAL TAVERNS. The Four Horsemen of the Apocalypse will arrive on four pedal taverns.

I think you should move to Madison, Wisc. I was there just recently, and it's really nice. Open a vape shop. Call it "Vape Canaveral," and thank me later.

How Should I Pick My Theme Song for the Year?

. . . .

PUBLISHED FEBRUARY 2, 2016.

Dear King,

How do you pick your theme song for the year?

—Brett in Cookeville

Depends on my goals for that year, Brett. By the way, how did you know I have a theme song for the year? Does everybody have one? Anyway, I like a song with a good beat—something that energizes me. I usually end up with a track from Survivor's *Vital Signs* album. That album's been very good to me. Since it came out in 1984, my theme song has been something from *Vital Signs* like 26 times.

We are all animals, Brett. We are programmed to SURVIVE and THRIVE. Every day is a metaphorical hunt for "meat" (cars, electronics, tailored clothes), and a regular hunt for real meat. That alarm clock on your bedside table is the meat-hunt starting gun. Have you ever seen the original *Rollerball*? It's a lot like that.

At the end of the day, whoever has the most "meat" (paintings, rugs, big bathtubs), and real regular meat WINS. I'm a man who doesn't like to lose, Brett—the music of Survivor helps make sure that I don't.

It's right there in the name. Survivor. If that name was a dog, it would bite the ass out of your pants. What's the main thing a person wants to do every year? Survive. Sure, you might want to go to a Broadway show, maybe drink a couple milkshakes. But I got news for you, Brett: Dead men don't drink milkshakes. The songs on the album *Vital Signs* will keep you on your toes, physically and spiritually, year after year. Survivor's "First Night" was my theme song from 1984–85, then again from 1987–94. It was also my theme song for last year. I love that song.

Check out this quote from "First Night":

And this night shall be the first night
And first nights were made for love
I can taste the action in the air tonight
Hearts are poundin' as the sparks ignite

If reading that doesn't make you want to run out and get rugs and electronics, you should have your blood pressure checked—you might already be dead! Get out of bed! TASTE THE ACTION and the pounding, sparks, etc.

Cinderella's "Shake Me" was my theme song in 1988. (I am unironically listening to "Shake Me" as I write this, and it still rules. Fun fact: Cinderella's singer, Tom Keifer, lives in Nashville.)

In 1995 I married my first wife Stephanie in the Florida Keys. We danced our first dance to "The Search Is Over," and that was also my '95 theme. We spent that whole year horseback riding and doing cocaine.

From 1996 to 2004 I owned a gym in Miami, and Steph was the most popular realtor in Dade County. My theme song was *Vital Signs*' "Popular Girl" for all of those years. It's a great workout song, it's great on a set of headphones if you're out on the street—probably the Survivor track that's most like a shot of espresso. A real mover.

Me and Stephanie divorced in 2004. She was having an affair with the wrestler Moondog Spot, who worked out at my gym. I had a few rough years after that. My theme song from 2005 to 2009 was Leonard Cohen's "Famous Blue Raincoat."

In 2009 I was in a work-release program (long story—the gym burned down) when I met my current wife Angela at the car wash. I was polishing her fender and she said, "Do you rub backs as well as you rub fenders?" We were married in 2010. "It's the Singer, Not the Song" has been our theme song every year since. Except for last year when it was "First Night." It's hard to keep track of this bullshit.

Still you wonder if you've got the clout
To make it happen in this cold-hearted town
And you're feelin' that you're trapped
You wonder should you just stop tryin'
Well take a message from the man
Who's not afraid to come on strong
When there's magic in the music
It's the singer not the song
When it's comin' from the heart
All the people sing along
It's the man behind the music
It's the singer not the song

Brett, "Take a message from the man who's not afraid to come on strong," and your cave will always have a huge bathtub.

Just the Tip; My Car Stinks

. . . .

PUBLISHED AUGUST 25, 2015.

Dear Advice King,

Is "just the tip" a good strategy?

—Adam in Chattanooga

A good strategy for what? What is "just the tip"? I mean, I think I know what it means, but what does it *mean*? Has anyone ever actually said that? I mean, SERIOUSLY said it? I think it's one of those things people say to each other at work, like "More Cowbell," or things about bacon.

"More Cowbell" is old now, but people used to say it a lot in offices. It's from a *Saturday Night Live* sketch. I have written a short play to explain:

INTERIOR, REAL ESTATE OFFICE, 2002

Two white men are drinking flavored coffee and eating huge donuts. Both men have brown hair and regular faces.

LARRY: This coffee is pretty good.
BILL: Yes, but it could use "MORE COWBELL," HAHAHA!
LARRY: HAHAHA
BILL: This donut has a *hole* in it. I like holes, HAHAHA!
LARRY: HAHAHA. Yeah, me too. I love holes. But we are married, so . . .
BOTH MEN TOGETHER: *JUST THE TIP!!!*

Building explodes.

THE END

I wonder what people say to each other in offices now. Do they still talk, or do they just exchange pictures of animals with block letters superimposed on them?* Did you know that if you build your "sense of humor" out of pop culture references then you are a corporate lackey? "More Cowbell," for example, is from a television show that broadcasts on a network owned by General Electric. General Electric is a tax-dodging multinational conglomerate that profits from wars. General Electric also designed the unsafe reactors at Fukushima. Turns out your "sense of humor" is bloody and irradiated. Make up your own jokes.

Adam, I don't know if "just the tip" is a good strategy, but it's a great way to sound dumb.

Your Highness,

I left my windows down in my car. Then it rained. Now my car smells like a dive-bar men's room. How do you get that smell out?

—Sean in Boston

Why does it smell so bad? It's rained in my car before, and it doesn't smell like a men's room. Are you absolutely sure no one urinated in the car? Are you a heavy drinker? It may have been you. Did it definitely rain?

If it really was rain, and the interior of your car smells like a bathroom, I can only assume one of the men on the assembly line urinated in your car. It dried a long time ago, you never noticed it, and the odor was re-activated by the rain. I bet your car is an older model. Probably from the 1970s or '80s. The assembly lines back then were like parties. Drinking, cocaine use, dice games and group sex were all common activities on the "line." The expression "line dancing" comes from automobile assembly lines. "Break" dancing was invented in 1976 by an auto worker dancing on his "break."

. . . .

* I have been informed by a millennial friend of mine that this thing is called a "meme." Figures. "Meme" is just the word "me" two times. These kids are hopeless. I bet they call trees "MEMEMEs" and shoes "MEMEMEMEMEs."

The problem with parties is that sometimes they get out of hand. Auto workers relieved themselves inside many of the cars constructed between 1972 and 1986. The Pinto was famously recalled because it smelled like urine. Ralph Nader wrote a book called *Unsafe at Any Peed*. There's a reason they call lousy cars "lemons"—it's because urine is yellow.

Put on goggles and a respirator. Fill the car with talcum powder. Pound it into the upholstery with your hands.

I Married into Cats

PUBLISHED APRIL 5, 2016.

Dear Advice King,

I married into cats. I love my wife, but the cats drive me nuts. They knock stuff off of shelves for no reason and meow relentlessly through the night. They also tear up documents and other important stuff. My wife loves these two cats. What do I do?

—Put Upon in Jersey

YOU MARRIED TWO CATS?! Well, you were asking for it. How did you end up . . . *Ohhhhh*, you married INTO cats. Wait, you got married IN two cats?! Wow! That is wild. How did you fit?

JK! (That means "just kidding" on the street.)

Yeah, cats. Cats and documents. Remember that indie-rock band "Cats and Documents"? I saw them in 1996 opening for "June of '44." They had a lady who played the saw.

What kind of documents you got? DMV stuff?

Cats. Some people are CRAZY about 'em. I mean truly crazy. Remember how people acted when The Beatles played on *The Ed Sullivan Show*? For some people, their cats are like The Beatles on *Ed*

Sullivan, except all day, every day. If your wife is one of those people, you are fucked. If your wife is one of those people, you'd better keep your mouth shut. She and the cats are probably already having meetings to decide what to do with you. I'm serious. If you absolutely must complain, make sure you do it when the cats ARE NOT AROUND. Wait until you and your wife are in the car. Cats can suck your breath. My uncle used to talk shit about cats, and one morning they found him completely deflated. He got a hairball in the mail the week before, so he should have seen it coming.

Were your wife's parents divorced? Remember in the 1970s, when men owned their own bowling ball and also left their families? Dads back then were always "splitting" because things at home were getting "too heavy" and it was starting to interfere with their drinking. I bet your wife's dad was one of those creeps. Cats act just like drunken dads: They are selfish, they withhold affection, they knock stuff off shelves. The only difference between cats and alcoholic fathers is (most) cats can't operate doorknobs—cats can't leave! If you think you are going to come between your wife and her furry alcoholic fathers, you've got another thing coming, "Put Upon." You and your precious documents will be living in a motel faster than you can say "wet food."

How many bathtubs do you have, "Put Upon"? Cats don't like water. You could keep your valuables in a submerged waterproof case. I had a friend who hated cats, and his wife had a cat, so he slept on a special bed he built in his swimming pool for eight years until one day he fell asleep on the couch after mowing the lawn and the cat sucked his breath. He had been complaining about the cat right in front of the fucking cat. I warned him, but he didn't listen.

Look on the bright side: Your wife could have 100 cats. I worked with a guy who had a hundred cats. I really did. I worked at the Associated Press from 1993 to 1997, and one of my co-workers had 100 cats. He was covered in cat hair. I mean COVERED. You would have needed a lint roller the size of a Volkswagen to clean him up. When he worked the night shift, he brought in a cot and he slept in it with two of his cats until he got caught. I have found that you get fired from most jobs if you're sleeping in a cot—with or without animals. He wasn't fired because we had a really good union. The kids in his neighborhood called him "Litter Box" and threw rocks at him until, one by one, they became short of breath.

Wear earplugs, laminate everything, and WATCH YOUR BACK.

On a serious note, I am sending all my love to my friend, *Scene* editor Jim Ridley, and his family. Jim is an amazing guy, and he has always been an inspiration to me. I love you, Jim!! Get well soon!!!

How to Catch Bigfoot

PUBLISHED JUNE 6, 2018.

Dear Advice King,

How do you catch Bigfoot?

—Chris in Eureka, Calif.

Cover the outside of all your windows with a fairly thick layer of SALTED peanut butter. Bigfeet love salted peanut butter, and Lord knows the only thing they like better than salted peanut butter is LOOKING IN WINDOWS. While Mr. Foot is licking the windows, quietly get on all fours behind the beast, and have someone push him over you. Once the monster is on the ground, throw a net on him. Now you have a Bigfoot. What are you gonna do with it? You'll have to get him an agent. He could be a judge on *The Voice*—he might even start dating Blake Shelton. Imagine that: a Gwen Stefani-Bigfoot-Blake Shelton love triangle. No one would even care. In 2018, "Blake Shelton, Gwen Stefani, Bigfoot in Love Triangle" sounds like a normal news story.

OK, let's get serious, Chris. I firmly believe that Bigfoot exists, and you *are* in a part of the country where you could actually catch one—the creature's habitat starts in the Pacific Northwest, and extends up through the dense forests of British Columbia. The first thing you are going to need is a shitload of plaster, because before you can capture *anything* you have to track it, and there is a law in the United States that says you have to make a plaster cast of every footprint you find that might belong to a Bigfoot. Hey, guess what, Chris—I'M BEING SARCASTIC. There is no fucking law that says you have to make a plaster cast of every goddamn Bigfoot print. And I think we probably could have discovered like 5 million Bigfeet already if these Bigfoot hunters FOLLOWED THE FUCKING TRACKS INSTEAD OF MAKING PLASTER CASTS OF THEM. ARE WE LOOKING OR ARE WE CASTING, FOLKS? Make a fucking decision.

I'm sorry I got so upset, but I truly feel like every Bigfoot gets away because these morons stop to mix plaster. Mixing plaster takes time, and Bigfeet aren't stupid. *They are half man*. While these clowns make plaster, Bigfoot slips away into his tunnel network. And if you are like "Tunnel network?" then I really can't help you, Chris. Because if you don't even know the basic public-domain facts, how do you expect to catch one of these hairy geniuses? Yes, tunnel networks. Thousands and thousands of miles of sophisticated tunnels full of salted peanut butter and rudimentary bunk beds. "But why haven't we found the entrances, Advice King?" BECAUSE THEY COVER THEM WITH BRANCHES, YOU DUMBASS. I'm sorry again, Chris. I'm just frustrated.

I know what you're thinking: "He shouldn't be yelling at me, I'm on his side! I'm a believer!"

Sure, you're a believer, and I'm glad—but believing on its own isn't enough. The last thing the cryptozoological world needs is one more dope running around the woods with night-vision goggles and a backpack full of plaster. Not only does it make Bigfeet lose respect for homo sapiens—which makes it even less likely that they will engage with us—but it's also NOT FUCKING SAFE. Many of the people who encounter Bigfoot report that it "looked like it may have recently eaten a huge powdered jelly doughnut." Here's the thing: Bigfeet don't eat jelly doughnuts. You know what they do eat? Idiots. Human idiots. That isn't powdered sugar and jelly, Chris—it's plaster dust and blood. Be careful out there.

What Should I Name My Craft Beer? And How Do I Make It?

. . . .

PUBLISHED APRIL 25, 2018.

Dear Advice King,

I'm thinking about trying to make a living brewing my own beer. How do you do it? What is a good name for a "small production" beer? I think the name is important. Thank you.

—Sully in Lawrence, Kans.

You don't even know how to make it? At all? I'm not trying to be a jerk, but that seems like a huge flaw in your business plan. I don't know how to make it either. I'm going to take my best guess at how it's done and then google it to see how well I did. You can play along, Sully.

Advice King readers: You can play along, too! Get a piece of scrap paper and write down how you think beer is made. Here's mine:

HOW I THINK BEER IS MADE

1. Get a big barrel and make sure it doesn't have any rats living in it.
2. Fill the barrel half with water and half with wheat stalks.
3. Put in like 5 cups of yeast—make sure the yeast says "ACTIVE" on the bottle.
4. Cover the barrel with a lid (or foil) and put it on a hot plate set on LOW.
5. Leave it on the heat for three months.
6. Stir for 5 minutes every day when you come home.
7. Put beer in bottles.
8. Name beer.
9. Bring bottles to store.

OK! Now I'm going to put on my Google Goggles™.

I was actually pretty close! They talk a bit more about "hops" and "barley" and a bit less about barrels, but I think I could make a decent (not great) beer using my recipe.* From what I can tell, the biggest problem with my beer is that it wouldn't be very fizzy. And it wouldn't have much alcohol, if any. It would probably taste a lot like "old wheat soup." Not a problem! Anheuser-Busch might have trouble mass-marketing old wheat soup, but in the small-production arena, "tasting like shit" is an asset: The worse it tastes the more "artisan" it is. If *you*—big dummy that *you* are—don't think it tastes good, it's because you have a low-class palate.

Liking things that taste horrible is a certified Advice King Power Move™.

Do you see what I'm saying, Sully? The good thing about "microbrews" is that even if they turn out horribly you can name them something that gives customers the impression that you made them taste like that on purpose. For example, my beer could be called "Chris Crofton's Flat-Bottom Boat Browne Ale." The "flat" in "Flat-Bottom Boat" would refer to the fact that the beer has no fizz. I don't even think a "Flat-Bottom Boat" is a thing, but it sounds like a thing—an "old-time" thing. That "e" on the end of "Browne"? Pure theater. By the time the suckers who buy this batch figure out there's no alcohol in it, I'm on to the next town. *Wink.*

If you don't feel like moving from place to place, and you can't figure out how to make the beer alcoholic, just add grain alcohol at the end. NOT TOO MUCH. *Wink.*

Here are some good names for the beer you don't even know how to make, Sully. Remember, the present day is so bleak people aren't just trying to get drunk—they trying to drink themselves into the past.

. . . .

* Send me YOUR beer technique and a SASE (self-addressed stamped envelope), and I'll send you a prize!

Anything that reminds people of the fun stuff they like to imagine the late-19th century was all about (square dances) and none of the real stuff (Civil War) is great small-batch-beer-name subject matter. Animals and things that are rusty are also good.

GOOD NAMES FOR SULLY'S MICROBREW

1. Black and White Picture Postcard of a Man with a Big Tree He Cut Down Lager
2. Rusty Pig Monocle Pilsner
3. One-Eyed Swimming Hole Square Dance Bitter
4. World's Fair Flume Ride Red
5. Friendly Gas Attendant Bock
6. Jumping Weasel Pocket Watch Porter
7. Rusty Mustache Yukon Gold Pan Moose Stout
8. Locomotive Railroad Steel Train Horse Beer
9. Man that Has No Sex Drive and Whistles Ale
10. Ferris Wheel Full of Owls Brown

What "App" Should I Invent?

PUBLISHED MAY 31, 2017.

Dear Advice King,

Have all the good "apps" already been invented? I want to invent an "app" and make a lot of money. Do you have any good ideas for "apps"?

Thanks!

—Darius Delgado, Glendale, Ariz.

Man, I really don't feel like trying to explain what "apps" are, but this column is read by millions of people, Darius, and not all of them are tech-savvy webheads like you and me. Some of my older readers even get mad if I talk about "television" or "cars."

Tinder is an "app." Uber is an "app." Instagram is an "app." Apps are tiny machines that are inside smartphones. Each machine does a little task or trick that is supposed to make life easier or more fun.

Imagine if someone figured out how to make ice cubes come out of a smartphone. A good name for that "app" would be Ice Machine™. Luckily for the people who make real ice machines, nobody's figured out how to do that.

FULL DISCLOSURE: I designed an ice cube app. The app worked, but by the time I got it inside the phone, the whole unit was actually a bit bigger than a regular ice machine.

I also tried to make an app where a cup of coffee would come out of your phone. I was going to call it Coffee Machine™. One solid piece of advice for anyone considering a career in apps is NO GODDAMN LIQUIDS. I was electrocuted about 700 times during the three years I worked on Coffee Machine™, and I never managed to produce a single cup of drinkable coffee.

Even if those apps had hit the market, the names aren't very good. Consumers like apps that have one-word names. Ice Machine™ should have been called "Cube." Or "Rocks." Or "Rox." "Rox" is an even better app name than "Rocks," because "Rox" looks more futuristic than "Rocks." People love to feel like they're living in the future.

"I HAVE A CAMERA IN MY PHONE! I CAN'T DIE!"—Everybody

I think there are plenty of good (dry) app ideas left, Darius! Here are some suggestions:

ADVICE KING APP IDEAS

1. SCALE™—Stand on phone. Phone displays weight.
2. HAMMER™—Pound nail into board with phone.
3. BOOKMARK™—Put phone in book.

4. LADIEZ™—Pictures of ladies. Not ladies to date. Regular, clothed ladies.
5. E-I-E-I-O™—Identifies cow, chicken, sheep, goat or pig from clear picture. Other animals get loud buzzer sound.
6. LINTBRUSH™—Outside of phone is sticky.
7. X-RAY™—Phone shows bones.
8. RATIONZ™—Jerky inside phone.
9. LIFTZ™—A phone in each shoe.
10. AISLE 4™—App that automatically tells you what aisle shit is in at the supermarket. This is actually a really good idea and I am dumb to put it in this column.

Meeting Women at the Gym

PUBLISHED SEPTEMBER 22, 2015.

Dear King,

I want to meet women at the gym. Any advice?

—Tom in East Nashville

Hello, "Tom from East Nashville." Meet women at the gym? Fuck if I know. I keep to myself at the gym. I put Survivor's *Eye of the Tiger* album* ("Eye of the Tiger" is the best song on that record BY FAR, btw) into my portable CD player—with skip protection, natch—and hit the elliptical HARD (for 20 minutes). The only two conversations I have had with women at the gym were both about "skip protection." Here's one of those conversations in the form of a short play:

* Fun fact: An image of the band is in the Tiger's eyes on that album cover.

INTERIOR, EAST PARK RECREATION CENTER, 2012:

WOMAN: Ha! I haven't seen one of those in a *while*! That's great! What are you listening to?
CHRIS CROFTON: Temple of the Dog.
WOMAN: Who?
CHRIS CROFTON: It has skip protection.
WOMAN: What?
CHRIS CROFTON: It has skip protection.

WOMAN walks away

THE END

That's a sad fucking play. I cried toward the end.

East Nashville, huh? The hippest neighborhood in the world. A neighborhood where even the hats wear hats, the tattoos have tattoos, the cocktails drink cocktails, and the motorcycles ride motorcycles that have tattoos and drink cocktails and wear hats. I thought gyms were out of style in East Nashville. Doesn't everybody do CrossFit? I call CrossFit "Americanacise." Dudes with beards running around carrying whiskey barrels and bench-pressing tree branches, barber chairs, old amplifiers.

"For today's first CrossFit 'set,' we bearded men (and women) will be going out to the woods and getting that abandoned 19th-century box factory up and running. At the end of the day, everybody gets a box."

Do any Americana ladies have beards? That would be Americana AS SHIT.

CROSSFIT DREAM: Running down the street carrying an ACTUAL ACRE OF FARMLAND. WITH COWS ON IT AND EVERYTHING.

FYI, thanks to this question I have now listened to almost the entire Survivor record *Vital Signs*. It's pretty fucking good. "Popular Girl" is the jam.

OK, here's the Advice King's Ten Tips for How to Meet a Woman at the Gym™:

1. Wear really tight gym clothes—ladies love a show. If you don't feel like you will make a "good impression" in those biking shorts, wear a cock ring—it will force blood into your dong, making it appear larger.*
2. Wear mirrored sunglasses.
3. Grunt loudly when you do "reps."
4. Take off your shirt and jump rope.
5. Say, "Can somebody give me a spot?" a lot.
6. Loudly complain to another male that the gym does not "have enough weights" for you to work out properly.
7. Vape, if permitted.
8. Put a Bluetooth in your ear and say, "I don't give a shit, just make it happen!" into it.
9. Neon, neon, neon.
10. When you are in between "sets"—sweating profusely, panting—walk over to the nearest woman and ask her if she likes *Boardwalk Empire*.

Should I Exercise while Drunk?

PUBLISHED OCTOBER 27, 2015.

Advice King,

I am 34 years old. I like to work out, but only if I'm having a few drinks. Is that healthy/safe? Only beer and wine . . . no hard stuff.

—W. in Nashville

* If you *do* decide to wear a cock ring, make sure your Lycra is fresh—Lenny Kravitz's pants split while he was wearing a "snake expander" recently, and everyone involved was traumatized.

Another gym question? I'm starting to feel like I write a column for *Muscle and Fitness* or *Tomorrow's Man*. FYI, I'm listening to Pablo Cruise's *Worlds Away* right now. Check out the dude who posted that on YouTube. He took a picture of the *Worlds Away* CD booklet and wrote "My beautiful picture" on it. Anyway, I think Pablo Cruise's *Worlds Away* is great workout music. I find that the more "produced" one's workout music is, the more productive one will be exercising to it. If you really wanna sweat, put on Styx's *Kilroy Was Here*.*

Why do you mention that you're 34 years old? Is it because you think you might be getting too old to drink and exercise? Or is it supposed to show that you are still young enough to get away with it? Drinking and exercising is a terrible idea no matter what age you are, "W." You will dump weights on some poor person's head. Right now I am picturing the mayhem you could cause in a public gym. You'd end up decapitating someone. In your stupor you'd mistake the severed head for a medicine ball and try to throw it to horrified onlookers before being tased and hogtied.

I admit that if you were 89 years old, drinking and exercising would be even worse. You would immediately rip your arms and legs off. Your kneecaps would fly out the window. Your torso would be found tangled in a Nautilus machine like a piece of paper jammed in a printer. A blood-spattered sign blinks . . .

PAPER JAM

PAPER JAM

PAPER JAM

I love "no hard stuff." That old trick. I used to be an alcoholic, "W." I know "no hard stuff" actually means "hard stuff and a little blow," and that concerns me. Do you have any idea how far a man will run when he's on cocaine? He'll run hundreds of miles just so he can meet new people to talk nonsense to. I snorted cocaine and left my house in Nashville for a short jog. I arrived in New Mexico three weeks later.

. . . .

* I'm fucking kidding. Don't *ever* listen to a Styx record, even as a joke.

I kept running and talking and snorting and running. I bored the shit out of people in five states with my meaningless coke jabber. I lost my job because I was gone so long.

Here's another cautionary tale for you, Drinky. In 1956 my great-uncle Larry went to the Moose Lodge in Youngstown, Ohio, to watch some stag films and have some beers. In addition to a color television, the Moose Lodge had a state-of-the-art exercise room. After reading the *Daily Racing Form* and having seven Schlitzes, my uncle made the fateful decision to try out the lodge's newest piece of equipment—the steam cabinet. Do I even need to finish this story? If you insist. Well, drunken Uncle Larry fell asleep in that cabinet. He slept for 10 hours. Uncle Larry was a tall man—6-foot-6, to be exact. When he emerged from that steam cabinet the next morning, he was 3-foot-4. Did I mention that Uncle Larry was a professional basketball player?

If you MUST drink and exercise, do it at home. Go ahead and drop the barbell backward through the sheetrock, expose your collarbones, shatter the fish tank—but don't make other people watch.

Investing in Marijuana, Pet Snakes, Banks and More

PUBLISHED DECEMBER 12, 2018.

Dear Advice King,

Should I invest in marijuana stock?

—Jean in Marietta, Ga.

Yes! Invest in reggae, cold cuts, condiments, Visine and sweatpants, too. And *stop* investing in sponges, detergent, toothbrushes, shampoo, soap and gymnasiums, because once every person in the whole world is high they won't use any of those things. Have you ever been to Humboldt County? It's an area of Northern California where people have grown and smoked marijuana for decades—it's also an area with extremely sticky counters. Pot people don't scrub™.

I think marijuana should be legal, and I think all the people in jail for nonviolent marijuana-related offenses should be freed. HOWEVER, if all the sane, fun-loving, empathetic people are stoned, then fundamentalist nutcases like Mike Pence will be the only ones sober (and clean) enough to run for office—and they'll be making the laws.

Invest in marijuana, but *use* it sparingly.

Dear Advice King,

I'm having a midlife crisis. Should I buy a pet snake?

—Lynn in Nashville

Hi, Lynn. You probably meant to type "convertible." You accidentally typed "pet snake." A snake is not a normal midlife-crisis purchase. Pet snakes are dreary. Unless you are planning to use it as part of a burlesque act. Are you having a midlife BURLESQUE crisis? That's a definite type of midlife crisis.

ADVICE: MAKE SURE THE SNAKE IS NOT GOING TO KILL YOU. Ten percent of women older than 40 are strangled by snakes during their burlesque acts. Ten percent die from complications associated with getting a tattoo of a big feather. The other 80 percent die of natural yoga causes.

Dear Advice King,

What should be done about this deer disease that has them drooling and wandering in circles? Is this the beginning of the end?

—James in Lancaster, Penn.

The BEGINNING of the end? This is the END, my friend. I don't know if you've noticed, but *everybody* is drooling and wandering in circles. At least the deer don't have a 24-hour news cycle to deal with.

Imagine if they did! Go ahead, imagine it.

Dear Advice King,

The time has come: I have GOT to change banks. But how can I find one that's good?

—Francine in Fort Worth, Texas

The main thing is to make sure the bank isn't made of wood. After that, I'd say that it should have free lollipops. And coffee! A lot of banks have coffee now.

I used to love hanging around the bank and drinking coffee. I'd ask about mortgages and credit lines and layaway plans. It turns out layaway plans aren't a bank thing. Anyway, you're probably wondering why I said I *used* to love hanging around the bank. Well, a few months ago while I was talking about (hypothetically) borrowing money to buy a big boat, I spilled my coffee on the manager's desk. Again. Then I wasn't allowed inside the bank anymore. I had to use the drive-thru—which is no fun compared to the inside. So I quit the bank, and I keep my savings* up a stuffed monkey's ass.

Annoying DJ Neighbors, Attempted Man Buns and Arctic Cruises

PUBLISHED AUGUST 8, 2018.

Dear Advice King,

How do I convince my neighbor who's an "aspiring DJ" to change career paths? Or to at least stop playing "Turn Down for What" on repeat.

—Alexa in Los Angeles

First of all, the city of Los Angeles itself is an aspiring DJ. Did you expect your neighbor to be some kind of serious person?

Secondly, have you considered the possibility that your neighbor might actually BE Little Jon, and that he is actually yelling "Turn Down for What"?

Thirdly, what "career path" would you suggest if you were going to suggest one? Is there such a thing as a "career path" in 2018?

Do you like when advice columnists ask YOU questions?

2018 CAREER PATHS:

1. Uber
2. Barista

* Fourteen dollars.

3. Lyft
4. Stand-Up Comedian
5. Uber
6. Lyft
7. Barista
8. Uber
9. Uber
10. Anthony Scaramucci

I think you're fucked, Alexa. Everybody in the world is an aspiring DJ. Except for old people. Move to Florida, where old people live. Become a bingo caller and get a ton of cockatoos. Name all your cockatoos Meghan Markle.

Dear Advice King,

I'm balding, but I'd really like to have a man bun. What should I do?

—George in San Francisco

Jump in a lake. Lake water is really good for hair follicles. The lake water that is the best for hair follicles is usually found in the middle of the lake. At night.

I'm pulling your dick, George. Lake water won't help you grow a man bun. I was trying to drown you because I think you are dumb.

I wonder where the expression "pulling your dick" came from. The Freemasons, probably. There's a lot of "dick play" in secret societies. When Freemasons meet up, I bet it's 90 percent dick pulling and 10 percent ideas for more tax cuts.

Have you seen a "man bun" on a balding guy, George? I have. It doesn't look anything like a bun. It looks like an unfinished sculpture of a hairball made by a mental case, which is no coincidence, because that's what it fucking is.

Dear Advice King,

I'm thinking about taking a trip to the Arctic Circle. There are luxury cruise ships that go all the way up there now. You can spend the day shopping and then get off the boat and see polar bears! Some people have been attacked by the bears, though. Should I be worried, or should I just go?

—Sally in Darien, Conn.

You ever heard of the motherfucking *Titanic*, Sally? It's not just a DVD in the giant fucking Tupperware thing in your basement—it's a real fucking boat. And it's really at the bottom of the motherfucking ocean. It was full of motherfuckers from Connecticut who were somewhere they didn't belong. They were shopping, too. They were on a big fancy boat, shopping for bumbershoots or medicine balls or whatever rich motherfuckers shopped for in 1912. They were doing this shopping IN THE MIDDLE OF A BUNCH OF MOTHERFUCKING ICEBERGS. Then the boat sank after it ran into an iceberg.

Then those Connecticut dopes were in the North Atlantic wearing hoop skirts and spats and monocles and top hats and holding bumbershoots and medicine balls, and boy oh boy did they feel dumb. Not only did they feel dumb, but they were being slapped by whale's tails, inked by octopuses, butted by manatees, stung by stingrays, pinched by lobsters—and then they all drowned.

Go, but watch your ass, Sally. Polar bears, octopuses, manatees, icebergs—AND HISTORY—are trying to tell white people something: Go shopping outside your own ecosystem, and you go shopping at your own risk™.

Should I Invest in Bitcoin?

. . . .

PUBLISHED SEPTEMBER 29, 2017.

Dear Advice King,

I'm in my late 30s, and I don't have any money set aside for my retirement. Should I invest in "bitcoin"? I've heard that it's the currency of the future.

Thanks in advance from a faithful reader!

—Eric in Chicago

Bitcoin? What the fuck is that? Can you buy a cup of coffee with it? Be right back . . .

Nope. Everybody at the coffee shop laughed at me. They said, "Get a load of this asshole! He wants to pay with BUTTcoins! Get him!" I started crying and running but I couldn't see where I was going because I was crying and I fell down and my pants ripped and all my REGULAR coins fell out my pockets. I tried to pick them up—I think I got most of them. Now I'm home with no coffee and my underwear is hanging out. My normal, real coins are wet with tears.

I just looked up "Bitcoin" on the ol' goog, and as far as I can tell it's a lot like those tickets you get out of a Skee-Ball machine—except Elon Musk talks about Bitcoin much more than he talks about Skee-Ball tickets. I'm assuming everybody knows what Skee-Ball tickets are. They ARE a form of currency, but they can only be used to purchase shitty prizes at arcades. And they are only accepted in the arcade where you're currently using the Skee-Ball machine. You can't take them to another arcade and get their shitty prizes—they're a one-arcade currency. Bitcoins are like Skee-Ball tickets, but the "arcade" where you can use them to get prizes is a thing called "the dark web." For those of you who don't know, the "dark web" is another whole internet that is supposed to be way cooler than the regular internet. I'm not fucking kidding. If the regular internet is a bar, the "dark web" is a speakeasy where I imagine the clientele looks like the customers at that *Star Wars* cantina. I don't know about you, but it's hard for me to imagine ANYTHING being cooler than regular old Yahoo.com.

For the purposes of this airtight Skee-Ball metaphor, the only difference between an arcade and the "dark web" is the prizes. You can use Skee-Ball tickets to get a plastic kazoo or a stuffed animal. You can use Bitcoin to get uranium or a hitman.*

The dark web definitely has more interesting prizes than your average Skee-Ball joint (outside of the storied high-stakes Skee-Ball parlors of post-war Singapore), but there's a big problem with both of these "currencies." I remember as a kid saving up Skee-Ball tickets to get a sock monkey. Before I could trade the tickets in, the arcade went out of business. The tickets were worthless. Where are you gonna spend your Bitcoin when the arcade closes, Eric™?

Does everyone understand "Bitcoin" now? Me neither. I'm not even sure I know what Skee-Ball is anymore.

The way world events are going, I'd say you'd be better off investing in the LEAST abstract things available, Eric—potatoes, boats, hand-crank dialysis machines, that type of stuff. Invisible coins that rely on a power grid for their very existence? No, thanks.

. . . .

* If uranium was one of the prizes at a regular arcade, it would cost AT LEAST 150,000,000,000,000,000,000,000,000,000 tickets.

Should I Buy a House?

. . . .

PUBLISHED MAY 26, 2021.

Advice King,

I've been saving up for 10 years to buy some property, but home prices are outpacing my ability to accumulate enough for a down payment. Should I keep trying, or give up on the American Dream of home ownership?

—Kristin in Charlotte, N.C.

Buy a "tiny house"! Get a tiny dog! Cry tiny tears!

I'm kidding. Only do the first two things.

The American Dream left town a long time ago, Kristin. It left on a horse called "NAFTA." "NAFTA" was accompanied by three other helper horses—"Citizens United," "Glass-Steagall Repeal" and "Gutting the Voting Rights Act." They were "dressage" horses. A "dressage" horse is a special kind of fancy horse that oligarchs buy with money that was supposed to go toward paying people a living wage.

To keep their minds off the fact that they moved American manufacturing jobs to countries without labor laws, oligarchs hire someone to teach these horses tricks. Most oligarchs say that when they watch their fancy horses do tricks they completely forget that the minimum wage has stayed the same since 2009.

I bet a red-hot oligarch joke is "If only I could teach that horse to fire the gardener!"

Soooo, "tiny houses." What are "tiny houses," you ask? Tiny houses are exactly what they sound like they are: tiny fucking houses. So why, you ask, do I keep putting "tiny house" inside quotation marks? Because houses that are way too small are being marketed specifically as "Tiny Houses" to trick people into thinking they are cute, special, whimsical, fun houses, instead of "THE ONLY HOUSES ANYBODY

CAN AFFORD." They are also marketed as "more sustainable" and "great places to practice mindfulness." I made up the last thing. But they really are marketed as more sustainable than regular-size houses.

But what does that mean?

"Sustainability" can only be achieved if EVERYBODY (or at least, almost everybody) is participating. As long as the absurdly large U.S. military keeps belching smoke, and the oligarchs keep the air conditioning running 24/7 in every mansion, guesthouse, boathouse, home theater, skating rink and tool shed they own, people living in "tiny houses" cannot be reframed as climate activists. They are nothing more than late-stage capitalism's victims. Except, that is, for a few eccentrics who choose tiny houses because they love feeling cramped—those people are having the time of their lives.

Here's a short play I wrote about a masochist living in a tiny house for fun:

THE TINY HOUSE I DESERVE, BY CHRIS CROFTON

Interior, broom closet

RESIDENT: I love this "tiny house"! I only wish it was smaller—it's not hurting my knees enough. That's right broom, hit me in the face. DO IT AGAIN, BROOM.

FIN

I'm not opposed to dreams, Kristin, but as long as the "American Dream" remains "owning multiple 10,000-square-foot residences," things will never improve—1,000 people will have 50,000 square feet and dressage horses—the other 300 million will have 75 square feet and a rain barrel. The U.S. military will make sure the climate is still fucked.

I propose revising the American Dream: Normal-size houses for everybody™.

ACKNOWLEDGMENTS

Thank you Mom, Dad, Gregory, David, and Pamela—I love you!

To Tracy Moore for suggesting that I write an advice column, and for the beautiful foreword. To the *Nashville Scene*. Jim Ridley, Patrick Rodgers, Elizabeth Jones, Adam Gold, Jack Silverman, Wendy Walker Silverman, and Steve Haruch. To the Vanderbilt University Press. Zack Gresham and Betsy Phillips. To Nicholas Gazin for the amazing illustrations. To David Dark. To Anna Hossnieh and The Daily Zeitgeist. To Richard Eoin Nash. To David Berman. To Gregg Turkington, Philip and Diana Cavanaugh, Larissa Nowicki, Mark Lonow and Jo Anne Astrow, and Daniel Lonow.

Thanks for the inspiration: John Denver, Prince, Jonathan Richman, Fugazi, The Wedding Present, The Jesus Lizard, PJ Harvey, Public Enemy, David Gates, Walter McDonough, D. Manus Pinkwater, Kurt Vonnegut, Flannery O'Connor, Charles Bukowski, Hunter S. Thompson, Steve Martin, *MAD Magazine*, and *Pro Wrestling Illustrated*.

Special thanks to all my friends and supporters in Nashville, Tennessee—I am forever in your debt.

CPSIA information can be obtained
at www.ICGtesting.com
Printed in the USA
LVHW010622020622
720217LV00003B/380

9 780826 504630